SPITFIRE STRIKES

SPITFIRE STRIKES

A NEW ZEALAND FIGHTER PILOT'S STORY

Johnnie Houlton
DFC

JOHN MURRAY

© Johnnie Houlton 1985

First published 1985
by John Murray (Publishers) Ltd
50 Albemarle Street, London W1X 4BD

Typeset by Inforum Ltd, Portsmouth
Printed and bound in Great Britain
by The Bath Press, Bath

British Library Cataloguing in Publication Data
Houlton, Johnnie
Spitfire strikes.
1. Spitfire (Fighter planes)   2. New Zealand—
Royal New Zealand Air Force   3. World War,
1939–1945—Aerial operations, New Zealand
I. Title
940.54'49931'0924   D792.N4
ISBN 0–7195–4178–6

CONTENTS

ILLUSTRATIONS

MAPS (*between pages 44 and 45*)

ILLUSTRATION SOURCES

ACKNOWLEDGEMENTS

I wish to thank those who have helped me in the preparation of this book: aviation historian and researcher Hugh Smallwood (London) for his extensive archives research yielding follow-up material of historical interest; Jeffrey Quill, for his comments on a Spitfire control problem encountered in 1943; Group Captain A.E. Thomson, OBE AFC RNZAF Base Commander Auckland and Flight Sergeant S. Clifford of Photographic Flight; Wing Commander J. Lanham, Commanding Officer of RNZAF Strike Wing at Ohakea and Peter Strugmell, Curator of the Ohakea Base Museum, for their very practical assistance. My thanks, also, to Davina Pryer of the Commonwealth War Graves Commission (Maidenhead); Group Captain T.C. Flannagan and Mrs Boyd of the Ministry of Defence Air Historical Branch (London); Tim Calloway of the RAF Museum Photographic Library (Hendon); the Staff of the Imperial War Museum Photographic Library and Documents Department (Lambeth); the Director, Research Department, National Meteorological Office (Reading); and the Staff of the Public Record Office (Kew). Pat Mentzer (Great Barrier Island), Joan Farrell and Jane Waugh skilfully produced the typescript from my convoluted drafts. My special appreciation for Vicki – my wife – in her ever supportive role, and as sounding board and critic.

Those who expect to reap the blessings of liberty must, like men, undergo the fatigue of supporting it.

Thomas Paine, *The American Crisis*, 1776–83

FOREWORD

by Air Commodore Alan Deere DSO OBE DFC & Bar

With his racy account of his experiences as a Spitfire pilot in the Second World War, Johnnie Houlton joins the ranks of those fighter pilots who, since the war, have exchanged guns for typewriters to record their personal accounts of the aerial battles of the time. The author has from time to time throughout his narrative introduced synopses of happenings in the war leading up to but touching on his own involvement on his particular front, thus enabling the reader to keep the wider picture of the war in focus while following the pilot's own story.

Though he had a short spell on operations in the UK, the author's first real taste of head-to-head combat was in Malta. What makes this part of his story interesting is reference to the on-the-ground hardships of the air and ground crews in respect of the Battle of Malta not, I believe, highlighted in previous personal accounts of this Air Battle. Tiredness is a major factor in battle, as I well know from my own experience in the Battle of Britain, and when it is aggravated as in Malta by sickness and lack of food it is a miracle so much was achieved by such a minuscule Air Force.

I first met Johnnie Houlton in 1943 when as a pilot in 485 (NZ) Squadron he moved to Biggin Hill where I was the Wing Leader. This part of the story is, for me, on home ground, so to speak, and I can fairly say that he has handled it well. In general I can vouch for the authenticity of most of what has been written, at least in so far as my memory serves me some forty years on. Specifically, I recall with some poignancy the day Johnny Checketts, the author's Squadron Commander, was shot down over France. At the time it was to me a great personal loss; to the Biggin Wing a tragedy for Checketts was a real 'ace' and a great inspiration to the younger pilots. Happily, as recorded later, he escaped capture and returned to fight again, as a Wing Leader.

Operations from Biggin Hill were clearly the core of the author's experiences, but it is to his credit that he keeps the reader's interest alive in the less glamorous year that followed leading up to the invasion of France. As an active participant, I shared the author's excitement of D-Day, and the awesome sight of the mighty Armada of invasion ships lives with me today. My operational career ended on that day, whereas Johnnie's was entering its last phase, a phase which he deals with in some detail, and to good effect.

It is a continuing source of amazement to those of us who fought in it that books on the Second World War still attract a wide reading public. In *Spitfire Strikes* Johnnie Houlton has succeeded in adding another link to this, as yet, unbroken chain.

AUTHOR'S PREFACE

Time condenses history into a selection of memorable events, and already the 1940 Battle of Britain is recognised as the first milestone on the road to the final defeat of Germany, when the Royal Air Force fighter pilots demonstrated that this enemy was not invincible.

It is now largely forgotten that six Hurricane squadrons based in France in early 1940 inflicted heavy casualties on the Luftwaffe – No 1 Squadron alone destroyed 100 enemy aircraft for the loss of only one pilot killed – and their efforts must surely have weighted the scales during the Battle of Britain which followed.

Similarly, the part of RAF fighters in the survival of Malta, and the real significance of the air battles over Western Europe and the Middle East, are seldom seen in their true context against the planned, strategic re-entry into Europe.

Hurricane and Spitfire pilots fought the Luftwaffe in the crucial battles of 1939 and 1940; and the Spitfire went right on to the end, universally accepted as the finest propeller-driven fighter of the Second World War.

I was privileged to fly with mixed squadrons – which were like a small League of Nations – as well as with the New Zealand Spitfire Squadron; but all were bound together by the common objectives and customs of the Royal Air Force.

The concept of this book is to record something of the atmosphere and incidents of that time, as experienced by the average

operational pilot; and into my own story I have woven experiences of other pilots, many of whom were – and are – my
friends.

Scanning the indexed names in Wing Commander H.L.
Thompson's war history *New Zealanders with the Royal Air
Force* has prompted memories of many friends and of half-
forgotten faces; of characters and clowns, of actions and
incidents, of good times and bad. I recall the vitality of
those days and the laughter, laced with sorrow on the passing of
one's friends. It also underlines the fact that, for every New
Zealand airman whose name was a household word, there were
hundreds whose efforts were comparatively unknown; and this
would apply equally throughout the United Kingdom and the
Commonwealth.

Although this book can represent only a very small part of the
whole picture, perhaps it will serve as a salute to the 'silent
majority' of Fighter Command, of whom so many failed to
return.

J.H.

1

PATHWAYS TO THE RAF

Home, until 1939 when I was seventeen, was in an outer suburb of Christchurch, New Zealand, with the Port Hills rising away from the back fence of our property. The solid brick house had been built by the owners of a brick kiln which had become derelict before I was born; the kiln was later demolished by relief workers during the Depression, and the rubble used to reinforce the banks of the Heathcote River. On our side of the street, there were only three homes, the balance being cow paddocks; and close by was a recreation ground which was rarely used, but was cropped for hay each summer. There were rabbits within a hundred yards of the house and, in autumn, the field mushrooms were literally the size of a plate.

My father was foreman for a building contractor, and our transport was a twin-cylinder Harley-Davidson and three-seat side-car, which he bought in 1927 for £125. During the Depression he was out of regular work for two years but, through odd renovation jobs and a large orchard garden, he managed to avoid having to take relief work.

Our family background was typical of most New Zealand families in those days, stretching back on both sides to Britain, which was still called 'Home'. On my father's side the name goes back to Lincolnshire, while his mother's parents emigrated from the Isle of Wight. On my mother's side the link is to Scotland and to Yorkshire.

One of my father's friends, Bill Park, was Custodian of the

original Canterbury Aviation Company at Sockburn, just south of Christchurch, and visits to the Park family were highlights of my boyhood. Sir Henry Wigram had formed the Aviation Company, which became the Canterbury Flying School during the First World War; and 180 pilots had been trained there for service with the Royal Flying Corps. In 1923 the aerodrome was purchased by the Crown to become Wigram Air Force Base, and Sir Henry donated £10,000 towards the cost, and subsequently gave another 83 acres of land. Part of the arrangement was that Bill Park was to be retained in his employment, so the Park family was raised in the aerodrome house, which eventually, during the expansion caused by the Second World War, was surrounded by Air Force buildings.

On those visits to Wigram in the late 1920s and early 1930s my older brother and I were able to roam through the almost empty hangars, to gaze at the few resident aeroplanes (which, today, would have pride of place in any vintage aircraft collection) and to breathe the heady aroma of burnt castor oil and acetone doped fabric.

There were Bristol Fighters, a few Gloster Grebes, Hawker Tomtits and Avro Trainers, and a Puss Moth. Later came the Vickers Vildebeests, Blackburn Baffins and Fairey Gordons.

One of the greatest days in the history of Wigram was in 1928 when Charles Kingsford Smith landed his three-engine 'Southern Cross' after the first successful crossing of the 1200-mile stretch of the Tasman sea. His flight had been well publicised in advance, and when 'Southern Cross' arrived overhead, escorted by Bristol Fighters, a mass of people was crammed onto the aerodrome, and also blocked the surrounding roads, demonstrating how aviation had caught the imagination of the New Zealand public.

In pre-school days my mother would take me to call on a very old Scots couple, and a spinster sister who lived with them. Nan Inkster was over ninety years old, tall and upright, and an unlikely but fascinating companion for a small boy who never stopped asking questions. It seemed completely natural that she should talk away to me in a way in which I could readily understand, and there was always a feeling of warmth in that small house. I can still hear her telling me, calmly and clearly, that later on I would fly in the air and there would be danger all round me, but that I would not be hurt.

School was Opawa Primary about a twenty-minute trot along the banks of the Heathcote River. High School was Christchurch Technical College, which was the largest secondary school in the city. The very existence of the pupils of my day had been generated in, or after, the convulsive violence of the First World War, and it cast its shadow across the face of all our families. Commemoration of the 1918 Armistice began at 11 a.m. on 11 November every year, as all traffic, trains and trams came to a halt. Every person stood in remembrance wherever they might be for two minutes of silence, symbolising the quiet on the battlefield as the guns had been stilled. As the moving notes of Reveille died away the tableau would dissolve, for the sounds of living to begin again. However, the New Zealand day of mourning is held on 25 April, the anniversary of the 1915 landings at Gallipoli by the Australian and New Zealand Army Corps (ANZAC). Returned servicemen paraded with contingents from all service organisations, marching to the Bridge of Remembrance for the Cenotaph Memorial Ceremony.

It is said that the outsider often sees more of the game, and it was certainly true that in New Zealand, in the 1930s, there was an early perception of what was to come. Hitler and the Nazi Party had begun to take effective control of Germany only in 1933; but inside two years it was obvious that the philosophy of *Mein Kampf* was being translated into action. Similarly, the intentions of the Japanese in the Pacific and the Far East were accurately assessed early on by the general public, one of the pointers being the frequent presence in New Zealand ports of Japanese ships loading scrap iron and steel. It was commonly accepted that some of that scrap was going to be returned in the form of bullets and bombs; and the much-maligned waterside workers went as far as using their industrial muscle against that brand of New Zealand export.

In 1934 Cecil Matthews – a senior pupil of Christchurch

Technical College – had broken the British Empire School Boys' record for one mile, in a time of 4 minutes 29.6 seconds. In 1936 he represented New Zealand at the Olympic Games in Berlin; but due to a foot infection was unable to reach top form. He was there, however, to see Jack Lovelock win the 1500 metres final for New Zealand, one of the great sporting achievements of that time. Also in 1936, our Form Master returned from a year's sabbatical leave, several months of which he had spent in Germany. He gave us a detailed indication of the resurgence of the German Armed Forces, the increasing arrogance and excesses of the Nazis, and the mood of belligerent optimism which was sweeping through that country. It was a strange feeling to have such a clear portent of the future settle in the classroom, half a world away from the scene of action. Ironically, it was during that same year of 1936 that a new school Assembly and Memorial Hall was opened, which displayed a large plaque recording the names of former pupils who had been killed in the First World War.

Also about that time a neighbour in the next street, Charlie Savage, designed and built a small monoplane which was fitted with a four-cylinder in-line Ace motor-cycle engine. It was a smart looking machine, but when he requested a permit-to-fly the Civil Aviation Dept refused, on the grounds that it was not an approved design and would not fly safely, even though officials had been aware of the actual construction. After months of frustration he towed the aircraft more than ten miles to New Brighton Beach, starting at dawn on a summer Sunday morning. The Club Captain of the Canterbury Aero Club flew and tested the machine, finding it to be satisfactory and with no apparent problems. Charlie Savage then made another application, producing photographs and the flight report by the Club Captain, and he eventually won the day. The aircraft was listed for many years in the Civil Aviation Registry as the Savage Monoplane.

In 1938 the School Cadet Corps established – in liaison with the Royal New Zealand Air Force (RNZAF) – a small radio operator section, which I promptly joined. Each Monday afternoon we went to Wigram, where we spent as much time polishing aircraft as learning to send and receive Morse code, but at the end of the year each cadet was taken for a short flight. So the first time I experienced the exhilaration of flying was in the rear cockpit of a Vickers Vildebeest, flown by Flight Lieutenant 'Nugget' Cohen.

For some years many New Zealanders had been making their own way to England to join the RAF; and in 1937 a direct entry scheme was inaugurated whereby trainee pilots were selected in New Zealand, given elementary training, and then sent on to England with Short Service Commissions. Bill Foster, Tony Dini, and Basil Peryman were senior pupils of the school who sailed for England under this scheme, and were amongst the 507 New Zealanders serving with the Royal Air Force at the outbreak of war in 1939.

In terms of trained manpower, and stocks of munitions and equipment, Britain and the Dominions were ill prepared for war, in comparison with the German forces. The reasons for this were political, and were reflected in government reluctance to allocate sufficient funds for large-scale expansion of the Armed Forces, at least until war was seen as inevitable. One factor which emerged at the eleventh hour, however, to help redress this imbalance, was the planning and immediate implementation of the Empire Air Training Plan. At the end of September 1939, when Poland had been overrun by the blitzkrieg campaign in which the German Air Force had played a major role, it was clear that British air supremacy was going to be essential for survival. For various reasons it seemed unlikely that large numbers of airmen could be trained quickly in the British Isles, so close to the main theatre of war. Prompted therefore by Viscount Bruce (then High Commissioner for Australia in the United Kingdom) and Captain Balfour (the British Under-Secretary for Air) the Empire Air Training Plan was ratified in December 1939 between Britain, Canada, Australia and New Zealand; with South Africa and Rhodesia joining in later. Each Dominion undertook to set up training organisations for specified numbers of recruited air crew, to be deployed under the operational command of the RAF. The staff work achieved by the RAF and Dominion Air Forces deserves the highest commendation. For example, the New Zealand Training Schools reached their full scheduled capacity under the Empire Plan before the end of 1940, and each of the Dominions continued throughout the war to select and train aircrew, including a large number of aircrew from the United Kingdom itself, to meet the immense operational requirements of all RAF Commands.

2

FRANCE: 1940

In 1939 I started work as a Public Service Cadet in Christchurch, and when the Declaration of War was made on 3 September we all knew that the pattern of our lives could never be the same again. My older brother, Charlie, was interested in radio theory and practice, so he joined the RNZAF as a wireless mechanic in 1940. My father's building firm was fully extended and, as mobilisation and training schemes began to accelerate long working hours, six days a week, became the norm.

A close friend of mine in those days was Dave Fraser, whose father was a veteran of Gallipoli and France. Many of his contemporaries from the First World War volunteered again for overseas service, and after a farewell party for some who were leaving with the First Echelon of the Second NZEF, Pop Fraser found a white feather in his pocket. Being a fiery Scots-Kiwi, he volunteered at a Recruiting Depot where no awkward questions were asked; and he sailed away for the second time in twenty-five years, this time leaving behind a wife and a family of five. He was to be posted missing following the Army withdrawal from Greece and Crete; but after many anxious months in the Fraser household, he was notified as a wounded prisoner of war.

On 10 May 1940 the German attack which led to the occupation of France and the Low Countries had opened with assaults on the frontiers of Luxembourg, The Netherlands and Belgium; while the airfields and communications in all those countries were heavily bombed. The lightning course of the German campaign culminated in the collapse of French resistance and the signing of the Armistice at Compiègne on 22 June 1940. There was widespread shock and anxiety as the Allied Armies were outflanked and outfought, and at the rapidity which ended the conventional concept of warfare. Despite the massive defeat on the ground and the withdrawal of the British Expeditionary Force it is worth considering again the part played by the RAF during the Battle of France, which has been largely over-shadowed by what followed it – the Battle of Britain.

As Wing-Commander H.L. Thompson in *New Zealanders with the Royal Air Force* has explained:

> From the outset the Royal Air Force in France, equipped with a handful of Hurricane Fighters and a few squadrons of relatively obsolete Battles and Blenheims, attempted to reply to the enemy's massed air attacks and hinder the advance of his armoured columns. . . . The support they could receive from the squadrons based in the United Kingdom was limited by the distance involved, and by the rapid dislocation of communications. Nevertheless, aircraft from Bomber Command operated over the battle area from the first day, while fighters from forward airfields in Kent maintained patrols along the Belgian and Dutch coasts to the limit of their range. Three Hurricane squadrons were also sent to France as reinforcements on 10 May, and during the next few days, as calls for further assistance increased, more pilots and the equivalent of six squadrons were sent across the Channel. In addition, fighter aircraft were dispatched each day to operate from bases on the Continent. But with the collapse of the Allied Front and the loss of airfield facilities that followed the German bombing, it was con-sidered unwise to strip Britain's defences further and commit the major resources of Fighter Command to the Battle of France. Later, however, as the Battle in the North approached its climax, a maximum effort was made by all three Home Commands to cover the evacuation from Belgian and French ports.

At the beginning of May 1940 there were 600 New Zealanders with the Royal Air Force, the majority of whom were flying with units of Bomber, Fighter, or Coastal commands based in the United Kingdom. However, in France there was now a significant representation among the bomber units and in the fighter and reconnaissance squadrons, with a few men serving in administrative posts or on ground duties.

During the air operations of May and June 1940, 44 New Zealanders lost their lives. 'Cobber' Kain, from Hastings, became widely publicised as the first recognised 'Ace' of the Royal Air Force in this war with a tally of 14 destroyed, before he was killed in a flying accident on 7 June 1940. Tony Dini was in the thick of the air fighting with 607 Squadron, flying Hurricanes which had only just replaced their Gladiator biplanes. He destroyed one Heinkel bomber and probably destroyed two more on the first day of the battle; but he also was killed in a flying accident, on the last day of May 1940.

The air-to-air combat successes of the RAF Fighter squadrons received more attention than the less spectacular but dedicated effort of the British Bomber force. The very high casualty rate of the bombers giving close support to the Army was such that Wing-Commander Thompson later wrote:

> Throughout the first week of the campaign the British Bomber squadrons in France attempted to reply to the enemy's air attacks and delay the advance of his ground forces. In doing so they suffered heavy losses. . . . Thirteen out of thirty-two Battles were lost in one attack on the first day. On the following day, of eight dispatched all failed to return. On 14 May a large-scale attack by some 70 RAF Bombers based in France was launched against bridges and roads near Sedan, and at least forty were shot down. . . .
>
> During the next few days the whole situation changed rapidly. The German armoured forces poured through the widening gap at Sedan and advanced westward towards the Valley of the Somme and the Channel Ports. Further North, the Allied forces in Belgium began their withdrawal, abandoning Brussels and Antwerp. With the enemy's rapid advance and his bombing of landing grounds, the Air Forces in France were forced to retire to less vulnerable positions in the rear, and from this time onwards a succession of moves, combined with failing communications and supplies, had their effect on operations from bases on the Continent. . . .
>
> Despite the adverse conditions under which they now operated,

the squadrons in France continued to fly an amazing number of sorties. The bombers, flying at a higher level, attacked bridges, troop concentrations, and armoured vehicles in a gallant effort to stem the German advance.

As the Battle developed over Belgium and France, RAF fighter support was flown by squadrons based in England; and the Spitfires of Fighter Command went into intensive action against the Luftwaffe for the first time. Then, as the defeat of the French Forces became inevitable, the classic evacuation was carried out at Dunkirk between 26 May and 4 June, resulting in 336,000 British and French troops being disembarked at English ports. This was seen, even as far away as New Zealand, in much the same terms as Winston Churchill saw it: 'Wars are not won by evacuations. But there was a victory inside this deliverance which should be noted. It was gained by the Air Force. Many of our soldiers coming back have not seen the Air Force at work; they saw only the bombers which escaped its protective attacks. They underrate its achievements. . . . There was a great trial of strength between the British and German Air Forces.'

I was just one of many airmen who, later in the war, were on the receiving end of bitter comments from soldiers who had fought through that campaign. They complained of the apparent absence of the RAF from the sky above, which was understandable to some degree, but hardly a fair comment in view of the facts. During the actual evacuation period alone the Germans, according to their own records, lost 189 aircraft, while the British losses during the same period were 131 machines, of which 99 were Fighters. As the Commander-in-Chief of the BEF afterwards reported: 'The embarkation of the force would have been well nigh impossible but for the fighter protection provided.' Indeed the RAF still fought on in France long after the army had departed.

Within a few weeks from the start of the shooting war in Europe, one of the three RAF pilots I knew personally from my school days in New Zealand had been killed on active service in

France, and one had become an injured prisoner of war.

Casualties suffered by the Royal Air Force during those battles in Belgium and France included over 600 aircrew, nearly half of whom were pilots. In addition the RAF had lost, from all causes, over 900 aircraft, including 306 Hurricanes and 67 Spitfires. On the other hand, the men who survived, particularly the fighter pilots, had acquired battle experience and confidence which were to prove of the greatest value in the air battles soon to take place over England.

Perhaps the most valid and significant assessment of the RAF effort in support of the British Expeditionary Force lies in the comments of the German High Command at the height of the battle. On 24 May 1940 the War Diary of German 19 Corps recorded: 'Enemy Fighter resistance is so strong that our own air reconnaissance was practically impossible.' On the same day General Halder, of the German High Command, noted in his diary: 'Now, for the first time, enemy air superiority has been reported by Kleist.'

After a pause of two months the vital daylight phase of the Battle of Britain was fought out over southern England and, close run as the result may have been, Fighter Command of the Royal Air Force achieved sufficient supremacy to turn aside the threat of invasion, and Britain was still in the war.

3

RNZAF TRAINING

From New Zealand, the pattern and progress of the war had at first seemed like a distant, giant kaleidoscope; but tangible links quickly began to form with the departure of soldiers, sailors and airmen. I had been transferred to Wellington by my department, and on 6 January 1940 was able to watch four great liners depart, carrying the First Echelon of the Second New Zealand Expeditionary Force to Egypt; a sombre occasion which was to be repeated many times in the course of the war.

At Easter 1940 I took my accumulated leave but, instead of hunting Wapiti in Fiordland, I spent three weeks cooking for eighteen men on one of my father's jobs, which was the building of a linen flax mill. Production of linen flax fibre had been given a high priority to meet the demand for aircraft fabric, and the men were working from 6 a.m. to 8 p.m., seven days a week. We slept in tents, and I operated in one of the old-time harvest-field cook-houses with a coal stove. Nobody complained about the food, so my efforts must have been an improvement on those of my predecessor, who had jibbed at eating his own cooking, and had taken his nourishment from a bottle.

On 2 May 1940 the New Zealand Army Second Echelon sailed for England, as a reinforcement against the expected German cross-channel invasion. Also, with the age limit set at eighteen-and-a-half for aircrew service, each RNZAF training course intake was now being filled, and a waiting list was building up.

In June 1940 the head typist from our Wellington office went
north to Auckland to say farewell to her brother, who was
sailing for England in *Niagra*. She returned to Wellington on
the overnight train and came straight to the office, to learn that
the ship had been sunk by a mine at 3.40 a.m. just a few hours
out from Auckland, but fortunately with no loss of life. *Niagra*
was carrying nearly £2.5m Sterling in gold, and half of the New
Zealand Army supply of small arms ammunition, which was to
help replace British losses after Dunkirk.

On 20 August 1940 SS *Turakina* was under attack from a
German surface raider and, by coincidence, not far beyond the
horizon from the town of the same name as the ship. Armed
only with a stern gun, she fought the raider for nearly three
hours, and two-thirds of the crew were killed. A German
national magazine later claimed that it was the Armed Merchant
Cruiser *Orion* which had sunk the *Turakina* and nine other ships
in the South Pacific, on a voyage lasting seventeen months and
covering 112,000 miles. The raider had sailed round the north
of the Soviet Union at the most favourable time of the year,
entering the Pacific through the Bering Strait.

At least three German raiders operated in the South Pacific
during 1940–1, and on 21 December 1940, 496 survivors were
put ashore by the Germans on Emirau Island (north of New
Guinea). These included captured New Zealand personnel
destined for the Fleet Air Arm (and not yet in uniform) who had
been forced to sign an undertaking not to serve in the Armed
Forces against Germany.

Through the last four months of 1940, however, all our
attention was focused on the crucial air battle over England,
with the daylight offensive against the RAF finally giving way to
night attacks against the cities and ports. My own eighteenth
birthday coincided with the first daylight raid on central London, and it was immediately followed by widespread night raids
on Birmingham, Bristol, south Wales, Liverpool and Clyde-
side. Coventry was ravaged on the night of 14 November, and
two nights later Bomber Command began its attacks on German
industrial targets. Just before Christmas 1940 Spitfires carried

out a low-level attack on an airfield in France, and the pattern of the air war was no longer confined to desperate defence in the daylight skies.

By the end of 1940 the number of New Zealanders serving with the Royal Air Force had increased to 1650, while 203 had been killed and 40 had become prisoners of war. Now that I was eighteen-and-a-half myself, in April 1941 my father gave his consent to my application to join the RNZAF as a trainee pilot. My reasoning was probably no different from that of anyone else, in that I was well tuned to the way of life we enjoyed in New Zealand, and rejected the proposition that a self-styled 'Master Race' should impose its will and its ways on us. It seemed quite certain that, if Britain fell, New Zealand would end up as just another occupied satellite of Germany.

During the eight weeks before I was called up the House of Commons and Westminster Abbey were bombed; HMS *Hood* and *Bismarck* were sunk; RAF Bomber Command raided the Ruhr on twenty consecutive nights; and daily Fighter Command sweeps were flown over the English Channel and northern France. On 22 June 1941 Germany invaded the Soviet Union – the first real turning-point in the course of the war.

As the German blitzkrieg smashed deep into Soviet territory, there was wild speculation in New Zealand on the ability of the Soviet forces to survive. In the months which followed we watched – in mild astonishment – the convulsions of British foreign policy which transformed the menace of the Giant Bear into a worthy comrade of the Lion.

Bill Foster, who had joined the Royal Air Force under the pre-entry scheme inaugurated while we were still at school, was lost on 8 June 1941 when his Wellington bomber crashed in the sea, just one week before I went into the RNZAF. Under the Empire Air Training Scheme the first step for an aircrew trainee was to enter an Initial Training Wing. The New Zealand ITW was at Levin, north of Wellington; and when I stepped from the train with several hundred other entrants I experienced, for the first time, the sensation of being part of a stream of energy forging along in one channel.

Soldiers, sailors and airmen are rightly proud of their own particular arm of the Forces; but there was always great mutual respect between the three Armed Services of New Zealand, despite the occasion early in his term of office as wartime Governor-General of New Zealand, when Air Marshal Sir Cyril Newall unwittingly opened something of a 'credibility gap' by beginning an address to a combined Services Parade: 'Men of the Army and Navy, Gentlemen of the Air Force. . . . ' It says a great deal for the understanding between the three Armed Services that, after the profanity and dust had settled, this phrase became top of the historic 'hit-parade' of Forces humour.

My particular course intake included some of the Fleet Air Arm recruits who had been rescued from Emirau Island, and who had finally, despite their signed undertaking, been given permission by the government to join the Air Force and fly on operations. After six weeks' Ground School at Levin, the course was split between the four Elementary Flying Training Schools (EFTS), and I was sent to Harewood on the outskirts of my home town, Christchurch. From that point on, our lives were to a large extent influenced by luck, the mascot of the day or a guardian angel – call it what you will.

Each instructor started with two pupil pilots, and each course was quickly and ruthlessly culled. Those of slow aptitude were soon grounded, and a maximum deadline of eight hours' dual instruction was allowed before making the first solo flight. Grounded pilots were given the option of remustering to navigator or air gunner courses, returning to civilian life, or transferring to the army if aged twenty-one or more. Military Service was still voluntary at this stage and twenty-one was, ironically, the legal age for voting, for drinking in a hotel, or for joining the army.

Many of the trainees who were washed out at the EFTS stage would undoubtedly have made the grade with a little more time, and some did pass pilot courses later, after completing operational tours as navigators or wireless operator/air gunners. Ruthless as the groundings were, it was probably the only way that the necessarily higher quota of navigators and air gunners could be filled.

At the EFTS we first encountered the Air Force problem of selecting the right people as instructors. In many cases pilots keen to get on to operational flying were held back and commissioned as instructors, while others who had the temperament for instructing were passed on through the system. Sometimes a reluctant instructor took his frustrations out on the pupil which, particularly at the elementary stage, could cause unnecessary tensions and, indeed, groundings.

We trained in the DH 82 Tiger Moth with noisy, open cockpits and a fairly primitive speaking-tube arrangement between instructor and pupil. One trainee had a bad-tempered instructor who often became incoherent in the air. After about six hours' dual instruction the pupil was even more fed-up than the instructor, and knew he was about to be grounded. With a torrent of abuse coming from the front cockpit our friend undid his straps and, standing up in the rear cockpit, leaned forward and clouted his tormentor hard on the top of the head. Back on the tarmac the pupil spoke words of wisdom in his instructor's ear, who saw the light and obligingly exchanged pupils with a colleague, and the trainee completed the course.

In my own case the first of many lucky breaks came my way at the EFTS when I reported to my designated instructor – Flying Officer Hopwood. We stared at each other in surprise: 'I thought I had seen the last of you years ago,' he said. As Heathcote County Traffic Officer he had intercepted me when I was fourteen, riding an unlicensed motorbike on the roads near home. After looking over the old bike, he pointed me towards an unused road, where the neighbours would have no cause to complain about the noise.

Don Hopwood was in his thirties, and an excellent instructor with a genuine interest in his job. I regret to say that I repaid his care by giving him a tremendous fright on my first solo, an incident which I believe was still talked about at Harewood at the end of the war. Checking the traffic around me as I came into land, I found two Moths making steeper, full-glide approaches above and behind me, so I turned aside to get out of their way. I was still cross-wind when the ground arrived, and my Moth bounced off one wheel up to about 30 ft and hung there wobbling, with the wings' slats flopping in and out as I rammed the throttle wide open. Don Hopwood had drummed into me that it was fatal to attempt to turn below flying speed, as the aircraft could stall and crash. One climbed and descended at 65 mph in a DH 82 and that, as far as I then knew, was flying speed! I therefore juggled the Moth along glancing from the air speed indicator to the Control Tower straight ahead, and when the needle touched 65 mph whipped the control stick over and pulled it hard back, literally running the aircraft wheels across the face of the Control Tower. The Controllers baled out down the back stairs, and the Chief Flying Instructor on the ground floor dived under his desk. A group of instructors on the tarmac hooted with laughter when the Moth rebounded but they soon froze, and when I rolled into the turn in front of the Tower Don Hopwood recognised the large identification number painted on the underside of the wings, and went into shock. Next time round I made quite a good landing, then had to explain myself to a white-faced instructor. I was desperately worried that I was going to be grounded, especially when I had to report to the Chief Flying Instructor. I saluted and stood in front of his desk while he just stared at me with an odd sort of expression; then told me to go.

One of the characters on our course was Pete Marshall. He was a few years older than most of us and always involved in any skylarking which went on. He also had a dry sense of humour. Pete kept quiet about the fact that he had previously worked for New Zealand Aerial Mapping Ltd and had flown 300 hours before enlistment. His instructor boasted that he had a special protégé in Pete, sending him solo after about an hour and a half of dual instruction.

On most Sundays we were free of duties, and my father would collect me, and some of the others, to go home for the day. Already lasting friendships were forming in the groups, and I teamed up with Corran Ashworth – known as 'Ash' – a man of considerable charm and ability, and a very good pilot. His instructor was called 'Butch' Baines, because of his tendency to turn purple when he wound himself into a rage. Ash trudged away from a Moth one morning grinning widely, but with a pale and subdued instructor. The flying exercise had been spinning, and recovery from the spin. Ash had pulled the nose of the aircraft up until it was stalled, but was not applying rudder (to cause the spin) to the satisfaction of his instructor. 'Boot it on – hard – like this' yelled Butch lunging at a rudder pedal. With the Moth spinning earthward he then roared: 'Right – recover and pull out.' He was one of those annoying instructors who sometimes kept his hands and feet on the controls while the pupil was in action, and after several turns in the spin he started raving at Ash to pull out. Ash yelled back, 'Get your bloody feet off the rudders.' The panic set in. Butch had jammed the sole of his flying boot between the rudder bar and the side of the cockpit, and there was no way it could be withdrawn. In desperation he released his safety harness, wrenched his foot out of the flying boot, then tore the boot forward and clear of the rudder bar with his hands. Ash corrected the spin and only pulled out of the dive 'scraping the daisies'. After they landed Butch actually apologised to Ash.

At the EFTS dire threats were issued if we should be caught doing anything in the air other than our designated solo exercises; but, as on every course, quite a number of us would meet, whenever possible, over the pine forest on the far side of the Waimakariri River, and battle each other down to the deck in mock combat, getting ourselves into and out of some strange situations.

At the end of the six-week course we had flown nearly 50 hours, and I had an average assessment. About half of our number then went on to Canada, while the remainder were split between the New Zealand Service Flying Training Schools. Ash, Pete Marshall, Dave Bennett, Johnny Lindup, 'Speed' Harris and myself were all posted to Woodbourne, near Blenheim, and there were to be thirty-three in that course altogether. Again there was an element of luck in this posting, for we flew Harvards which had only recently arrived, while those at Ohakea still trained on Hawker Hind biplanes. With retractable under-carriage, hydraulic flaps and a variable pitch propeller driven by a 550-horsepower engine the Harvard was an ideal, high-performance trainer for single-engined aircraft roles; while the other part of the course trained on twin-engined Oxfords.

Half of each day was again spent on flight training, and half at lectures; and as we moved on into summer the hardest part was to stay awake during lectures, in the heat of the day. In mid-October we all managed to pass the ground school examination and a flight test by the Chief Flying Instructor. My own flight test was a dismal affair, as I was the first victim on the morning after a late-night party in the Officers' Mess. The CFI started roaring when he arrived on the tarmac, and was still snarling when he walked away. In the meantime, while concentrating on trying to hear what he was bellowing from the back cockpit, I had first flown in front of an Oxford while I was supposed to be doing steep turns; then turned, on aerodrome approach, in front of another Oxford which was making a low-level pre-cautionary landing approach. The great man marked me 'below average' and commented: 'Not much air sense and does not keep a good look out.'

At that stage we lined up in the dining room to collect and sign for our wings, which was certainly more agreeable than having to endure the sort of graduation parade inflicted at some stations in the Empire Air Training Scheme.

Ash and I shared a room, and there were some sterling characters on the course. Bill 'Blocko' Jones and his close friend Gordon Hudson were in a constant state of warfare – which had begun at their EFTS at New Plymouth. There the boys had just rolled Bill up in the corridor mat when his friend Hudson arrived and took a running jump onto the trussed carcass. Unfortunately he landed on the back of Bill's head, flattening and breaking his nose against the floor, and Bill's name was 'Blocko' thereafter.

The course comedian was Frank Fahy, invariably last to bed, last on parade and broke between pay-days. One morning he

came into land with his wheels up and his flaps down, so the
Duty Pilot gave him a red light to send him round again. Frank
dropped his wheels and picked up his flaps then reversed the
procedure about twelve times, until he just went in and landed
with the wheels up and the warning horn blaring in the cockpit.
When asked for an explanation he said he was fed up with
playing games with the Duty Pilot, and it was lunchtime anyway.

On a cross-country flight, via Ohakea to New Plymouth and
back, Frank and his flying partner detoured to Hawera, Frank's
home town, beating the place up in a big way. For good measure
they buzzed the Control Tower as they left New Plymouth and
so, on return to Woodbourne, an impressive number of disciplinary charges awaited them. Frank was supposed to face these
charges the day we left Woodbourne on final leave, but he
simply joined the exodus from the camp and went home, turning up again in Auckland when we assembled for embarkation.
The Air Force took the easiest way out, and just made sure that
he boarded ship for England.

It was strictly forbidden for pupils to carry passengers, but
some of the Oxford trainees showed a touching confidence in
their fellow Harvard pilots, by sitting in the back cockpit during
night circuits and landings. I spent an hour with Pete Marshall
one afternoon in his Oxford and flew it into land from the
right-hand seat, while Pete lowered the wheels and flaps. At 50
ft Pete took his control wheel, easing the nose down a little, so I
dropped my hands on to my thighs. At the moment of impact
we both grabbed for the controls, and Pete had the problem of
mastering the shuddering series of bounces, and then having to
report a heavy, heavy landing so that the undercarriage could
be checked. It was probably the only bad landing that was ever
laid at his door.

The Station Commander, Group Captain Grid Caldwell,
New Zealand's best known fighter pilot from the First World
War, had a down-to-earth approach to pilot training. He was a
well-built man with a shock of black hair, who radiated vitality
and confidence. Beside the airmen pilots' dining-room there
was a small bar operated by the pilots themselves, and this was

believed to be the only facility of its kind within the Empire Air Training Scheme. Grid Caldwell had set this up on his own initiative, on the basis that the bar was the centre of mess life on active service, and that it made good sense to include exposure to controlled use of alcohol during Flying Training. As far as I know the privilege was never abused, but we did hear later that the bar had been shut down by Air Force Headquarters.

On one navigation exercise over the rugged Marlborough Sounds I pressed on too far into deteriorating weather, which closed in behind me. Circling in a narrow valley I estimated the compass bearing of the direct route to the aerodrome, and the distance, then, using the blind flying instruments, climbed up into the clouds, still circling, until I was 1000 ft or more above the highest peaks shown on the map. It was a really rough ride from severe turbulence in the cloud, and after the estimated time I let down to break cloud in the Wairau Valley about two miles from Woodbourne. The pilots ahead of me on the same exercise had put down at Nelson or at a landing drome at Takaka, and those behind me had turned back in time. The Navigation Officer said a lot of rude things, convincing me that, in my state of over-confident inexperience, I had been an accident waiting to happen by the 'stuffed cloud' route.

Our last weeks included advanced training in bombing, gunnery and formation flying; and the armament phase was carried out from the landing ground beside the Range at Lake Grassmere. At the end of each day aircraft and ground crew returned to Woodbourne, and to avoid travelling the dusty road in the back of a truck, an amazing number of ground crew would pack themselves into and on to the large Fairey Gordon biplane used for drogue (target) towing. This practice came to a sudden end when the Fairey Gordon was seen coming into land back at Woodbourne with an airman draped on the wing, and another clinging to an undercarriage strut.

The few instructors and Staff Pilots at Lake Grassmere were not bothered about finesse or formality, and the Harvards absorbed all the energy and enthusiasm with which they were hurled around the sky. All of us experienced, for the first time,

the phenomena of G force and of blacking out when pulling out
of a dive on to the air-to-ground target. Gravity demands that
one's body should continue on down, but as the aircraft zooms
up only loose body parts and one's blood can continue to move
towards earth. So as blood is dragged down from the brain
vision fades out; if high G forces are applied a visual black-out
can be followed by unconsciousness, until the blood supply is
restored to the brain.

In low-level bombing, with the 5-lb practice bombs, it was
not too difficult to be reasonably accurate; but dive-bombing
was a different matter. Releasing the bomb in a 60-degree dive,
as instructed, meant that the nose of the aircraft had to be lifted
above the target (which was then obscured) before release of the
bomb which took a curved path (or parabola) downwards. Ash
managed to sort out that problem by half rolling and diving
vertically on the target, scoring direct hits every time.

At the conclusion of our training one-third of the course
members were commissioned, and the rest of us became Sergeant
Pilots. This was one practice (following the RAF war-time
system) of which most of us – including those commissioned –
totally disapproved. Later experience confirmed the negative
effects of such an arbitrary division, which appeared to be based
on the status of the College or High School which had been
attended, or on age. Our argument was that nobody could
possibly know, in advance, how any individual would shape up
in action; but by commissioning a proportion at that stage of
training, actual and visible authority and leadership rights were
being unrealistically awarded. The proper method would have
been to commission all or none at all, and to promote only on
operational merit. We were probably our own best critics,
perhaps because of the tendency of young men to make judge-
ments in black or white, with no shades of grey. There was
usually a consensus in any group of those who were most likely
to succeed in particular roles; but I believe we recognised that
the ability to fly an aircraft was one thing, while the elevation of
every third person above his fellows, at this stage, was something else altogether. Given that this was the system, however,

the Air Force made no mistake in my case, since I knew there was no reason why I should be advanced ahead of anyone else on the course.

The day we left Woodbourne Grid Caldwell had each course member into his office for a brief talk and farewell. I found him with tunic unbuttoned, smoking his pipe; and when he learned that I hoped for the day-fighter role in the United Kingdom he laughed, and said: 'The best advice I can give you is not to shoot till you see the whites of his eyes.'

The word went out that one of the newly commissioned course members had requested to be retained in New Zealand as an instructor. He certainly kicked and struggled – right up to the moment when a cut-throat razor dragged off one-half of his moustache!

At the end of our initial flying training on Tiger Moths at Harewood there had been a lively course-farewell party at a Christchurch cabaret, with the result that when Ash and I went home the next morning we were still suffering. My mother asked if we had a course mascot, and I said a pink elephant would do nicely, right then and there. At the end of our final leave she presented to me a magnificent animal in pink velvet, with a gold sash and a jewelled headband. For some reason which now escapes me, I named him Butch.

4

OPERATIONAL TRAINING

During our time at Woodbourne the RAF bombing offensive on Germany had continued to build up; fighter sweeps over France had also continued, with considerable losses on both sides; while HMS *Ark Royal* was sunk after delivering aircraft reinforcements to Malta, and the see-saw of the Desert war had begun; but Hitler's armies had failed to take Moscow. During my nine-day final leave, along with my brother Charlie who was also under orders for embarkation, we heard the news of the Japanese attack of 7 December on Pearl Harbor, followed by the shock report of the sinking of HMS *Prince of Wales* and *Repulse* by Japanese aircraft off the coast of Malaya. The war had suddenly become more personal.

We sailed from Auckland on 13 December 1941 in the *Rangitiki*, bound for England via the Panama Canal; but it was not a happy thought that we were heading for the other side of the world just when Japan had begun the long-expected aggression in the Pacific. The ship sailed alone, initially heading well to the south of New Zealand, then east and north-east up the coast of South America.

My brother was also on board with a group of radio mechanics and armourers; and segregated in the lower decks there were a number of German Jewish refugees, many of them in family groups. They had made their way to England before the war started, and had since been interned as enemy aliens. They had then been dispatched from England in the *Rangitiki*, but first the Canadian, and then the Australian and New Zealand governments declined to take charge of them, so now they were on their way back to England without having been allowed off the ship. We talked with some of them, and found that most were well educated and possessed valuable skills, which they professed to be ready and willing to use for the Allied war effort. These unfortunate people were still on board when we left the ship on arrival in the United Kingdom.

In Panama we first experienced the generous hospitality of the Americans, as there were many United States Forces units in the Canal Zone, as well as the American civilians who operated the canal system itself. Ash and I visited Albrook Field, a military aerodrome on the outskirts of Panama City, where we sighted some Airacobras – a rear-engined fighter which proved something of a disaster, and later had to be taken out of service.*
The Americans flew us round part of the Canal Zone in a light aircraft, plied us with coffee and doughnuts in the Officers' Mess, then drove us back to the ship. The American pilots we met there were career officers. Shock and anger over the Japanese attack on Pearl Harbor had generated a bitter determination in the Americans, and we were impressed, and relieved, to get some inkling of the retribution which Japan could expect; and that our part of the world could also expect the protection of US Forces.

The day we arrived in Halifax, Nova Scotia, a large convoy sailed for England; and three days later the surviving ships returned, after meeting a concentrated U-boat attack. The *Rangitiki* joined the next convoy and our passage was uneventful, apart from some heavy weather, and the fact that the bar ran out of bottled beer half-way across the Atlantic. A deputation complained to the purser, who indignantly claimed that 24,000 dozen had been disposed of since leaving New Zealand; and that supply was supposed to last right back to New Zealand.

---

* Bell P-39 Airacobra's engine was in the rear fuselage with a 10-ft shaft extension forward under the cockpit floor to drive the propeller. A cannon fired through propeller hub (plus two .50 machine guns on top of the nose firing through propeller disc).

'Don't be stupid,' said one of the deputation, 'they're only pint bottles.'

Our arrival in England coincided with the fall of Singapore on 15 February, and the outlook was as bleak as the weather which greeted us. In London the bomb damage was stark and the city was in tones of grey, with ice and slush underfoot; but we felt at home there, as so many buildings could be readily recognised, just as the buses, the taxis and the Underground already seemed familiar. We were quite shattered by the reality of rationed food in the restaurants, but were warmed by the welcome we found.

Our party joined many thousands of other aircrew in Bournemouth, all awaiting postings to flying duties. Every nationality in the Commonwealth was to be found in Air Force uniform. Most were still in groups of their own countrymen, but it was the start of an integration process whereby the Service became the common denominator, regardless of one's country of origin.

We were billeted six to a room in a commandeered hotel called Bath Hill Court, and there was a RAF dining-hall nearby. The food was so shockingly prepared and spoiled, however, that most of us ate at the various restaurants and tearooms around the town. A RAF Warrant Officer once took it on himself to wake us in the small hours of the morning, by beating a fire shovel with a poker in the corridors; but he disappeared after Chook Raymond kicked him down two flights of stairs and into the goldfish pond. Some of the administrative people seemed to have the idea that their jobs required them to act like beggars-on-horseback. Roll calls were ordered for 9 a.m. and 1 p.m. each day but these were ignored, as they interfered with our breakfast and lunch arrangements. An order was then posted that aircrew not present at roll calls would be held back from postings to flying duties, so the next morning there was almost a full attendance in the courtyard. A pompous Pilot Officer called those present to attention, and a corporal called the roll. When Raymond was called, Chook responded from the bedroom window above, still in his pyjamas, and that effectively broke up the first and last full parade.

The overall attitude of the RAF was very reasonable, however, and we were not just confined to hanging around Bournemouth. After a week's leave which most of our contingent used to get to know our way around London's West End, Ash and I spent a day in Christchurch, in a visit of nostalgia for my home in New Zealand. It was a fine, mild day which we enjoyed just ambling around the town. In the early afternoon we called at a small pub on the outskirts, and were surprised to learn that – until wartime shortages took effect – the proprietor had brewed his own ale in an odd-shaped building behind the hotel. He had served in France alongside the New Zealanders in the First World War, and toasted us with three dusty bottles of the final brew of his magnificent Nut Brown Ale.

The Lady Frances Ryder Organisation arranged leave visits for Dominion personnel in whatever part of the country one nominated, and we were able to stay as guests of an estate manager on the fringe of the New Forest; where we were also made very welcome. There were indications too that full-blooded romance was abroad. Two of our party were setting off for the West Country as house guests – arranged under the Lady Ryder scheme – when one of the pair was summoned to meet relations in the north of England. The other proceeded as planned, to find that his hostess was a vivacious and attractive war widow of independent means, with an equally attractive sister. Being a polite young man of handsome presence he played the part of the person glad to be pressured to please in an intricate 'ballet de trois' until – in self-defence – he sent himself a recall telegram. Ironically, his friend returned to report that his relatives had gathered round in very large numbers but, as theirs was a strictly teetotal family, he had been driven to 'drinking in the wardrobe'.

A personal effort to forge a closer Commonwealth relationship backfired on me at a London dance. I was dancing with a gorgeous Irish girl, whose soft, lilting voice was most intriguing. To stimulate the conversation I breathed in her ear, 'And what part of Scotland do you come from?' She stopped in her tracks, took one step back, then slapped my face and stalked off the floor.

After several weeks of killing time Paul Langston and Alf Dryden fell for a call for volunteers to be temporary flying instructors, on the understanding that they would be released for operational flying after six months. They only managed to get out of Training Command eighteen months later, with masses of flying hours which were of no real use to them at all, and both were soon killed in action.

In March Ash, Blocko Bill, Noel Faircloth and myself were posted to an Advanced Flying Unit at Watton in Norfolk for a three-week refresher course, as we had not flown for three months. The aerodrome was totally fog-bound for the first week; but after that we flew the Miles Master Mk II, a light two-seat trainer with an 840-horsepower Bristol Mercury engine, giving it a very good flight performance indeed. Canadians were predominant on the course, with a sprinkling from the other Dominions including two tall Australians who had just completed a short commando-style course to fill in time. Emerging from the local hostelry into a cold, starlit night we faced a long walk around the perimeter to the aerodrome gate, but the Aussies used their new-found skills to take a short cut. Walking between these two Anzacs I heard one say across my head 'Shall we?' and when the other said 'Yes, let's', they grabbed me from each side and tossed me face down on the rolled barbed wire, then pounded across using my back as a stepping stone, hauling most of me out by the belt of my tunic as an afterthought.

At Watton we had a lesson in just how little one knew about the next fellow, when strangers from all parts of the world were brought together in one unit. My room-mate was Paul Goffen-baugher, a quiet, pleasant, well-built American with curly hair, snub nose and big brown eyes. He entered his name for a boxing tournament which was being staged on the station, and all the course went along on the night. The final bout was announced as an exhibition match between a Lance-Corporal from the Dublin Fusiliers, who was middle-weight champion of the British Army, and Sergeant Pilot Paul Goffenbaugher of the United States of America, serving with the Royal Canadian Air Force. The Irishman appeared with an army great coat over his shoulders, and the crowd jeered when Paul climbed into the ring wearing a crimson dressing gown with a gold collar, and 'Golden Gloves' in gold on the back. He knocked the tall Irishman cold in the centre of the ring, then walked the un-conscious body across the ring with an awesome tattoo into the mid-section, and the bout was over in the middle of the first round. It transpired that Paul had fought his way into the semi-finals of the Golden Gloves tournament, and was rated fourth in his class in the USA.

When the weather did finally allow us to fly, we were able to work off some of our built-up frustration in flinging the Masters around the sky, and making mock attacks on any aircraft in sight. At that time the daylight fighter offensive had intensified over northern France, with reports of RAF losses mounting. Enemy air attacks on Malta had built up to a ferocious level. Bomber Command had dropped its first 8000-lb bomb (on Essen), seven out of twelve Lancasters were lost on the first daylight raid which was directed at the German MAN factory at Augsberg, and the Luftwaffe retaliated with raids against Exeter, Bath, Norwich and York.

On 7 April 1942 our small party of New Zealanders reported to Hurricane Operational Training Unit No 55 at Usworth, between Newcastle and Durham. We were again fortunate, in that the Station Commander, Wing-Commander W.D. David, DSO DFC, was an experienced operational pilot who showed a genuine interest in our progress as we trained to be fighter pilots. The instructors were all ex-operational pilots themselves and went beyond their normal duties in conditioning us for the job ahead. There was no parade ground nonsense, but a friendly atmosphere in which we were encouraged to ask questions and were given common-sense information. Squadron Leader Mike Baytagh was the Chief Flying Instructor, with an easy manner and a good sense of humour.

Many of the Operational Training Units (OTUs) experienced high accident rates, but at 55 OTU the staff made considerable efforts to ensure accidents would be kept to a minimum. On our first day Wing-Commander A.F. 'Bush' Bandidt – an Australian in the RAF – introduced us to the right and wrong ways to crash-land a Hurricane. He informed us that the aircraft were Mk I Hurricanes of Battle of France and Battle of Britain vintage, and were all pretty well clapped out. We could expect engine failures, and possibly engines seizing up and catching fire. If the aircraft did catch fire and you had enough height – then jump for it! In a forced landing, make no attempt to turn to take avoiding action when near the ground. Once committed, just go straight ahead . . . the aircraft would take a heavy impact on the nose, but would crumple if side-swiped into the ground or a solid object. He passed around a book of photographs which was over two inches thick, showing every 'prang' while the OTU had been functioning. On each photograph was written the cause of the accident, the action taken by the pilot and the result. It was graphic stuff, and certainly indicated that most straight-ahead crash landings were 'survivable'.

The next morning, as we cycled to our dispersal area, we saw a Hurricane begin its take-off run on the grass field but obviously – from the flat sound of the propeller – in coarse pitch, the minimum power setting. When the pilot realised he could neither get airborne nor stop, he selected 'wheels up', and slid straight on through a brick hut which removed the wings. The fuselage came to rest amongst some trees. Bush Bandidt arrived in his car while the dust was still settling, helped the unhurt pilot out of the cockpit, then pointed out to us that, while the pilot had been careless, he had proved one of the points of the Flight Safety Lecture.

The Hurricane was a very stable aircraft and a great pleasure to fly. It had a strong undercarriage, which defied our various efforts to wrench off the wheels or ram them through the wings. The worst problem was poor visibility on many days, arising from cloudy conditions and the industrial haze, while barrage balloons lurking around Newcastle and Durham compounded the problem.

At the end of April the whole training unit moved to Annan (between Dumfries and Carlisle) to a new aerodrome with paved runways. On the further side of the Solway was Silloth, another training unit where crews were being trained on Lockheed Hudsons. These aircraft had a reputation for engine failures on take-off, and the mud flats at the end of the aerodrome had been labelled Hudson's Bay. One of our instructors was Flight Sergeant Goode, an English pilot who had been operating in Malta, where the air battle was still very much in the news, with the RAF fighters heavily outnumbered. Goode commented that one advantage, in Malta, was that enemy aircraft recognition was not a real problem.

There was a mixture of English, Canadian, New Zealand and Australian pilots on the course, a stocky Rhodesian and a giant Nigerian; and another, half-American and half-French, who had won his wings in the French Air Force. We all got along together very well. At some memorable parties in the mess and in the nearby towns we met Alec, an Australian army sergeant, who had brought some equipment from his London base to an Australian Forestry Unit, which was camped near Carlisle. Alec had been sending signals for six weeks to his London unit, postponing his return, because of various mythical ailments which kept developing in his large diesel truck, so our group had transport laid on to get us back to camp most nights of the week.

After we returned from a dog-fighting exercise one morning I found Ash banging his forehead in agony against the back wall of the dispersal building. Although he had been operated on before enlistment to open his sinus cavities, these were again becoming restricted. Air trapped in the sinus passages could not equalise to the pressure of the outside air with rapid changes in altitude, thus causing violent pressure and pain. This was now happening to him quite often, but Ash refused to report to sick quarters, as he was sure to have been grounded.

There were a few forced landings during the course due to engine failure, and Jock McCauley ended up in hospital with burns, after demolishing the stone walls on either side of a Cumberland country road, when his engine caught fire at low altitude. As the end of the course came near, the instructors were happily predicting this would be the first course ever to get through without a fatal accident, but two days from the finish an English Pilot Officer hit power wires while force-landing, and was killed.

During the last week each pilot was thoroughly worked over by an instructor in mock air combat, and I drew Flying Officer Jean Morai, a Belgian fighter pilot who had a bitter hatred of all things German. He was an experienced pilot from pre-war days, and very keen on the ploy of initiating attacks in a dog-fight from the top of a loop. Our advice, from experienced fighter pilots, was that to do formal aerobatic manoeuvres in a dog-fight was to issue an invitation to be shot down, and our practices confirmed this. However, Jean was an enthusiastic instructor, so I obliged him by 'shooting him down' twice, using his favourite gambit. This had an unexpected outcome. When the end-of-course postings were announced I was one of two pilots posted to Spitfire squadrons, while Ash and the other New Zealanders were sent to 253 Hurricane Squadron. It proved impossible, moreover, to have the posting changed. But it is an example of how a single incident can lead to a distinct change of direction in one's life.

5

KENLEY

On 7 June 1942 I reported to 485 (NZ) Squadron at Kenley, arriving on the same day as Sergeants George Moorhead and Max Sutherland, who had trained at a Spitfire OTU. 485 Squadron had been formed in March 1941 and had been in the thick of the fighter sweeps and early bomber escorts over France. Flying Mk V aircraft, the Spitfire squadrons had been fighting a war of attrition against the Messerschmitt Me 109 fighters of the Luftwaffe. While these two opposing fighters were fairly evenly matched in performance, the Royal Air Force was now suffering the same disadvantage as that experienced by the German fighter pilots over England in 1940. This was, quite simply, that the fighters had a very limited range of action, and thus could spend only a brief period over enemy territory before having to turn for home. When increasing power from cruising conditions to full throttle for combat, the fuel consumption doubled; so the risk of running out of petrol over hostile territory or over the Channel was ever-present.

The RAF squadron totals of enemy aircraft destroyed had steadily increased but their own losses were considerable; and 485 Squadron had been no exception.

Early in 1942 a new factor loaded the dice very much in favour of the Luftwaffe, when the Focke-Wulf FW 190 went into service alongside the Me 109. The FW 190 out-performed the Spitfire Mk V in practically every aspect. It was faster, it had a superior rate of climb, and it accelerated faster in a dive, with a fuel system which maintained full flow when the nose was pushed sharply down – when, under the same conditions, the Spitfire Mk V engine would cut out for a second or so. Adolf Galland, one of the top German fighter pilots, is said to have told Hermann Goering, during the Battle of Britain, that he would like to have a squadron of Spitfires under his command; but when I joined 485 Squadron the pilots would gladly have exchanged the Spitfire Mk V for the FW 190.

Squadron Leader Reg Grant was the Commanding Officer of 485 Squadron; a tough, thick-set character from Auckland. He had flown with 145 Squadron as a Seargeant Pilot, destroying three enemy aircraft and being awarded the DFM, before joining 485 Squadron. Casualties were heavy, and when Reg was commissioned he was promoted rapidly, becoming Squadron Commander after four months, which was something of a record. The squadron had been on offensive operations almost continuously for over a year, and there must have been a fairly high level of fatigue amongst the old hands. The frequency of operations had been slowed down, and in the dispersal hut most were preoccupied with a card game called 'Shoot'. I never did figure out the rules of that game, but it seemed to cost one pound each time a player opened his mouth.

One of the Sergeant Pilots showed me around a Spitfire, but otherwise we three newly arrived pilots just sat around for several days. I began to wonder if the others did not want to bother too much with new pilots, on the assumption that we were unlikely to be around for long anyway. Cynical as that thought may have been, the daylight offensives had taken a distinctly defensive bias because of the depredations of the FW 190. Nor was the situation improved by the battle formation used by the Kenley Wing, and presumably by other RAF units. The squadron flew in three sections of four, with each pilot weaving his way along behind the leader at 50-70-yd intervals. The idea was to guard against surprise attacks from behind and below, with each pilot having a clearer view to the rear each time he turned, first one way, then the other. The degree of weaving progressively increased, back through the section, with the unfortunate tail-end Charlies zigzagging well out to either side of the mean flight path. As each weaving aircraft was covering more ground than the one in front, the rear pilots had to use more and more throttle – and more petrol – to keep up; so that those at the rear, already at greatest risk from attack, also ran the greatest risk of running out of petrol. I knew that the Malta pilots flew in sections of four in wide line abreast, which had proved to be a sound formation; while the Germans used a system of loose pairing, which was also effective.

My Flight Commander, Mick Shand, was taken aback when he found I had never flown a Spitfire; then he sent me off to fly his own aircraft, which carried the letters OU-V. Whereas the Hurricane had been agreeable to fly the Spitfire was a delight, and seemed just to slip smoothly along. As I throttled back to come into land the airspeed fell off very slowly, compared to the Hurricane, as though the aircraft was reluctant to leave the air. In fact, I made two overshoots before adjusting the approach path to land comfortably on the shorter of the two runways. Mick just grunted, when I confirmed that his aircraft was OK, and went back to the card game. Hec Leckie remarked that Mick had been complaining the aircraft was clapped out. Perhaps he had been hoping I would prang it, and win him a new machine.

The Station Commander was Group Captain 'Batchy' Atcherley, a well-known name in the Royal Air Force between the wars. He was a first-rate example of the autocratic and eccentric English career officer, who regarded the Royal Air Force as his rightful domain, and he ruled Kenley Station very much as his personal kingdom. Striding around the aerodrome with his large Alsatian dog, he would occasionally startle the ground crew by climbing into a Spitfire at random, and fly it without helmet or parachute, but with his service cap turned back to front. Once, when flying a Miles Magister trainer, he spotted an aircraft carrier at anchor in Scottish waters and decided to call on the Royal Navy for afternoon tea; but the aircraft lift was descending when he landed, and the Admiral was not amused.

I was disappointed in the atmosphere of 485 Squadron, which

seemed to project an inner and outer circle effect. Later I found this was not uncommon in squadrons of a single nationality. Over ninety per cent of New Zealanders during the war flew with mixed RAF squadrons and, as a general rule, there was a more ready sense of comradeship in an outfit which included a range of nationalities.

In my second week on the squadron a party was laid on for the pilots by a local magnate, who was an expatriate New Zealander; and word came down the line that anybody who failed to turn up could expect a posting to Training Command. We three new boys duly went along to one of those thrashes where nobody was introduced to anybody else, and I managed to put up a decent black when a middle-aged gentleman informed me that I was 'just a clumsy bloody colonial'. Had I known he was our host I might have phrased my reply more politely.

Doug Brown was an experienced NCO pilot, and a jovial extrovert who went out of his way to bridge the gap in the crew room. When Sergeants Jack Yeatman and Matt McLeod returned from leave they also livened up the atmosphere. Jack was a happy six-footer, while Matt was only about my size (5ft 6½in.). Jack had also trained on Hurricanes before his posting to Spitfires.

During June there were few operations for the squadron, and I was kept busy with practice flying – including the dreaded weaving formation – and a few convoy patrols in the Channel. Then early in July the squadron was taken out of Eleven Group for a six-month rest period at Kingscliffe, a satellite station of Wittering in Twelve Group. Practice flying continued, with the occasional convoy patrol, and I flew on a low-level 'Rhubarb' operation – pairs of aircraft operating within pre-selected areas – inside the enemy coast near Ostend. We went in a section of four – in line abreast for a change – with Mick Shand leading, and I flew No 2 to Dick Webb, who was a supernumerary Flight Lieutenant. We split into pairs before crossing the coast, and as we raced in over the sandhills at low level I felt a rhythmic jolting on the controls, then a stream of pretty, green balls started to shoot past the port wing tip. I still recall the enormous shot of adrenalin which flashed from fingertips to chest, as I wrenched the aircraft to port through the flak path, dived down to zero feet and started jinking. As my pulse rate subsided, I realised I had made the correct, split-second reaction without conscious decision; a happy thought in that training and mental programming had paid off. The point is that the only safe evasive action against attack from behind and to one side is to break hard *into* and across the line of fire. Natural instinct is to turn away from the attack, but that gives the attacker an easy shot from astern, frequently with fatal results.

Dick Webb and I located a train and, in accordance with recognised procedure at that time, made a pass over the locomotive to warn the Belgian crew, who promptly locked the brakes on and jumped. After two attacks each, with 20 mm and .303 guns, the locomotive was left enveloped in steam. Then we found and shot up another locomotive before heading back home. Dick made a long, flat approach on the first attack; and the turbulence from his slip-stream knocked my wing down as I followed him in, wiping off the airspeed indicator pitot head (below my port wing) on a tree; so I kept well clear of his slipstream the next time round.

We flew into Martlesham Heath (near Ipswich) for a week of air-to-air gunnery practice; but as the aerodrome remained fog-bound throughout our stay, no flying was possible.

Most of the pilots were billeted out in private homes in Ipswich, and one afternoon I set about lighting the gas calafont above the bath at my billet. My ignorance of the correct procedure was only exceeded by the explosion which blew me through the doorway and up against the stairhead. My eyebrows and front hair were scorched off, and the top and bottom of the heating cylinder had blown out, depositing a generous layer of rust in the bath. As I threw open the cracked window two neighbouring ladies were shrieking at each other that it was definitely a bomb which had gone off, even though the siren had not sounded.

Towards the end of July a general signal was issued, calling for volunteers to go out to Malta. I had long been fascinated by the Malta battle, its progress and its tactics, ever since it began in June 1940, shortly after Dunkirk. So I decided, along with Jack Yeatman and Matt McLeod, to put my name in the hat.

6

SIEGE OF MALTA

The Malta battle had begun with the original defence fighter force of three Fleet Air Arm Gladiator biplanes named Faith, Hope and Charity.*

In 1940 the Air Officer Commanding Malta was Air Commodore Maynard, a New Zealander who had served with the Royal Naval Air Service and Royal Air Force in the First World War. He had a considerable talent for improvisation and half-hitching stray bits and pieces of equipment, a gift which was also to become one of the hallmarks of the Second New Zealand Expeditionary Force in the Middle East. He 'borrowed' the Gladiators from the Fleet Air Arm, and they were flown by flying-boat pilots; then he latched on to four Hurricanes which were in transit to Egypt. The first engagement over Malta on 11 June 1940 set the pattern which was to persist for more than two years – when three Gladiators took on ten modern bombers and five fighters. The Malta battle ebbed and flowed, but dramatically developed in intensity in early 1941 when the Luftwaffe joined Italian forces in the assault, and the real bombardment began. Meanwhile a meagre trickle of Hurricanes had been flown in to reinforce the defences.

By May 1941 the whole of the Middle East looked like a huge

---

* Four of eight crated fleet reserve Sea Gladiators were taken over by the RAF and formed a Fighter Flight in April 1940. One crashed and was used as spares to keep others flying.

disaster area; with the Navy evacuating the Army from Crete, Rommel rampant in North Africa, and Malta coming very close to being neutralised as a strike base for naval and RAF anti-shipping forces. As happened over Western Europe, however, the pressure was eased when Hitler began regrouping his forces for the attack on the Soviet Union and all Luftwaffe forces operating against Malta were withdrawn from Sicily. At the same time Air Vice-Marshal Sir Hugh Pughe Lloyd took over as Air Officer Commanding Malta, and continued with the organisational and command work which had been so well initiated by his predecessor – who had been promoted to Air Vice-Marshal in February 1941. Air Vice-Marshal Maynard had also, by special award, been created a Companion of the Order of the Bath, in recognition of the RAF defence of the Island.

It is rare that unanimous appreciation is expressed for a military leader by the men under his command; but every person I have met who served during the 1942 peak of the Malta battle has, without exception and without reservation, named Sir Hugh Pughe Lloyd as the architect of the ultimate success which was achieved.

The drama of the sustained air warfare over a tiny island only seventeen miles long has possibly overlain the vital strategic significance of Malta, linked by sea and air to both ends of the Mediterranean, with every area of the Middle East conflict thus within range of its bombing and torpedo-carrying aircraft and of its naval assault force. The battles in the Western Desert – and indeed the whole of the North African campaign – hinged on the ability of both sides to ship munitions and supplies across a narrow stretch of sea, and the position of Malta was the key factor. Had it not been for the sea and air anti-shipping offensive maintained from Malta, even at the height of the blitz, Rommel would almost certainly have succeeded in reaching Alexandria in 1942, instead of running out of fuel only sixty miles from his goal. While Rommel's supplies were exhausted, the reinforcement and re-supply of the Eighth Army was able to proceed at full swing, leading to victory at El

Alamein and to victory in North Africa. In short, had Malta fallen, the Allies might well have lost the war.

I saw the siege of Malta as a direct parallel to the position of Britain after Dunkirk, where survival depended both on air superiority to ward off invasion and on keeping the sea lanes open for essential supplies; and to rebuild strength for the offensives. The situation was, in effect, a microcosm of that in the United Kingdom; but concentrated onto a very small platform, with none of the amenities and back-up facilities which were readily available in Britain. The waging of modern war depends on the full involvement of all the people, with leadership in a common direction; and the Island's resistance was a unique example of a Combined Operation in which the Royal Navy, the Merchant Navy, the Army, the civilians and the Royal Air Force were all indispensable and inseparable. New Zealanders had a very personal stake in that struggle, through the commitment of the Second New Zealand Expeditionary Force in the Middle East.

The first Spitfires went into action in Malta in March 1942, fifteen Mk Vs having been flown in from an aircraft carrier, just as the battle was moving into its most critical phase. In February and March 3000 tons of bombs had been dropped on Malta, and an officer of the Royal Artillery suggested that the BBC news bulletins should cut a long story short and say: 'During the last month Malta had six "All Clears", one of which lasted for twenty-five minutes.'

The February 1942 convoy of supply ships failed even to reach the vicinity of the Island, but in March the Navy fought through with two out of four supply ships from Alexandria; and one other, the *Breconshire*, drifted ashore near Hal Far Aerodrome.

In April 7000 tons of bombs were concentrated mainly on Grand Harbour and on the three airfields; where 3000 soldiers toiled to repair the damage quickly, and airmen sweated in the open-topped blast pens to keep the Royal Air Force flying. Three hundred civilians alone were killed in that month, when King George VI awarded the George Cross to the 'Island

Fortress of Malta'. Three groups of about 170 bombers then raided Malta each day, escorted by Me 109 fighters, against which the RAF could seldom muster more than ten Spitfires and Hurricanes. On 20 April 1942 forty-seven more Spitfires flew in from the United States aircraft-carrier *Wasp*, only to be greeted by concentrated bombing on the ground. By the end of the following day's fighting only seventeen of these aircraft remained serviceable.

At the end of April the situation was desperate; but as the heavy German aircraft losses and expenditure of bombs and fuel had taken supplies away from their forces in North Africa, the Luftwaffe assault faltered in early May. This easing of the attack was a bad mistake by the Germans, for it gave Malta time to prepare and rehearse what was to become the climax of the battle.

In three days a Combined Operational plan was worked out: to protect the arrival of more Spitfire reinforcements, and a single ship carrying ammunition and petrol. The aid of the Army was enlisted, and details of the plan were explained to all pilots, ground crew, soldiers and sailors. From dawn on 8 May 1942 all rationing restrictions were lifted on the use of anti-aircraft ammunition, and the full complement of Royal Artillery Units stood to their guns.

In the early afternoon of 9 May the first of sixty-four Spitfires from *Wasp* began to arrive. (When it was my turn to fly into Malta three months later in August, the identical reception system was used.) As each Spitfire came to the end of the landing run, an airman appeared out of the dust and, jumping onto the wing, directed the pilot into a blast pen built of stone blocks and dirt-filled petrol tins, each pen being already stocked with petrol and ammunition. Airmen assisted by soldiers tore into the job of refuelling and arming the aircraft, while the pilot stretched his legs, or was replaced in the cockpit by an experienced Malta pilot. Refuelling was done by hand, with four-gallon tins being passed along a human chain; while the armourers fed in the belts and drums of ammunition. The system was so well planned and rehearsed that some of the new

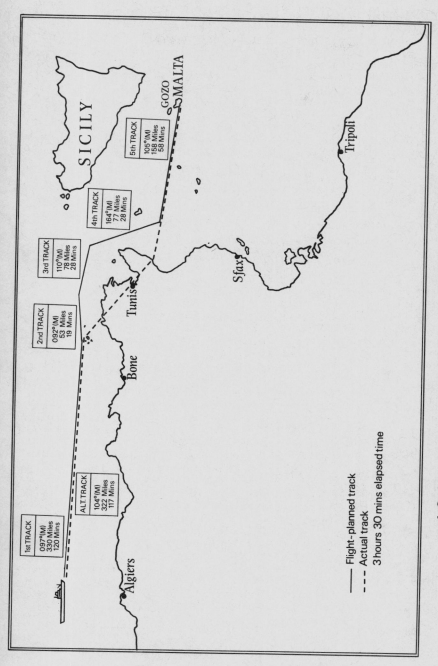

1st TRACK	2nd TRACK	3rd TRACK	4th TRACK	5th TRACK
097°(M)	092°(M)	110°(M)	164°(M)	105°(M)
330 Miles	53 Miles	78 Miles	77 Miles	158 Miles
120 Mins	19 Mins	28 Mins	28 Mins	58 Mins

ALT. TRACK
104°(M)
322 Miles
117 Mins

SICILY

GOZO
MALTA

Algiers

Bone

Tunis

Sfax

Tripoli

——— Flight-planned track
– – – Actual track
3 hours 30 mins elapsed time

1 Style of map issued to Author aboard HMS *Furious*, August 1942

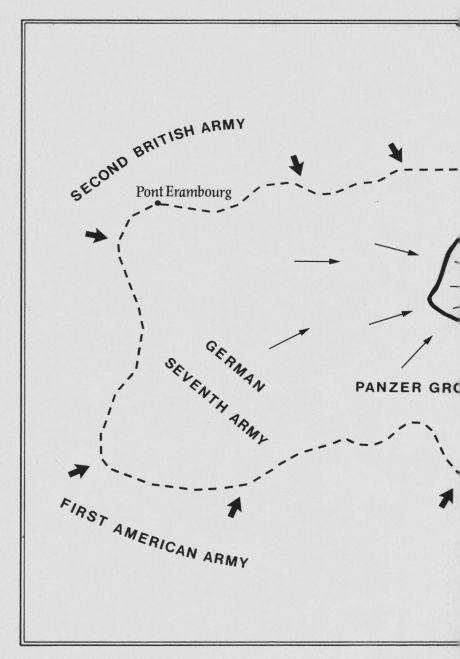

2 The Falaise Pocket: site of concentrated attacks
   by RAF 2nd Tactical Air Force

(33 miles)

Vimoutiers•

PANZER ARMY

uise

Trun•

'CORRIDOR OF DEATH'

Mont-Ormel•

St Lambert•

•Chambois

Villedieu les Ballieul•

•Occagnes

RBACH

Argentan

THIRD AMERICAN ARMY

- - - German Front evening 16 August
—— Allied Front evening 19 August
➤ Allied Thrust
→ German Retreat

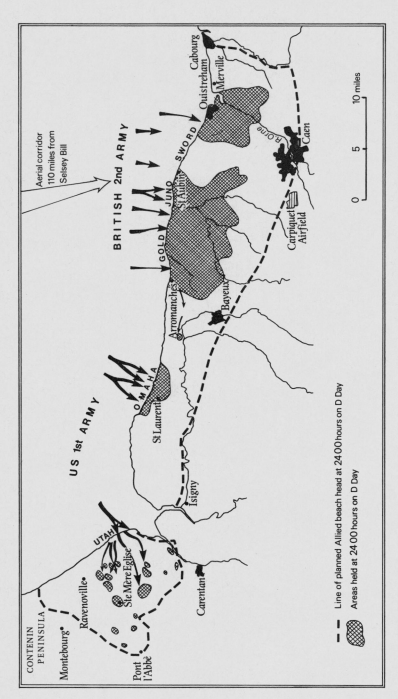

CONTENIN PENINSULA

Montebourg●
Ravenoville●

UTAH

Ste Mère Eglise

Pont l'Abbè

Carentan

Isigny

U S 1st ARMY

O M A H A

St Laurent

Arromanches

Bayeux

GOLD

JUNO

St Aubin

BRITISH 2nd ARMY

SWORD

Ouistreham

Merville

Cabourg

R. Orne

Carpiquet Airfield

Caen

Aerial corridor 110 miles from Selsey Bill

Line of planned Allied beach head at 24.00 hours on D Day

Areas held at 24.00 hours on D Day

0   5   10 miles

3 The Normandy Landings, 6 June 1944

aircraft were airborne again in nine minutes, and every aircraft was ready for action in well under half an hour. Some pilots had to land while a raid was in progress, or under attack by Me 109s hunting around the airfield. Several Spitfires were shot down when making their final approach to land.

Nine enemy bombing raids came in that day, but they met steadily increasing resistance during the afternoon, as the new aircraft joined the action. Nine enemy aircraft were definitely destroyed – one by the guns – with about twenty damaged or probably destroyed.

The climax began early the following morning when HMS *Welshman*, a 40-knot mine-laying cruiser, entered Grand Harbour loaded with ammunition and petrol, to be unloaded in a five-hour non-stop effort by naval shore parties and garrison soldiers, while the raids still kept coming in. But on this day – and for the first time – the Royal Air Force was able to meet the Luftwaffe on something closer to equal terms. The attacks came in six waves spaced throughout the day, each of which was mauled by the Spitfires and by the mighty ack-ack barrage over Grand Harbour. A mood of elation swept over the defenders as the air battles raged overhead; and airmen and soldiers stood on the air raid shelters cheering just like fans at a Cup Final. At the end of the day the Spitfires and Hurricanes had destroyed fifteen enemy aircraft, while the gunners had accounted for eight more, for the loss of three Spitfires destroyed, but only one pilot killed.

The Battle of Malta carried on for another six months of chronic shortages – particularly of food and petrol – with regular bombing and strafing, but never again did the enemy regain his former degree of air supremacy over the Island.

Throughout this book I have endeavoured to write mainly about men I knew or talked with personally at one time or another, and I think the silent majority of the Malta boys would agree that this episode by Ray Hesselyn* says it all – a fitting

---

* *Spitfires over Malta* by Paul Brennan, Ray Hesselyn and Henry Bateson (1943).

remembrance from one of their own:

We scrambled at 3 o'clock, climbing south of the Island getting to 26,000 feet with the sun behind us. Woody called up and said: 'Hello Mac. There's a big plot building up but it's taking time to come south. Keep your present angels and save your gravy. I will tell you when to come in.' We stooged around until he gave us the word. Then we sailed in. . . .

Suddenly, glancing behind, I saw four 109s coming down on me. Three of them overshot. The fourth made his turn too wide and I got inside him. I was slightly below when I attacked from 200 yards, firing perhaps twenty feet ahead of him in the hope that his aircraft and my bullets would arrive at the spot simultaneously. They did. I kept on firing as I was determined to make certain of him. He caught fire. Black smoke poured out, he rolled on his back and went into a vertical dive and straight into the drink.

As he crashed it struck me suddenly that there might be something on my tail. In my excitement I had forgotten to look, but luckily none of the other 109s had dived down on me. Woody now reported that the 88s were diving on Takali, and I pulled up to 10,000 feet. The next instant the 88s were diving past my nose, and the other boys were coming down from above to attack them. I picked out one and went for him, and as I pressed my gun button his rear gunner opened fire. I fired for about a second when my port cannon packed up. Luckily I was travelling fast. This prevented my aircraft from slewing from the recoil of my starboard cannon, as I was able to correct with rudder. I concentrated on the 88's starboard motor and wing-root and could see my shells hitting. Bits were flying off him and flames began spreading as he continued in his dive; he was well ablaze when he crashed.

Returning to land I had my first experience of being beaten up in the circuit. A great pall of smoke and dust from the bombing was hanging over Takali. I made a couple of dummy runs over the airfield and could see that the landing path was well cratered. Just then I sighted six 109s above at 5,000 feet, waiting to pounce. The other boys were kicking about the circuit waiting to try and get in. I beatled up Imtarfa Valley, skipped round some windmills at the top and swung down a valley on the other side. Again and again I thanked my stars that the Spit was such a manoeuvrable aircraft. Each time I was attacked I turned violently and the shells and bullets swept past behind me. It was a nerve-racking business. With all the violent twisting and turning I began to feel very sick. My neck ached from constantly twisting from side to side looking back, and from holding it up while doing tight turns against the extra gravity force. Eventually Mac said that we were to go in and he would cover us.

I started a normal circuit about 300 feet above the airfield, put my wheels and flaps down, did weaving approach and, as my wheels touched ground, felt a sigh of relief. I taxied to my pen, forgetting to put up my flaps. All I could do when I got there was to lie back in the cockpit and gasp for breath. The ground crew had to help me out of my aircraft and, dazed and dizzy, I groped my way along the wing out of my pen.

I met Laddie as I was wandering over to dispersal. Both our tunics were soaked with perspiration. We looked up to see how Mac was getting on. He was making his approach about 50 feet up when suddenly two 109s darted out of the sun. Their shooting, however, was poor and whipping up his wheels Mac turned sharply into them. The 109s overshot him, carried on and beat up the aerodrome. Mac made a quick dart, put his wheels down and managed to get in. He landed with two gallons of petrol – at the pace we were using it, sufficient fuel for only another two minutes in the air. I had five gallons; the others about the same.

7

MALTA CONVOY

Sixty or more pilots assembled in the briefing room at the embarkation centre in England. It was announced that, as only forty-eight pilots plus a few reserves would be needed, those with the lowest number of operational hours would return to their previous units. For this reason I had been taken off the list for Malta, but as the pilot sitting next to me had urgent family problems, I was able to take his place. Our contingent was a good-natured and exuberant cross-section of the Empire, and all but about half a dozen were NCO pilots.

The hangars on HMS *Furious* were already packed with Spitfires when we went aboard. Apparently *Furious* had originally been designed as a battle-cruiser, then was altered during construction to become a carrier. She thus had a conventional bow, called the Lower Flying-Off Deck, below and ahead of the flight deck. We were quartered in a mess flat just aft of that deck, and on the same level, and were briefed on the system used when going to Action Stations. This involved doubling round the ship in one direction only, going up ladders on one side and down ladders on the other side; an efficient exercise which positioned everybody in his proper place in only a few minutes. The first time the bells sounded I headed, against the tide, directly towards my supernumerary Action Station at one of the Oerlikon guns about fifty feet away, so half the ship's company just knocked me down and hurtled over my cringing body.

I found it very difficult to sleep in the mess flat, as the air was soon stifling with all scuttles shut to darken the ship; so after two bad nights I camped in the Oerlikon gun pit out in the open, and slept like a proverbial log. We all turned in fully clothed, with life-jackets to hand: stretched out on a safari bed it was wonderfully peaceful to watch the night sky swing to the movement of the ship, and the war seemed very far away. We went to Action Stations half an hour before dawn each morning, so I was already on the job in the gun pit anyway.

With an escort of four destroyers *Furious* made a fast passage to Gibraltar; then laid alongside for several days, whilst the other ships for the Malta convoy assembled.

Gibraltar was crammed with sailors and soldiers bent on painting the small town red, and our Air Force contingent was soon absorbed in the throng. I was already impressed with navy team work in the ship, and it was good to see how well the navy looked after its own, whether ashore or afloat. If a sailor was in trouble or had passed out, the patrols took charge; not just to get him into more trouble in his ship, but for his own protection. On the outskirts of the town one patrol picked up a sailor who was badly cut about the face, and barely conscious. While two sailors took the injured man off to a First Aid post, the balance of the patrol went off to a small blood-splashed basement bar which, apart from the barman, was deserted. Ignoring the barman, the patrol systematically demolished the place; and in ten minutes there was not a single bottle, glass or item of furniture still in one piece. The patrol's attitude was that as this place had a reputation for organised robbery and violence, and as it was impossible to prove charges, they would put it out of business for a while.

There was no black-out in Gibraltar unless an air raid was imminent, and at night it seemed strange to see a surging mass of uniforms packed into the brightly lit streets and bars. From one of the narrow roads running across the lower face of the Rock I had a good view of the town and the bay, with the lights of La Linea clearly visible at the Spanish border; but my luck nearly ran out when I tried to avoid an on-coming vehicle.

Forgetting that traffic kept to the right I moved the wrong way
and collected a badly split lip, a wobbly tooth and a very swollen
nose. The next day I walked round past the aerodrome on the
Isthmus to Cataline Bay – for a swim – then drifted off to sleep in
the sun. That was another mistake, as I woke with a badly
sunburnt back. It seemed I was on one of those down-swings,
where everything has to be done the hard way.

The carrier sailed again during darkness, and daylight revealed we were in company with the merchant supply ships and
capital ships of Operation PEDESTAL – the August 1942 convoy to
Malta, with Spitfires flying off carriers en route – heading east
into the Mediterranean. Fourteen fast merchant ships were the
heart of the convoy, and their cargoes were probably more vital
than the Spitfires at this stage since food, petrol and ammunition were almost exhausted in Malta. A certain amount of fuel
and ammunition was being taken in by submarine, and by
transport aircraft at night; but the daily expenditure of fuel and
ammunition far exceeded this rate of supply.

There were two battle cruisers – HMS *Nelson* and *Rodney* –
and four aircraft carriers – HMS *Furious, Indomitable, Victorious*
and *Eagle* – with a large screen of cruisers and destroyers. In fact
it was more like a fleet than a convoy, a stirring sight as these
powerful ships moved steadily along in two lanes.

There were still some surplus pilots, and again I was dropped
off the list, but luckily I was again able to change places. We
were briefed by the carrier's Flying Control Officer on the
technique for take-off and some Malta pilots, who would be
leading sections into the Island, went over the route to be
followed and the procedure on arrival. Each pilot was issued
with a strip map made up from old French maps, marked
with the track headings and distances to be flown. The Spitfires were fitted with 90-gallon long-range tanks slung under
the fuselage, which doubled the fuel tankage and range of the
aircraft; but added an unseemly bulge to the graceful belly of
the Spitfire. As the ammunition boxes were empty, we were
able to fill that space with chocolates, sweets and cigarettes
bought in Gibraltar or at the ship's canteen, and a small kit

bag of personal gear was tied into the radio compartment.

The flaps on a Spitfire have only two positions – up for take-off, and down for landing – but to provide extra lift for take-off slim, wooden wedges were positioned between the flaps and wings. By selecting flaps down and up again after take-off, the wedges would fall free.

The Fleet Air Arm spokesman advised that if any aircraft proved unserviceable after take-off, the pilot should bale out ahead of a destroyer which, if not too busy, would pick him up. One Australian voiced a rude comment on that suggestion, so the navy man said that a landing could be attempted on one of the larger Fleet carriers – a successful Spitfire landing had, in fact, been made on *Wasp* earlier in the year by one of the Malta-bound pilots.*

We were to fly off the carrier in batches of eight, from a position about one hundred miles north of Algiers; and as it took some time to arrange each section of aircraft into position, the Captain invited pilots waiting their turn to watch from the bridge on top of the Control Tower or Island. *Furious* was in the right-hand lane of the convoy, but as the wind was from the port or left-hand side, *Furious* changed positions with *Eagle* in the left lane – in order to avoid disrupting the other ships when she turned into wind to fly off the Spitfires.

I was to be in the last section to fly off. From the Control Tower I saw four brown puffs rise from *Eagle*, which I assumed was gun fire: but they were, in fact, torpedo hits from a U-boat. *Eagle* just keeled over on her side, and sank in a matter of minutes. It was like watching a silent newsreel, but helplessly, with the grim knowledge that a thousand men were in peril right before one's eyes. Incredibly, the number of casualties proved to be quite low, which had to be due to the very high standard of navy training and discipline. As the destroyers charged in to hunt the U-boat and to pick up survivors, suddenly we became intent on parting company with *Furious* just as

---

* P/O Smith (Canada) landed back on USS *Wasp* in May 1942 after slipper tank fuel feed problem. Awarded US Navy Pilot's Wings to commemorate his feat.

quickly as we could. We had been warned of suspected enemy spying activity in Gibraltar, on the doorstep of neutral Spain, and we believed that the torpedoes had been meant for *Furious*.

The ship had now worked up to 30 knots into a fresh head wind, and we had chocks behind our wheels at the take-off position to stop the aircraft from being blown over the stern. As one of the pilots ahead of me opened up for take-off it was obvious, from the position of his elevators, that he was holding the stick hard back. I watched in horror as the Spitfire skidded across the deck to the left and plunged over the side, flipping over as it disappeared from sight. There was just a patch of foam to be seen as the ship raced by, and the unfortunate pilot must have gone straight down with his aircraft.

After take-off Al Stead, from Dunedin, drew the short straw as his engine would not pick up fuel from the long-range tank. Jettisoning the auxiliary tank he lowered the wheels and made a low pass over *Indomitable*, which turned into wind and showed him a green light.

The RAF method of landing in a very short distance is to stalk the landing strip at low level and low speed; but Al nearly flew into the hangar, as the ship pitched up on a big swell. Next time he sideslipped to the deck and landed safely. *Indomitable* carried a squadron of Sea Hurricanes and one of Grumman Martletts, and the Fleet Air Arm pilots were delighted to have a Spitfire delivered into their hands. The argument over who was going to fly it in action, however, was resolved when a night-landing Hurricane crashed into it, and both aircraft were pushed over the side.

Furious returned to Gibraltar after flying off the Spitfires. As the convoy approached the Straits of Pantelleria (known as 'Bomb Alley') it came under very heavy attack by aircraft from both North Africa and Sicily, and the remaining Fleet Air Arm pilots from *Victorious* had their hands well and truly full. Early in the action Al Stead was in the bottom hangar when *Indomitable* took two direct bomb hits which burst in the top hangar, causing heavy casualties, damage and fire; and a near-miss which also caused extensive damage. Al was petrified, he said, but full of admiration for the way the crew fought the fires, and dealt with a very hazardous situation.

Only four of the merchant ships reached Malta, one being the American tanker *Ohio*, which was 'cameled' in with decks nearly awash, and a destroyer lashed to each side.

The navy also repelled surface attacks by the Italian navy and, apart from *Eagle*, a number of cruisers and destroyers were lost from air attack when outside the range of the Malta Spitfires. The men of the Royal Navy and the Merchant Navy paid a grievously heavy price to keep 'aircraft-carrier Malta' afloat.

With a 50-knot head wind blowing straight down the deck my own aircraft was quickly airborne, and when the last of our group joined up we set off eastwards, climbing slowly to 12,000 ft in line abreast formation. Reaching the Galite Islands two hours later, we turned to take a short-cut across Cape Bon Peninsula. On that leg of the journey one of our number vanished from his position at the outside of the formation, and we never did learn what happened to him.

With about fifty miles to go, we descended to sea-level into the thin, brownish-tinged haze which was often a feature of the area. Sections of Spitfires covered our approach against marauding Me 109s, and we landed at Takali after a flight of three and a half hours. Airmen and soldiers swarmed over the aircraft as soon as the propeller stopped turning, and a Malta pilot was already waiting to step into the cockpit. They all had a good laugh when I emerged, with my swollen lip and clutching my pink elephant mascot; but I was exhausted, and all I wanted to do was crawl under the wing and lie down.

8

BULLY BEEF AND BED BUGS

For the first few days newly arrived pilots were quartered in Rabat, a small town perched on a low hill over looking Takali aerodrome. There we picked up the general outline of what went on in Malta, before being allocated to a squadron. Takali had two fighter squadrons, and Luqa airfield, a few miles to the south-east, also had two Spitfire squadrons, as well as accommodating Wellington bombers and torpedo-carrying Beauforts. Hal Far – in the south-east corner of the Island three miles from Luqa – had one Spitfire squadron and a Navy Flight of Swordfish torpedo-carrying aircraft.

There was an immense concentration of bomb damage on and around the airfields and in Grand Harbour, which itself was littered with sunken or damaged ships. Hundreds of houses built from local, soft limestone blocks were in ruins; but this same stone was easily worked and provided, ironically, a ready supply of filling for the bomb craters, while the stone construction of the buildings at least posed no fire hazard under bombing attack.

In early July, six weeks before Operation PEDESTAL, the increasing number of Spitfires on the Island had led to a change from purely defensive action when the raids arrived, with Spitfires now more free to go forward to intercept enemy attacks before they crossed the coast. In the first ten days of July 1942 over one hundred enemy aircraft had been shot down, for the loss of less than a quarter of that number in Spitfire pilots. In mid-July Air Vice-Marshal Lloyd handed over to Air Vice-Marshal Sir Keith Park, a New Zealander, and the outstanding Commander of Eleven Group in southern England during the Battle of Britain. He continued the development of more aggressive tactics by the Malta-based forces. The regular German bombing attacks had now given way to fighter sweeps by Me 109 and Italian Macchi 202 aircraft in stepped-up formations, operating at between 20,000 and 30,000 ft.

Greatly improved radio location equipment now gave the Malta Operations Room a high degree of accuracy in plotting incoming raids, which was well utilised by the Chief Controller, Group Captain A.B. Woodhall (the 'Woody' of *Reach for the Sky* fame). Woody's calm, imperturbable voice was our only link to the ground, and he inspired almost fanatical faith and confidence in his ability to control and direct the Spitfires for maximum results and minimum losses. The four squadrons based at Takali and Luqa operated as forward defence, their pilots being the first to be scrambled for interceptions. 185 Squadron at Hal Far continued in its Island Defence role, being mainly used to patrol the aerodrome areas when a raid was plotted on the board in the Operations Room.

In Rabat I was introduced to a gangling, fair-headed Sergeant Pilot wearing an Australian side cap, who ambled around looking mostly up at the sky. He was George 'Screwball' Beurling of the RCAF, who had already destroyed 14 enemy aircraft while flying with 249 Squadron from Takali. He was a unique, self-contained fighter pilot with complete mastery of his aircraft and of the complex art of aerial gunnery. He preferred to hunt alone, and was uninterested in promotion or in leading a formation of fighters. I gathered from what he said that, for these reasons, he had quickly found himself out of favour in a Canadian Squadron in the UK; but he was in his element in the Malta style of combat where pilots flew in sections of only four aircraft, and he was free to use his own initiative. He was amused to find that he was becoming an embarrassment to the higher echelons, as he was now the highest-scoring pilot on Malta; but he refused on principle to accept a commission, having been passed over for commissioning at his SFTS.

About two weeks before I flew into Malta, an incident occurred which probably qualifies as the first aerial hi-jacking.* A Beaufort from Luqa ditched after attacking an enemy convoy off Greece, and an Italian Cant float plane picked up the crew from their rubber dinghy. The Beaufort pilot was a South African (Lieutenant Strever), the navigator was English, and the wireless operator air gunners were Sergeants Brown and Wilkinson, New Zealanders from Timaru and Gisborne respectively. The Cant crew went to the island of Corfu for the night, and the prisoners were very well treated there, being given an excellent dinner followed by a lively party, and they slept in comfortable beds. The next morning they were put aboard the same Cant with the same crew – who were flying to Italy to go on leave – together with a corporal escort armed with a pistol.

During the flight west towards Italy Wilkinson suddenly flattened the Italian navigator with a punch to the jaw, hurdled over his falling body, and seized the escort's pistol. Lieutenant Strever then used the pistol to disarm the pilot, and the Italian second pilot was persuaded to fly the float plane south towards Malta. As the Island appeared ahead three Spitfires attacked the Cant, and a burst of fire through the wing prompted a hasty water landing, just as the Cant's engines were running out of fuel anyway. A launch towed them into Grand Harbour, which was one of the most bizarre arrivals the battered Port had ever seen.

The British crew apologised to the Italians for their lack of courtesy, in return for the hospitality they had been shown on Corfu; but the Italians seemed to cheerfully accept the reversal of their roles.

Jack Yeatman went to one of the Luqa squadrons, having learnt on arrival at Malta that his friend Matt McLeod had just been killed in action. I was duly posted to 185 Squadron at Hal Far airfield and was made to feel at home from the moment I

---

* See *Aeroplane Monthly*, vol. 11, nos. 7 & 8, July/August 1983; also Roy Conyers Nesbit, *Torpedo Airmen*, William Kimber, 1983.

entered the crew room. The CO was Major Swales (South
African Air Force) and my Flight Commander was Ken Charney – ex-602 Squadron in the UK – who had lived in Argentina
before going to school in England. There were Canadians,
Englishmen, two Americans, one Australian and one other New
Zealander on the squadron, and the variety of backgrounds
ensured that discussions were always interesting. Gray Stenberg, from Auckland, was the other New Zealander on 185
Squadron; and he was also one of the highest-scoring fighter
pilots on Malta. Gray was an amusing, volatile type. When I
arrived he had just been grounded for a week, after beating up
the aerodrome in his Spitfire. I gathered that the grounding was
not really a disciplinary action, but aimed at slowing him down,
so that he would depart from Malta still in one piece.

I was briefed on the local situation and learned that, while
the Maltese people were doing a fine job for the services –
including the many manning the anti-aircraft guns – a certain
amount of fifth column activity, or sabotage, was suspected.
This was not really surprising, in view of the mixture of nationalities living on the Island; and the fact that the Italians had
operated the airline services into Malta right up to their declaration of war.

While Malta was a fighter pilot's paradise as far as air fighting
was concerned, the reverse was true of our living conditions.
Food supplies were strictly rationed to a few ounces of bread –
supposedly nine but more like five ounces per day per man –
with half a tin of bully beef. Tea, sugar and butter was eked out
between issues, and staples such as potatoes were never seen.
We slept in commandeered quarters on the waterfront of Kalafrana Bay, and NCO pilots had their own mess, which was a
sensible move in that half the squadron pilots were at readiness
at all times, from dawn to dusk. We paid high messing fees to
enable the cook to buy extra sugar or tea on the flourishing black
market, and he devised a number of ways to deal with the bully
beef – but which was still just bully beef. An old, decrepit bus
with no glass in the windows took pilots to and from the airfield;
and in a gully beside the road stood the burnt-out skeleton of

one of the old Gladiators. From daybreak each morning four pilots sat strapped into their aircraft on the line at the edge of the airfield, four more waited beside their aircraft in the blast pens, and four more waited in the crew room. If the first section was scrambled the next one came on line, and those in the crew room moved into the pens. If there was no activity, sections changed places after two hours, which was certainly long enough to sit frying in the cockpit.

Ken Charney explained the Malta line-abreast formation, which was certainly simple and effective. Pilots flew about two hundred yards abeam of each other, and the section of four could turn to either side, or reverse its direction, without losing contact. Each pilot scanned the sky above, behind and below his neighbour; reporting any aircraft sighted to the section leader, who would normally call his instructions back on the RT. In combat each four would split into two pairs, thus attempting to at least maintain mutual cross cover. Enemy fighters would normally appear above the section, and Ken stressed the importance of carefully counting their numbers, if there was time, to avoid unpleasant surprises if the enemy should split up.

There was no practice flying in Malta, and the first scramble I flew on was uneventful; but on the second one Control had just reported twenty-plus bandits passing over the Hal Far area, when the RT was completely jammed up as the Takali boys went into action to the north. Watching across Ken Charney's tail I saw him waggling his wings, then half roll away down after a Macchi 202 which dived under him from head-on, so I went with him. The Macchi pilot pulled up again and turned in front of Ken, who got in a long burst to send the Macchi over on its back and into the sea. Back in the crew room Ken asked me what I had seen; then he quietly told me that another Macchi had made a head-on firing pass at me, which was why he had waggled his wings, being unable to warn me because of the RT chatter. Thereafter I made a point of looking ahead much more often.

A built-in problem in Malta was 'Malta Dog', a form of

diarrhoea which afflicted all new arrivals and often persisted for months on end. Attacks were sudden, painful and unavoidable; and coupled with the minimal ration scale meant that most of us lost weight steadily, thus further reducing resistance to sickness. Climbing away on a scramble one morning a Canadian voice on the RT called: 'Black One from Black Two, I'm going down – got the dog', then about ten seconds later: 'Black Two rejoining – too late.'

One of the Americans on 185 Squadron was Sergeant Weaver, from Oklahoma, who claimed that he was 100 per cent American, but born of 100 per cent German parents who had settled in the States. He was restless on the ground, highly aggressive in the air, and had already shot down five enemy aircraft and been awarded the DFM. He was tall and powerfully built, with a thatch of blond hair which grew straight up in a thick crew-cut. After a raid by German Ju 88s and Italian Cant bombers, Operations reported that a Cant had force-landed, but no pilot had claimed it. Weaver had fired a short burst at a Cant, so he lodged a claim; but the remarkable George Beurling nominated the number and location of the few strikes he had made on a Cant, commenting that it was so lightly damaged he had not bothered to mention it. It turned out that the Cant in question carried the identical strikes which Beurling had itemised.

Fresh water was in short supply, and there was no hot water at all; which made hygiene a myth, and helped to spread the various complaints around. While we were half-starved the mosquitos, sandflies, bed bugs and fleas fed very well; and I was soon reminded that bites and stings had unpleasant effects on me, while several of the Canadians reacted in the same way. The tiny sandfly – only a fraction of the size of the New Zealand variety – was particularly virulent, and the fighter pilots were supposed to be issued with special fine-mesh sleeping nets, which the sandfly could not penetrate; but the Medical Officer told me that supplies of these nets had run out.

Bridge playing was the popular pastime in the crew room and in the messes, with marathon games running on for days on end.

It was surprising how often the scores would even up over a prolonged period of play. Our NCO Pilots' Mess hosted challenges from the Officers' Mess, and one evening we broke off for supper as a new hand was dealt. On resuming, the opener bid a grand slam, which precipitated a quiet evening into a violent screaming match, as the other three players wildly protested their own bids. Each player had a full suit in his hand, and it would need a computer to work out the odds against such a fall of the cards. A spluttering noise from the corner revealed the joker who had substituted the rigged hands of cards and, naturally enough, it was one of our Australian friends.

We had a bar which was largely ornamental, for no supplies of beer or spirits were available. The local vino (called Ambete) would turn the lips purple, and had other devastating effects on the system; it was not recommended for the uninitiated, and was known locally as 'Stuka Juice'. While on board the carrier on the way out to Malta, all the NCO pilots had been allocated a daily ration of neat rum; but as many of the pilots turned it down, I had been able to collect two quart bottles of this 'Nelson's Blood', which I handed over to the mess. Well watered down, and fairly dispensed while it lasted, it provided a suitable antidote for the bug bites.

During the latter part of August and the first weeks of September there was a lull in the bombing against Malta. Enemy activity was confined to sweeps by twenty or thirty Me 109s, and I flew about every third day on scrambles, as sweeps were plotted by the Operations Room. The squadrons based at Takali and Luqa were now regularly meeting the enemy Me 109 forces between Malta and Sicily, and we saw only small formations high above us, as they turned over the Island and dived away for home.

Meanwhile, in the UK the United States Eighth Air Force operated for the first time when twelve Flying Fortresses, escorted by RAF Spitfires, mounted an attack on the Rouen railway yards. The costly Dieppe raid took place, provoking a major battle between the Luftwaffe and RAF Fighter Command; and this coincided with the beginning of the Battle of

Stalingrad. Since early July Rommel's forces and the Eighth Army had been holding static positions at El Alamein, as each side built up its supplies and troop reinforcements.

On 17 September 1942 our section had been scrambled to patrol the eastern end of the Island, and when control advised that Me 109s were around Hal Far we went into a steep dive from 23,000 ft. Passing through 7000 ft, and with no warning whatever, I was hit with the most excruciating and indescribable pain in the forehead, and was blinded by a glaring white light, as if I was looking into the sun. Punching myself in the forehead and screaming in agony, I wanted to die then and there; but the Spitfire literally retrieved the situation, without any help from myself. I had gone flying with a slight head cold and the sinus passage had blocked in the dive, causing tremendous internal pressure which distorted the bone structure above my left eye. It was impossible to trim a Spitfire Mk V to fly hands-off in a steep, high-speed dive; and when I took both hands off the control column, the aircraft reared out of the dive and climbed up again. My vision cleared, and when I was back at about 11,000 ft the pain became bearable. Letting down slowly I returned to Hal Far to find I was stone-deaf in the left ear, which lasted for three days; and also had a sizeable lump on my forehead, which has never quite disappeared. I realised then what Ash must have gone through many times with his blocked sinuses, and could only salute his fortitude.

Three days later I flew again, to find I was blacking out in quite moderate turns. By this time I had lost over a stone and a half in weight, while the insect bites had become a suppurating mass on my arms, legs, face and ears. Ken Charney chased me off to see the young Medical Officer, who refused to look me over outside his morning sick parade hours. I reckon he was on borrowed time anyway, for Ken made some phone calls and the MO was told to pack his bags for Cairo via the next submarine. Meanwhile, an ambulance took me to Imtarfa Military Hospital where I promptly acquired a case of tonsillitis, three days before my twentieth birthday.

Again I was very fortunate, as the hospital Medical Officers decided that the problem arose from under-nourishment, accentuated by a too persistent case of Malta Dog; and I was assigned an unrestricted diet, in a ward of twenty airmen who had digestive problems. The food was marvellous, and included dehydrated potatoes, dried egg, spam, fresh green vegetables, dried-milk puddings, cheese and fresh fruit. The final touch was that everyone in the ward was given a bottle of Guinness each evening and, as some of the patients could not keep it down, the Ward Corporal and I used to polish off the spares over a game of cards, and I slept very well indeed.

Many of the airmen in the hospital were quite ill, having been exposed to danger, disease and short rations for up to two years, living and working in the most primitive conditions. Talking to those in the ward, I realised just how much worse their living conditions must be, and how endless the conflict must seem to men cut off from civilised amenities for so long. As NCO pilots we at least had the privacy of our own mess, and could afford to pay for extras, when available. Also, we were unlikely to stay on Malta for more than a few months anyway. I was embarrassed when several walking patients appointed themselves as a sort of personal valet service, even to the extent of making my bed each morning, and delivering my meals. The Ward Corporal pointed out that, for a very long time, all their efforts had been concentrated on keeping their aircraft serviceable for their pilots to fly, and this was their way of helping me to get back in the air as fast as possible, as a substitute for taking care of their own aircraft.

As the build-up of the opposing armies in Egypt approached its zenith, the Luftwaffe mustered its strength for another full-scale blitz on Malta, which began a couple of weeks after I had arrived in Imtarfa Hospital. The first raid consisted of 58 bombers escorted by fighters, but the forward interception system worked well, and the Spitfires destroyed eight bombers and seven fighters in the first encounter. The Germans used a total force of 600 aircraft in this blitz, against which Malta could now field 60 Spitfires, but bombers and fighters did still get through to attack the airfields and Grand Harbour.

As Imtarfa Hospital was on the top of a low hill beside Rabat,

exactly one mile from the boundary of Takali airfield, it suddenly became a very unhealthy place to be living. The Ju 88s
sometimes passed directly overhead in a shallow dive on to
Takali, and one could look up and watch the bombs leaving the
aircraft. When the Spitfires attacked during this final run-in a
lot of bombs were jettisoned, causing us some nervous moments.
In an earlier blitz a hospital block had been demolished, killing
a considerable number of off-duty medical staff. When the
attack began on 11 November I had already put on nearly a
stone, so I began to agitate to be released from hospital. It was
another ten days before I was examined by the Chief Medical
Officer, who gave me the option of going home to New Zealand,
or back to the United Kingdom; but he was persuaded to release
me back to 185 Squadron. The blitz stopped the day I said
goodbye to my friends in the ward, and on the following day –
23 October 1942 – the Eighth Army attacked at El Alamein.

This proved to be the last blitz against Malta, but in it 80
people were killed by bombing, and 469 buildings were destroyed or damaged. No airfield was rendered unserviceable for
more than half an hour, however. And on every night, except
one, the Malta torpedo-carrying aircraft and bombers had continued their strikes against Axis shipping. In twelve days the
Spitfires destroyed 132 enemy aircraft and probably destroyed
another 64, while the guns accounted for eight more; against
a loss of 31 Spitfires.

I was very happy to rejoin the squadron and to find that, despite
usually being last squadron up, the pilots had achieved a respectable number of aircraft destroyed and damaged. George Beurling had been awarded a bar to his DFM and he had destroyed
29½ enemy aircraft when he finally accepted a commission on
the direct order of the Air Officer Commanding, Sir Keith
Park. Beurling was wounded in the foot in October; and survived when the Liberator he flew out in as a passenger overshot
the airstrip at Gibraltar and had crashed into the sea. Earlier we
heard that he sometimes made an inverted approach to land,
rolling over at quite low level to put the wheels on the runway.

Our American Sergeant Weaver set out to emulate the man-oeuvre. First he tried a pass across the aerodrome inverted, and at very low level; but forgot to put the gun button to 'Safe'. Pushing on the control column to keep the nose up he hit the gun button, sending a decent burst over the head of Sir Keith Park, who was visiting the Flying Control position. After being grounded for a week, Weaver was shot down on his next sortie, force-landing on a beach in Sicily.

German activity had abruptly declined to sporadic raids by fighter-bombers and fighter sweeps high above the Island, as the Desert war peaked; while Malta-based anti-shipping strikes continued at full pressure. When the 185 Squadron line-readiness section scrambled to engage a German fighter sweep, I flew in the standby section which followed them up; but the Me 109s were already heading for Sicily. Danny, one of the Canadian pilots, had his aircraft shot up, and Sergeant Saunders destroyed a Me 109 in their brief encounter. The next day we again scrambled against a plot of twelve enemy fighters. The RT went berserk as the Me 109s pounced out of the sun onto the leading section, as it emerged from the haze at about 10,000 ft. Sergeant Saunders was shot down and killed but when we, in our turn, flew into clear air, there was not an aircraft to be seen.

With the fuel and general supply situation relieved, in November we began flying standing patrols and also convoy patrols over shipping, which was now getting into Malta free of constant air attack. The hammering the Spitfires had been taking in combat and under primitive ground conditions began to take its toll, however, and the squadron lost two pilots drowned in ditchings after engine failures.

The surface of Hal Far aerodrome was rough as a result of the filled-in bomb craters on the surface, and the finely ground stone-dust covering the surface sometimes caused malfunctions in the aircraft and their guns. The surprisingly high number of aircraft serviceable each day was an eloquent tribute to the dedication of the ground crews, despite their physical debilitation and the chronic shortage of servicing facilities.

The dust on the airfield also posed a hazard on each scramble.

Once, as I watched a section of four scramble from the line in the usual echelon starboard, our Australian Flight Sergeant's aircraft lagged behind the leader, to be enveloped in the dense plume of dust fanning out behind. His Spitfire reared up above the rolling, brown blanket; but stalled and crashed into a tangled heap, inflicting severe injuries on the pilot.

When the Allied troops under General Eisenhower landed in French North Africa on 8 November 1942, the writing was obviously on the wall for the Axis forces. A week later, therefore, Air Vice-Marshal Park directed that Malta Spitfires should now take the offensive, beginning with sweeps over Sicily by full squadrons, instead of operating in separate sections of four aircraft. At the same time four aircraft of 185 Squadron were fitted with ingenious bomb-carriers which had been designed locally and made up in the Malta naval dockyard.

On 28 November I flew one of four Spitfires which carried a 250-lb bomb under each wing to dive-bomb Gela Aerodrome in Sicily, while eight more squadron aircraft flew cover for us on the run-up to the target. This is believed to be the first time that Spitfires operated in the fighter-bomber role. Major Swales had by now returned to the UK, and our new CO climbed right up to the cloud base of 12,000 ft on the run-up, before peeling off to dive at the target. We quickly lost sight of each other in the prolonged dive and, as the airspeed built up, I had to use both hands to hold the nose down on the target, before releasing the bombs in the direction of some aerodrome buildings, then I headed back at high speed towards Malta.

A faint call from Malta Control reported bandits at 10,000 ft in the area and, as I shot out low over the coast I saw eight Ju 52 aircraft in close formation below me, heading for North Africa. The Ju 52 was a three-engine transport aircraft with fixed undercarriage which had been used effectively in the Battle of Crete, and was reputed to carry about fifty armed troops. Calling a sighting report to the Squadron Leader – and to come and give me a hand – I attacked in turn each of the three aircraft on the left of the formation, starting with the rear one. As the 20-mm guns fired only one round I had to do the best I could with the four .303 machine guns, and was surprised by the amount of return fire from the formation. At least some of the aircraft had upper gun turrets, and it also appeared that some irate passengers were using automatic weapons through the windows. The first Ju 52 dropped below the formation and turned towards Sicily, and the next two were still descending steeply towards the sea when the Me 109 escort came diving down, and I ducked into a handy cloud.* The return fire had taken some effect. There was a bullet through the mirror above the windscreen, and an oil line in the engine had been grazed, causing oil to flow back over the cowling and the cockpit cover.

Back at Hal Far I was astounded when the Squadron Leader said he had heard my radio call and had sighted the transports; but that our task had been to drop bombs – not to go chasing after enemy aircraft. My response to that made it clear that I was unlikely to succeed as a career diplomat. Sir Keith Park later questioned me on the incident and it seemed that, while Malta radar had picked up the fighter escort at 10,000 ft, the transport formation at low level had not been detected. About one week later a telephone call from Headquarters advised that the 'Y Service' had confirmed at least one Ju 52 crashing into the sea. 'Y Service' was a unit which specialised in monitoring enemy RT communications, and was a useful source of information for Intelligence.

Allied Forces in the desert were bringing more and more weight to bear against Rommel, and Malta Headquarters reported that more airlifts were being made by German transport aircraft from Sicily, carrying troop reinforcements and fuel. Another report came in that a build-up of German fighters was suspected on the airfield at Lampedusa, a small Italian island half-way between Malta and Tunisia, and about one hundred miles from Malta. I was one of a section of four, led by Flight Sergeant Walker, detailed to make a reconnaissance of the

---

* German records show that three Ju 52s were lost between Biserta and Reggio that day as a result of fighter action, one crashing in flames. They all belonged to Transportverbände Einsatz Mittelmeer Afrika and were from K.Gr.z.b.V.,S.11 (Brindisi).

aerodrome. The plan was to fly past the island at 6000 ft, then turn about and dive low across the aerodrome, and on back to base.

Our briefing from Headquarters advised that no Allied aircraft would be anywhere near Lampedusa, and that we should be on the lookout for enemy aircraft from the island. But what began as an interesting sortie ended in a kind of personal nightmare.

The patrol went as planned as we turned and dived in wide line abreast over the aerodrome, where only a couple of twin-engined Italian aircraft were to be seen on the ground. As we crossed out very fast at 200 ft a violent barrage of light flak chased us. I glanced ahead and saw a single-engine aircraft with floats flying low to my left, visible in the bright glare of the sun off the water, and about 500 yds away. Giving a quick call to the Section Leader, I turned in and down, opening fire at 200 yds. For once both cannons fired, pounding into the sea ahead of the target, while the pattern from the four machine guns was churning the surface slightly behind it; so I pulled through to hit the wing-root, cockpit and engine area with the machine guns. Simultaneously I glimpsed a roundel on the fuselage and recognised the target as a Hurricane, with long-range fuel tanks under each wing, which I had mistaken for floats. I broke away, and screamed over the RT to the other pilots who were turning into attacking positions. From start to finish the sighting and the attack were over in about six seconds; then began forty-five minutes of the ultimate form of self-torture for any fighter pilot. The Hurricane was well riddled in the wing-root and lower cockpit area, a sizeable chunk of the wing leading edge was missing and the pilot's airspeed was down to 120 mph as he nursed the aircraft along, right down at sea-level. I realised that the Hurricane came from a small Royal Naval Air Service unit at Hal Far which operated anti-shipping Swordfish and also possessed a couple of Sea Hurricanes.

Malta appeared out of the haze after what felt like several lifetimes. The Hurricane pilot lowered his wheels and landed straight in at Hal Far, slithering round to the right and stopping in a great cloud of dust on the edge of the field. By the time I completed a circuit and landed, the ambulance was disappearing towards the camp hospital, which screwed my anxiety level right off the clock again. I arrived at the hospital breathless and knocking at the knees to find the Naval Lieutenant Pilot unhurt, which testifies to the benevolence of both our guardian angels on duty that day. He had been returning from a courier flight to Headquarters Middle East. To relieve the boredom of just stooging along over hundreds of miles of ocean, he had detoured to Lampedusa to strafe shipping in the harbour beside the aerodrome. Pulling out from his last attack the wing of his Hurricane had hit the mast of a schooner, and he was just staggering away amongst a storm of flak when we arrived on his back. He said his worst moment was when the tyre of his starboard wheel had blown apart beneath his right foot, and he had no idea he was being attacked by a fighter until I pulled up alongside him.

The Lieutenant very decently said that he had asked for trouble by attacking the harbour without orders; and we both had enormous strips ripped off us by the authorities, in my case for 'bloody awful' aircraft recognition. A check on my aircraft showed that the 20-mm guns were, in fact, incorrectly harmonised well above the machine guns, which had been the best of good luck for both of us.

In mid-November the siege of Malta was finally raised, when a large supply convoy from Egypt reached the Island intact. Since the beginning of 1942 alone the Navy had lost three cruisers, nine destroyers and two aircraft carriers in reinforcing Malta, while a total of 744 fighters had been ferried into the Mediterranean by the carriers during the two-year siege.

Rations now began to improve, easing the incidence of disease and the effects of under-nourishment; but it really became clear that the battle was over when some enterprising souls – we heard they were soldiers – got the brewery back into production. The second issue was four one-pint bottles of beer per head, which arrived on an afternoon when Zip Zobell, a Canadian Sergeant, and myself were amongst those off duty until noon the next day. Neither of us had been to Valletta, and the euphoria created by this brew carried us on to the rattletrap civilian bus, and into the bars and dives of Valletta night life.

It was a case of the blind leading the blind, as there was no moon and a strict black-out prevailed. Early on, having extricated ourselves from a small bar where the natives were unfriendly, we blundered into an art class in a night school where a young man was modelling a head of Mussolini, which we insisted on improving by wiping off the ears and nose. Further along we joined a boisterous party of Greeks celebrating a family wedding. Most of the group had fled from Greece when the army pulled out; and they had fond memories of the New Zealanders, which they demonstrated with loud and lavish hospitality. I awoke in a dormitory surrounded by cheerful sailors, who assured me that I had really enjoyed the rest of my night out with the navy. The morning bus back to Kalafrana had four square wheels, and Zip was also suffering much pain when he showed up at lunchtime.

Ken Charney had returned to the UK while I was in hospital, and as pilot reinforcements were now plentiful, a general dispersal of squadron pilots had begun. I was attracted to the Desert Air Force style of operations, but realised it would be a mistake to stay within range of man-eating insects, so I elected to return to the UK.

One of my regular bridge partners had been Geoff Guy; a steady, pipe-smoking English pilot who refused to be flustered in any situation. He was one of those who just simply went missing, between Sicily and Malta. My last flight with 185 Squadron was a search for Geoff; but the sea was empty.

The Liberator being used as a transport took off from Luqa at 2 a.m. and the Polish pilot flew at 16,000 ft for most of the six-hour flight to Gibraltar. Without protective clothing or oxygen the Malta pilots on board were frozen into semi-consciousness for most of the journey. I reflected wryly that the physical discomforts of my arrival and departure had been well matched by the conditions during my stay. On the other hand I had taken a small part in the tail-end of the Malta saga, which was now already passing into history.

I left Malta with a clear philosophy towards air fighting which I endeavoured to practise for the rest of the war. This was really a matter of simple arithmetic. It made good sense – and good economics – to shoot down one with no loss. It made no sense at all to shoot down one aircraft but to lose one pilot or more in return. I had learnt some part of the fighter pilot's trade under the enlightened style of leadership in Malta. This included the principle that sub-section leaders had built-in responsibilities for the safety of an inexperienced Number Two, otherwise the balance sheet could well be bad news – particularly for the unfortunate Number Two.

In Gibraltar the story was going round that one of the courier flights between Gibraltar and the United Kingdom had ended in some trouble for the crew. Courier aircraft regularly flew night flights carrying dispatches and VIP passengers each way; and this had become something of a 'milk-run', free from molestation by German night fighters.

Gibraltar was 'ration free' and 'duty free', so a brisk trade had developed into the UK with cigarettes and the like concealed inside items of aircraft equipment, which Customs Officers were not permitted to examine. Then a Lockheed Hudson (medium bomber) courier aircraft had been intercepted by a Ju 88 night fighter over the Bay of Biscay; but after the air gunners had fired the top layers of belted .303 ammunition from the panniers, chocolate bars and cigarettes had proved to be no substitute for bullets.

I talked in Gibraltar with soldiers from British regiments who had fought up and down the Desert with the Eighth Army. They made no secret of their admiration for the achievements and reliability of the New Zealand Division in the Middle East and they also envied the relaxed, informal but effective link between officers and men which was another hallmark of the New Zealanders. This became symbolised by the well-known complaint of a British Officer to General 'Tiny' Freyberg VC, who commanded the New Zealand Division. When this officer objected that New Zealand soldiers on leave in Cairo did not salute him, Tiny Freyberg advised: 'Try waving to them, I'm sure they will wave back.'

As with all New Zealanders serving with the Royal Air Force, I followed the exploits of the Second NZEF with great interest and admiration; and the word had filtered through that the Division had established the right command structure from the top down. An officer who proved to be incompetent in action was removed or demoted, and a considerable number of men were actually commissioned in the field. The Army command policy throughout the fighting units precisely paralleled our thinking when one third of our Course had been commissioned at Woodbourne.*

After stocking up with luxuries in Gibraltar, six ex-Malta pilots sailed in one of a convoy of troopships returning from the French North African theatre. The only other passengers were crewmen from Royal Navy ships which had been sunk while supporting the landings. Some of these men had survived as many as four sinkings since the war began, and they were understandably jumpy at travelling as passengers in a merchant vessel; but I was struck by their conviction that there would be no real worries as soon as they picked up another navy ship.

Seeing a group of Customs Officers boarding from the pilot launch as we steamed up the Mersey, the Naval contingent cursed their luck – and ours. I recalled that Service equipment

---

* In 1955 I joined the Officers Club in Hamilton (south of Auckland) and made many friends amongst the predominantly ex-Army members. Colonel Playle DSO was the President, a man of few words with an outstanding record of war service. If anyone addressed him as Colonel or 'Sir' he would go red in the face and growl: 'The name is Joe.'

Phil and Morrie West were identical twins who had been Captains in the pre-war Territorial Army, and then in the wartime Home Forces. They had dropped their rank and joined the Division in the Middle East as sergeants, to be commissioned again in the field, returning to New Zealand as captains. Their younger brother Geoff went overseas as a Sergeant Pilot and was flying Number Two to Douglas Bader on the sortie when Bader was obliged to bale out over France. Geoff then fought with distinction in Malta during the height of the Battle, and returned to New Zealand as Squadron Leader West DFM.

was supposed to be exempt from examination, and our Air Force group hastily tossed out the bulky flotation pads from our 'Mae West' style lifejackets, stuffing the vacant space with silk stockings and other choice items. With the jackets draped over our shoulders, it was hard not to laugh as the disbelieving Customs men pawed through the contents of our kit bags, rudely dumped out on the deck.

9

SCOTLAND AND CORNWALL

I arrived back in England from Malta right on Christmas 1942, and spent two weeks' leave in London, shivering my way from clubs to pubs, where the warmth and hospitality inside banished the raw cold of that grey winter outside.

As always, London was the cross-roads for thousands of service people from all parts of the world, some in groups of their own nationality, others intermingling in briefly bound friendships before moving on, each to his own destination.

I was amused to see a demonstration of private enterprise in a Charing Cross pub where a party of New Zealand naval ratings were raffling a fat Christmas turkey at half-a-crown a ticket. A little chap in a shabby raincoat scuttled out of the crowd to claim his turkey. Several pubs later the same turkey went to the same little man, as the sailors raked in some spending money.

The widening scope and intensity of the war was brought home by the much greater number of service people, including Americans, now to be seen in London; and the fact that I ran across only one familiar face. He was a Canadian pilot from the refresher flying course before we moved on to operational training units early in 1942. He was sitting alone in the New Zealand Forces Club, and as he turned towards me I jokingly asked if he had a stiff neck – as he moved his head and shoulders together – before I saw he was wearing a plaster collar. Hawkins was a dead-pan type who did not say much, and he handed me some newspaper clippings which explained his stiff neck. He was flying with a Spitfire squadron when his aircraft was badly shot up over the French coast. The engine seized up and the elevator was jammed solid, with the aircraft diving steeply towards England. He managed to jettison the cockpit hood; but he could not pull up, roll the aircraft over and bale out in the recommended way. He started to force his way out of the cockpit but, with his body only half way out, the parachute streamed from his seat pack and caught on the rigid radio mast behind the cockpit, ripping and tearing itself to pieces in the violent airflow. He operated the quick-release catch on his parachute harness, and the whole lot was plucked away. He then twisted himself round and managed to grasp the base of the radio mast, then swung his body out and up on to the top of the fuselage. But he could not hang on to the mast against the blast of the airstream, which blew him straight down the fuselage and pinned him against the vertical tail fin.

Hawkins's weight at the tail reduced the diving angle, and he just rode the crippled Spitfire all the way down to the Channel at about 150 mph. As the nose of the aircraft hit the water the tail flipped up, catapulting him up and away like a rag doll, to splash down with an almighty thump which broke his neck and knocked him out. A Royal Air Force High Speed Rescue Launch raced in to fish him out, and with his head carefully wedged between sandbags, he was rushed to hospital.

When I met him in the Club he was classed as 'walking wounded'; his vertebrae tied up with silver wire and his torso encased in plaster. Hawkins expected to be cleared again for non-operational flying only, but figured he had used up most of his luck anyway.

I spent a couple of hilarious days with a carefree group which included a most attractive Australian WAAC who was over six feet tall, and was introduced as 'The Boundary Rider's Sister'. After walking her back to her billet in a commandeered house she looked down at me and said: 'Go up two steps, Kiwi, and I'll kiss you goodnight.'

I also met a husky Australian Flight Sergeant who had one hand in plaster and the other heavily bandaged and who was the target of some ribald comments. He had ditched his Spitfire in the Channel after being shot up on a bomber escort into France, as he was unable to bale out because the canopy was jammed shut. The Spitfire was a difficult aircraft to ditch successfully at any time, and in the choppy conditions it dived straight to the sea bed in fairly shallow water, close to the English coast. As water spurted into the cockpit he threw off his safety harness and parachute straps to attack the canopy with his fists, in a frenzy of super strength bursting the canopy clear and popping to the surface. He was now bemoaning the fact that he was unable to buy a Tatts ticket (Tattersall's Australian lottery), and was having trouble holding his pint glass.

After two weeks I was posted to a new Search and Rescue squadron being formed up in the north of Scotland, where the railway line ends. As I had what amounted to a phobia of being shuffled off into backwaters away from operational flying I strongly suspected that this outfit was not for me.

After freezing for three days on the snow-and-slush-bound aerodrome at Castletown, two more pilots arrived together with the squadron leader – who delivered a mind-boggling pep talk to the effect that this was going to be the very best unit in the whole of the RAF . . . 'best foot forward . . shoulders to the wheel' etc. He then proudly announced that our first aircraft was expected any day. I put a leave pass in front of the squadron leader for his signature which he handed back, saying that leave would come later. Next morning a Walrus Amphibian aircraft (flown by a navy sub-lieutenant) ground its way into the circuit, landed and trundled up to the dispersal area. Despite my admiration for the rescue work carried out by the Walrus crews I stared in disbelief at this old-fashioned biplane with its wooden pusher propeller, and its fuselage built like a mini-submarine.

After lunch the squadron leader detailed me to start conversion training on the machine, but in an eleventh-hour attempt to delay the evil moment I protested that, where I came from, Commanding Officers led from the front. So the squadron leader duly climbed into the monster, the sub-lieutenant flew a demonstration take-off, circuit and landing; then handed over to the squadron leader at the dual controls. We saw the Walrus head off down the runway and lurch into the air, turn quickly to land again, and stop at the dispersal area. The sub-lieutenant fell out of the hatchway helpless with laughter, then the squadron leader emerged clutching the control wheel. Apparently the squadron leader had the machine pounding along at flying speed when the sub said: 'Righto, pull her off now', and as his pupil pulled back, the control wheel came off in his hands.

The CO progressed to his office in a daze. I slipped the leave pass in front of him, which he signed like a lamb. Thirty minutes later I checked out of the guard house, hitch-hiked to Thurso, and caught the night train to London where I made straight for the RAF Postings Unit. For ten days I haunted RNZAF Headquarters in the mornings and RAF Postings in the afternoons, with a variety of compelling reasons why I should go back to an operational squadron instead of being cast away miles from anywhere and in such an unsuitable role.

It seemed that I had been trapped by the edict that six months was the maximum tour of duty in Malta at that time, to be followed by a mandatory period of six months clear of front-line operations. But on the tenth day the authorities gave in, and signalled RAF Castletown that I was posted to 602 Squadron, in Ten Group. Every hour of the dreary two-day journey back to Castletown to obtain a station clearance was worth it; then all the way back again to London, and west to 602 Squadron at Perranporth in Cornwall.

I looked into the New Zealand Forces Club in London on the way, and met Marty Hume and Evan (Rosie) Mackie from 485 Squadron, Evan being en route to the Middle East. 485 Squadron had moved south again into Eleven Group after its rest period in Twelve Group, and was once again being hammered by the FW 190s in sweeps and escorts over France. But there was good news too – the squadron had been given a definite undertaking for early re-equipment with the new Spitfire Mk IX, and would then be able to fight on more equal terms.

When I arrived at 602 Squadron on 30 January 1943, I was delighted to find that the CO was Squadron Leader Mike

Baytagh, the genial Irishman who had been Chief Flying Instructor of my Hurricane OTU early in 1942. I settled in with a very happy squadron of mixed nationalities, which included a Polish Sergeant Pilot called Charlie Zerionoski, who had been a boxing champion in Poland. He was a cheerful type with the constitution of an ox, who drank only neat whisky and in copious quantities; but seemed only to get happier in the process, and never passed out or fell over.

Three weeks later Mike Baytagh showed me a signal in which 485 Squadron 'Request Posted' me back to that squadron. He explained that the CO of a squadron could request a pilot from another unit, but the decision was left to the pilot concerned. I did not really want to leave 602, which had such a tremendous atmosphere; but we were only doing convoy patrols in Ten Group, so I accepted the posting and rejoined 485 Squadron on 18 February 1943 at Westhampnett, a satellite field of Tangmere RAF station in Sussex.

10

TANGMERE SECTOR

Reg Grant was still CO of 485 Squadron, but in seven months there had been some changes, particularly amongst the Sergeants. There was an air of enthusiasm and energy abroad, despite the fact that 485 Squadron still flew Mk V Spitfires in the weaving formation, and the FW 190 was still on top.

During the squadron's rest period in semi-operational Twelve Group, several low-level 'Rhubarb' operations were flown by sections of four aircraft, which could be costly and for little return. Headquarters were generally reluctant to authorise this style of offensive operation, but when fighter sweeps or escorts were in abeyance, boredom and impatience soon set in. In that sort of climate it was inevitable that unauthorised low flying and beating up would flourish as pilots gave way to frustration, increasing the risk of aircraft accidents and unnecessary casualties. So the occasional 'Rhubarb' did act as a safety valve and, even though the casualty rate was high, some damage was done to the enemy in occupied territory, and no doubt it was a boost to civilian morale to see Allied aircraft overhead at low-level. The Luftwaffe probably had a similar problem, but their response was the hit-and-run-raiders (usually FW 190s) which spasmodically bombed and strafed the beach fronts at Brighton and Bournemouth, which were still holding-areas for large numbers of RAF aircrew.

A bunch of FW 190s had jumped a 'Rhubarb' section led by jovial Mick Shand who was shot down and taken prisoner, while Sergeant Norris (later reported killed in action) was posted missing, and Tommy Tucker's aircraft hit a stop bank during the hectic scrap, denting the underside of his engine cowling.

Doug Brown and Murray Metcalfe had shot up a train and some barges in the Ghent area on another 'Rhubarb', but Doug's aircraft took a 40-mm shell in the tail on the way out, while the canopy virtually exploded and ejected itself clear of the cockpit. The aircraft was momentarily stalled, elevator control was considerably impaired and airspeed reduced. It says a great deal for the toughness of the Spitfire, and for Doug's strength and ability, that they made it safely across 100 miles of sea to Martlesham Heath. The starboard tail-plane and rudder were a horrifying mess, but fortunately the elevator itself had escaped serious damage.

Reg Grant's younger brother Ian had joined 485 Squadron, but when the squadron tangled with FW 190s on 13 February Ian had been killed, and Tony Robson taken prisoner. Reg destroyed the FW 190 which had attacked Ian; while Marty Hume also destroyed one, and Doug Brown damaged another in the same engagement.

Doug Brown, George Moorehead and Max Sutherland had been commissioned, while the sergeants who had joined the squadron at King's Cliffe included Chalky White, Bluey Meagher and Tommy Tucker. Early in March Reg Grant had the four of us sign applications for a commission and, from his remarks, I gathered that Reg did not agree with the system either. As soon as a NCO had proved reliable in action, Reg expected him to be commissioned without delay. The next move was an interview with the Station and Sector Commander, followed by a final interview with the Air Officer Commanding. Chalky and Blue went off to Tangmere – the parent station – and returned with some unprintable comments. Chalky was first to be seen by the Station Commander, and confirmed that he had, indeed, been a professional sheep shearer in New Zealand and Australia – only to be told by the Group Captain that the standard of officers was getting far too low in the RAF, he intended to see that it improved, and could not recommend him for a commission. Chalky agreed he had shot nothing down, and pointed out that the FW 190 was a tough proposition for the Spitfire V. The Group Captain then asked if he had ever fired at an enemy aircaft, and Chalk said: 'Yes – I opened fire on a 190 yesterday at five hundred yards, and closed in to a thousand yards.'

So the Group Captain dismissed him and it was Bluey's turn. Blue was born in Tasmania, but brought up in the coal-mining and saw-milling area of the West Coast of the South Island of New Zealand, where he had his own carrier business before joining up, and had been a prominent amateur boxer. The Group Captain handed out the same comments to Blue, who told him what to do with the commission and walked out.

Reg Grant was disappointed that his recommendations had been over-ruled, but we gathered that the matter was far from closed. A week or so later Blue neatly dispatched a Me 109 during a bomber escort, and when Group Captain Paddy Crisham took over as Tangmere Station and Sector Commander shortly afterwards, we each had an amiable talk with him; followed by an equally pleasant interview with the Air Officer Commanding Eleven Group, Air Vice-Marshal Sir Hugh Saunders. The AOC had been Chief of Staff of the RNZAF from 1939 to 1941 at the time the Empire Air Training Scheme had been implemented, and was a gifted and respected senior officer. While we were en route to the United Kingdom from New Zealand on *Rangitiki* we had been anchored off Bermuda for two days, and the Air Vice-Marshal had thoughtfully signalled a personal 'Good Luck' message across from his own ship, in which he was returning to the United Kingdom.

Successfully passing these interviews did not, however, mean that the commission was then allocated. For one thing the Air Force had geared its accommodation for a ratio of officers to sergeants, so actual promotion had to wait until casualties or postings made room in the Officers Mess. Also, a squadron commander could hold back promotion by his own edict, for any reason at all. On the plus side, once the sergeant had signed the application his commission was back-dated to the date of signing; and if he should be shot down in the meantime, the commission was normally awarded at once – as prisoners of war officers did have certain advantages, and could not be obliged to join work parties for the benefit of the enemy.

Day-fighter squadrons were, in theory, also available for night operations as well, presumably if there should be a revival of the 1940–1 style night bombing of English cities. It was generally accepted, however, that the Spitfire was not really suited for night operations, as glow from the exhaust stubs on each side of the engine cowling dulled the pilot's night vision; and there was also the increased risk of landing accidents.

Early in April I flew on a 'Fighter Night' exercise, which involved twelve Spitfires heading off at five-minute intervals to fly circular patrols around a vertical searchlight beam near Reading; with each aircraft stacked up at 500 ft vertical separation. I was first off, and after two circuits at 12,000 ft around the vertical beam, the light went out, and another one shot up several miles away. After circling that one, it too went out, and another appeared – and so on – as I chased the elusive lights round the night sky. My exasperated calls on the RT did not come through on any channel, as the set had packed up. Also, as there was no moon and patches of low cloud, I soon had no idea of my actual position. When the patrol time expired I confidently let down to the south through broken cloud, to find the coast; and received a rude shock to find myself amongst the Portsmouth barrage balloons. By the time I groped my way back to Westhampnett and landed, all the other pilots were already back in the Messes, or on their way to bed.

In the morning I complained bitterly about the fiasco of the disappearing searchlights, but nobody wanted to know. I gathered I was being given full marks for an imaginative story, after being stupid enough to get myself lost.

The squadron's operational role, from February to the end of June 1943, was confined to Channel patrols, and to close escort for small formations of medium bombers attacking strategic targets in France, Belgium and The Netherlands.

High cover and straight fighter sweeps were now being flown by the high-performance Spitfire Mk IX, while the Mk V aircraft such as ours flew alongside the bombers, usually at around 12,000–15,000 ft. The high-flying squadrons were seeing more action, successfully drawing the German fighters; and activity at our level with the bombers was mostly from enemy fighters making a fast, diving pass but rarely staying to play. Apart from the Me 109 shot down by Bluey Meagher in April, no one else managed to score during this period; but Bill Denholm was shot down and killed in the same month, on a close-escort sortie.

After take-off the squadron flew in close formation – at only a few hundred feet – to a rendezvous point on the south coast to circle until the bombers arrived, then headed out into the Channel – still at low level to avoid radar detection. If the bombers were late, close escort squadrons had to continue turning in fairly tight circles in close formation, which was hard work in bumpy conditions; and one could well be soaked in perspiration before setting course from the rendezvous. The bomber forces were small at that time, usually twelve or twenty-four Venturas, Mitchells or Bostons; and at a predetermined point across the Channel the whole formation began a fast climb to operating altitude, with the close-escort Spitfires ranging beside the box of bombers.

The tactical plan was similar for each sortie, with one track outbound – including the climb to altitude – a turn of about 90 degrees onto a short bombing run, then a third track back to England from the target area.

Any RAF bomber force was right on time and on track all the way, but the American formations were frequently late, wandered well off course, and flew considerable extra distances. This posed serious fuel problems for the short-range Spitfires. It seemed that navigational training in the States was more on the lines of very long-range flights over vast tracks of land, whereas these short-range sorties demanded constant accuracy in fixing, close map-reading and timing.

On the return journey there could be anxious moments if too

much fuel had been used in combat, or in following the meander-
ing of the bombers; and I ran my tanks dry twice in one week.

The gauge was showing about five gallons on arrival at base in
the first incident, but the engine stopped as the tail came down
on landing. Four days later, however, we crossed in at Manston
where my gauge showed a comfortable margin; but it took a
sudden drop after two-thirds of the journey back to Tangmere.
The electrically operated gauge in a Spitfire had to be actuated
by a push button and was normally very reliable, but this time it
gave several wildly differing readings before steadying close to
zero. I made one pass at Friston (the emergency landing strip on
Beachy Head) which was obscured by low cloud, then pressed
on for Shoreham, flying at the main cloud base of 2000 ft over
Brighton and Hove, keeping within gliding distance of the
beach. Shoreham's grass field was just in sight when the Merlin
engine quit, and it was an eerie sensation gliding on down in
complete silence. The wheels thudded down into the locked
position without the use of the emergency pressure cylinder, the
propeller stopped windmilling as I touched down, and the
aircraft rolled to a halt only twenty yards from a petrol bowser.

Every squadron pilot was naturally looking to the day when
we would transfer to Mk IX Spitfires, but there were real
compensations in being based in the Tangmere sector. Operational air crew were allowed a small ration of petrol for private
motoring, which was one of the most inspired decisions during
the war, giving a degree of mobility and freedom which was a
great lift to morale. There were already a number of squadron
cars, and on arrival at Westhampnett I bought a BSA motor-
cycle to add to the stable, which proved to be a very good
acquisition indeed. A few days later I met Vicki Orsborn, the
most attractive girl who was later to become my wife. She was a
very keen and relaxed pillion rider, and we were able to roam far
and wide through the glorious countryside of West Sussex and
Hampshire throughout that spring and early summer.

The squadron shared Westhampnett airfield with 610 Squadron. One of its Flight Commanders, Johnny Johnson, later
became the recognised top-scoring pilot in Fighter Command.

Flying Officer Colin Hodgkinson, also of 610 Squadron, was an ex-Fleet Air Arm pilot who had lost both legs above the knee. He had been accepted into the Royal Air Force with his artificial legs, only after he reminded the medical people that they had cleared Douglas Bader to fly again with tin legs. Colin drove a Ford 10 car fitted with special controls; but he had no problems in flying a Spitfire.

486 (NZ) Typhoon Squadron was on Tangmere, and Squadron Leader Des Scott, from Greymouth, was appointed in command at the end of March 1943. Scottie had completed two tours on day and night flying Hurricanes – starting as a sergeant pilot; he was a cool and imperturbable type, who quickly became something of a legend in the Tangmere sector. While we were jogging along on close escorts to the medium bombers, the Typhoons of Eleven Group were heavily committed to strafing and bombing attacks against enemy shipping, harbour defences and the like; while rocket-firing Typhoons were also becoming part of the low-level armoury. The Typhoon was very fast down low, rugged, heavy and well armed with four 20-mm guns; but the casualty rate was high, from the very proficient German light flack which normally protected the targets.

486 Squadron was constantly in the thick of the action, and every Spitfire pilot was well aware of the cauldron of flak into which the Typhoon pilots were plunging again and again. We all regarded the Typhoon boys as very special. In addition, the Typhoons frequently tangled with FW 190s at low level, and with some enviable success.

A Royal Air Force rocket-firing Typhoon squadron was also based alongside 485 Squadron in the Tangmere sector for some time, and Warrant Officer Jimmy Wetere was an outstanding exponent of their particular form of offensive. The rocket-firing aircraft were especially vulnerable, because of the necessity to cease taking evasive action and to maintain a steady flight path for several seconds through the firing point, in the thick of the flak, to allow the rockets to accelerate clear of the launching rails under the wings. At the end of six hectic weeks there had been almost a total turnover of pilots on that squadron, but Jimmy Wetere was still in action.

Harvey Sweetman, a foundation member of 485 Squadron as a Sergeant Pilot in March 1941, was now in March 1943 one of the 486 Flight Commanders, having flown a very large number of sorties, with considerable personal success with both squadrons.

Air sea searches for survivors from crashed aircraft, or for pilots who had baled out over the Channel, were frequently and diligently flown, but all too often the searchers had to report that nothing had been seen. At daybreak one April morning Doug Brown and I were scrambled by Tangmere Operations to intercept a damaged Stirling returning from a raid, and the Operations people gave an impressive demonstration of their accuracy. Doug and I were vectored well out into the Channel below a layer of stratocumulus cloud at 2000 ft, then Control turned us round, to track along below and behind the target. Sure enough, the Stirling emerged from the cloud dead ahead of us flying on two engines, and continued to lose height right down to sea level. As Doug reported the sighting and alerted the Search and Rescue Unit at Shoreham, we could see the slipstream from the Stirling's two surviving engines fanning the surface of the sea. The Stirling made an enormous splash as it ditched about five miles short of the English coast, and disappeared altogether for several seconds, before surfacing again with its tail section broken right off. The crew succeeded in launching their rubber dinghy and all but one scrambled aboard; but the odd man seemed to be in difficulties, and was swept rapidly away westward by the powerful current. We were circling to keep him in sight when Doug startled me by calling on the RT that he was going to try and drop his own dinghy to the unfortunate one in the water below. Doug is a big man, and he must have performed some strange contortions in the cramped Spitfire cockpit, releasing his safety and parachute harness to drag the single-man dinghy clear of the square pack underneath him – we actually sat on our dinghy packs, which were fastened to the face of the parachute pack.

At about thirty feet, with flaps down and speed back to 100

mph, Doug hurled the dinghy from the cockpit at the appropriate point, but it wrapped itself around the tail plane. For one
horrible moment Doug almost went straight in as his aircraft
dipped sharply, before the dinghy was torn free by the slip-
stream. The Walrus amphibian duly arrived on the scene to
rescue all the Canadian crew, who later turned on quite a party
for Doug when they caught up with him. RAF Stores Branch
also caught up with Doug, presenting him with several accounts
demanding payment for 'one dinghy: pilot's for the use of'. To
cap that, it was later learned that another fighter pilot had been
decorated for a similar dinghy drop.

The squadron later used Bradwell Bay as a forward refuelling
point on a sortie escorting Mitchells to Flushing. The intense,
heavy flak damaged one bomber which dropped out of the
formation on the return journey, and we covered the aircraft
until it ditched close to the English coast. This time the aircraft
landed in a few feet of water over the mud flats, and the crew
climbed out onto the wing without even getting their feet wet.

March 1943 was the second anniversary of the formation of
485 Squadron, and Reg Grant arranged a party in the Station
Hall at Tangmere, carefully ensuring that the squadron would
not fly the next day. The complete air crew and ground crew
complement of the squadron had a memorable evening. It was
understood beforehand that the pilots would look out for the
ground crew, and their antics could well have been a model for
the Goon Show. Next morning one of the fitters said to me: 'We
had a great time last night – I can't remember a thing.'

The area around Chichester and Tangmere was certainly Air
Force country. Tangmere had been home station for some
famous RAF squadrons between the wars. There were already a
number of temporary airfields in use with more being built, and
the Air Force population was absorbed into the social life of the
area, revolving to a large extent around the fascinating range of
hotels and country pubs which are so much a part of England.
The motor-cycle was the ideal way of exploring the countryside,
and Vicki and I reckoned that eventually we had called at every
pub within a twenty-mile radius of Chichester. A particularly

favoured spot of ours was an old, thatched pub in the vicinity of Goodwood Racecourse, where the prizes in the evening darts game were freshly scrubbed carrots from the proud landlord's garden.

Vicki was in 'B' Watch of the WAAF Force of the Tangmere sector Operations Room, one of four watches which manned the Operations Room on a continuous basis. There were many beautiful women in the four watches, and they all did a very capable and conscientious job. Many pilots and bomber crews owe their lives to the high standard of controlling and homing services maintained by the Operations Rooms, and Tangmere was second to none. It was therefore something of an insult when a newly arrived 'Queen Bee' (Senior WAAF Officer) lined all the girls up and harangued them on discipline, dress, make-up and moral standards; ending with the statement: 'Look at me, I am over forty, and still a virgin'; which drew a prompt riposte from the back of the room; 'And that's nothing to be bloody well proud of either.'

I was surprised to learn how active the Operations Room could be after the day-fighter operations had ceased at dusk. Apart from detection of enemy night intruders – which by now were fairly rare – there was considerable involvement in controlling of our own night fighters, which were increasingly active as intruders over German-occupied territory, and in providing Homing and Search and Rescue services for RAF bombers which strayed into the area.

When I first met Vicki the Operations Room was in a commandeered school on the outskirts of Chichester, while the girls were billeted in Bishop Otter College, an imposing stone building some distance away. Shortly after a new Operations Room was put into service at Bishop Otter College itself, a hit-and-run Dornier bombed the recently vacated facility in the school. In view of the quite accurate local information with which prisoners of war were often confronted by German Interrogating Officers, I doubt if the bombing of the old site could be written off as just coincidence.

Vicki had gone into the Tangmere Operations Room during

the Battle of Britain, and during the winter snows of 1940 the women slept in the drafty administration buildings at Fontwell Racecourse. She recalls how they used to pile all their clothing on their beds, and still shivered through the night, with snow backed up against the doors. To raise funds for RAF Welfare the Operations people, in April 1943, staged a Variety Show in one of the Chichester theatres, which was a great success; presenting a range of talent and originality which was quite remarkable. The performers planned and produced the entire, two-hour show with no outside professional assistance, and clearly enjoyed what they were doing every bit as much as the audiences which packed the theatre. At the end of the show young servicemen were plucked from the audience and positioned in front of the curtain, nervously facing the audience; and as the orchestra began a waltz the curtain slid up to reveal a gorgeous young woman dressed in a ball gown behind each man, who was then persuaded to dance. Vicki sang some of the songs of those days such as 'Deep Purple', 'I'm in the Mood for Love', and 'Moonlight Becomes You' and her low, husky rendition brought an enthusiastic response from the audience.

Since the beginning of 1943 the news from North Africa had all been good, culminating in the final capitulation of Axis forces in mid-May. We were most interested in the increasingly effective part played by the Desert Air Force, which had established a great reputation for working closely with the Army, yet had been equally effective in dealing with the Luftwaffe forces above and beyond the battlefields. Word was filtering back of the success already achieved by Evan Mackie. He had left 485 Squadron for the Desert in February 1943 as a Flying Officer, and was appointed a Flight Commander in 243 Squadron in early April with his score then at four enemy aircraft destroyed. On 3 June he was promoted to Squadron Leader as CO of 243 Squadron, just before they moved to Hal Far in Malta in readiness for the Sicilian landings. Hap Harrison, another ex-485 Squadron sergeant, who had elected to go out to the Middle East theatre, was also beginning to climb the ladder; and they were certainly seeing more action than we in the Tangmere sector in the first half of 1943. Bluey Meagher also departed for the Middle East in May 1943, and the replacement Sergeant Pilots on 485 Squadron during this period included Terry Kearins, Frank Transom, Bill Strahan, and Mac McGuiness.

Terry Kearins had started out in an early course in New Zealand, training on Vincent biplanes*; but had been held back along the way through an error of judgement, in which he had left the tail of a Vincent sticking out of the home farmhouse roof. Frank Transon was tall, raw-boned and rugged, having been brought up on a steep hill country farm bear Taihape, where even the sheep hang on by their eyebrows. He and his brother Jack had put in a six-week stint once on the farm, when their father had left them in charge with a long, long list of fencing and other jobs to be done. On his return the old man made grudging noises of approval as Frank and Jack, working from daylight to dark, had cleared away every job. Then he asked where the two dozen 'killer' sheep had been moved to from the home paddock: 'We ate the bastards', was their reply.

Bill Strahan had also started out in an early course, and while in a Royal Air Force non-operational sector early in 1942 was detailed for an Army Co-operation Exercise; making low-level, simulated attacks on gun posts. The exercise was completed when the eager-beaver army officer in the back seat of the Miles Master said: 'Let's do one more, and make it good – the Brigadier's just arrived.' Bill this time hit a strong down-draught pulling out of the attack and the Master mushed badly, the propeller hitting the gun mounting, with spectacular results. Bill managed to pull up high enough to pick a ploughed field in which to crash-land, telling the 'brown job' to open his canopy and run like hell as soon as they landed, as the Master was a wooden framed aircraft which could quickly become kindling wood. The passenger took Bill at his word and ran, but the impact slammed Bill's canopy forward to jam it tight, and the air intake under the nose cowling rolled back in the ploughed dirt, forcing Bill's seat right up and wedging him against the

* The Vincent was the later version of the Vickers Vildebeest.

canopy, but with strength inspired by visions of incineration he managed to force the canopy open and escape.

The stiff-necked attitude of the RAF Group hierarchy led to a court martial, which handed Bill a sentence of 112 days' Detention with loss of rank. Disgusted, Bill demanded his release from the RAF by which, quite unknowingly, he invoked a special regulation which applied to servicemen from any of the Dominions. It transpired that 'Dominion Troops' attached to any United Kingdom outfit who lost rank by court martial could demand to be repatriated, and this had to be granted. So Bill was offered the alternative of returning to New Zealand, or doing three months on a night fighter unit as a Training Controller in the Operations Room – which he accepted.

Presumably this repatriation arrangement was the result of Dominion governments seeking to intervene against the rigid harshness which could be imposed by British Commands against volunteers from the Dominions. It never did make sense, in wartime, to deal out such harsh penalties to men who had joined and sailed half-way round the world to fight; and it was punishment enough, in the case of keen pilots, to be grounded for a period. The mindless repression and brutality of the Detention Barracks had the effect of crushing morale and initiative, and in my view was quite wrong for incidents arising out of over-enthusiasm or high spirits. It was unfortunate that the NZ Government failed to make the facts known to New Zealand aircrew serving overseas; or at least to insist that a court-martialled person be informed of the alternatives open to him, when convicted of a charge.

When a new Mark of aircraft was in the advanced stages of its development, the various prototypes were flown and assessed by good, average pilots from operational squadrons. This was a very practical policy, complementing the technical expertise of the design staff and the outstanding ability of the manufacturer's test pilot, who lived with the aircraft through every stage of its conception and production. Shortly after settling in with the squadron Bill Strahan was nominated for an assessment exercise on a prototype Spitfire Mk XIV, and we were most impressed with the performance figures he quoted. As we had only flown Mk V Spitfires at that stage, the comparison was even more dramatic.

With a 2035-horsepower Griffon engine driving a five-blade rotol propeller the Mk XIV had a fantastic climb rate in excess of 4500 ft per minute from ground-level, and a speed of 450 mph at 26,000 ft. It was a measure of the intensity of aircraft development being carried out that, while the new Spitfire Mk IX was being delivered to squadrons in early 1943, the greatly advanced Mk XIV had already reached the stage of prototype assessment by operational pilots.*

Sergeant Mac McGuiness was another new arrival during this period, a happy-go-lucky type from Coromandel, with a gift for getting himself into trouble without even trying. For some strange reason, at that time pilots were being issued with a parachute on being dispatched from OTUs to squadrons. Mac arrived at 485 squadron four days adrift, via London, but minus his parachute. So his greeting was to have enormous strips torn off, be threatened with an immediate posting to the Hebrides, and told that the lost parachute would cost him £100. That night he sat in a corner of the Mess muttering and moaning: 'Poor old McGuiness – nobody loves him – poor old McGuiness always in the shit – poor old McGuiness, far from bloody home', until Chalky White roared at him to quit crying into his beer and join the boys at the bar, which he did. Mac was great company, a very funny fellow and normally quite irrepressible. He reminded me of Frank Fahy from Woodbourne days.

A week or so later two Military Policemen collected Mac and escorted him back to his Spitfire OTU to be court-martialled (together with another ex-trainee from the same course) for flying under the Severn Bridge in their Spitfires. There was nothing unusual about trainees flying under that particular bridge, but in the case of Mac and his friend they had been

---

* The Spitfire Mk XIV had a fully retractable tail wheel and all-round vision – or teardrop style – canopy. Less than 1000 were built, and 610 Squadron was the first to be equipped with the Mk XIV, in January 1944. Later in the war Doug Brown was to command 130 Squadron, flying the Mk XIV.

flying in formation at the time, a man working on the bridge piers had fallen into the tide, and inquiries had pinpointed the two culprits. Mac was not told of the 'Dominion Troops' angle either, and had to do six months' detention in the infamous glasshouse.

'B' Flight Commander replacing Mick Shand was Johnny Pattison. Johnny was one of the few men still flying who had fought in the Battle of Britain and, from his enthusiasm for getting on with the job, one could be excused for thinking he was just getting started. Johnny had been shot down in September 1940 at the peak of the Battle of Britain and spent nine months in hospital, which left him with a noticeable limp. He joined 485 early in 1942, but in April was shot down for a second time, and rescued from his dinghy floating in the Channel. He could always be predicted to do the unpredictable, and one mild evening in April 1943, when all the 485 pilots booked for dinner at Harry Blogg's King's Beach Hotel at Pagham, the bars of the hotel were packed tight. Johnny Pattison surveyed the mass of large army bodies, dropped to his hands and knees and burrowed his way between a forest of legs, then popped up in front of mine host to have his order promptly filled.

In the third week of May Jack Rae rejoined 485 Squadron as a Flying Officer, having first flown with it as a Sergeant Pilot in July 1941, when the squadron was at Redhill. He scored two Me 109s and one FW 190 destroyed, with three Me 109s and one FW 190 probably destroyed in that hectic period on Spitfire Mk IIs and Vs, before he left (from Kenley) to fly into Malta from the USS *Wasp* on 20 April 1942. I was delighted for a number of reasons when Jack appeared, not the least of which was that his success as a fighter pilot and his vibrant personality polarised the enthusiasm of those less experienced, and particularly that of the sergeants.

Jack Rae's name had been prominent in the crucial period in Malta, between April and August 1942, frequently coupled with reports about other leading pilots such as George 'Screwball' Beurling, Ray Hesselyn (New Zealand) and Paul Brennan

(Australia) also of 249 Squadron, which was recognised as the crack squadron on Malta during that time.

Jack was shot down by a Me 109 on his second sortie in Malta, baling out at 17,000 ft about seven miles off the coast, but fortunately the breeze drifted the parachute to the Island. Apart from a wounded leg, he had real problems on landing when an agitated civilian baled him up with a shotgun, showing hysterical readiness to shoot Jack as a German airman because he had swastikas drawn on his 'Mae West' lifejacket. (These indicated his personal tally of aircraft destroyed.)

Jack's experience then in hospital was the opposite of the attention I was to receive at Imtarfa a few months later. As a sergeant he was put in a ward with a mixture of civilians and Other Ranks, in charge of a navy nursing sister who must have been first cousin to a battleship. It was bad enough being ordered to stand by his bed for morning inspection, but as the place was dirty and attention to his wound minimal, Jack kicked up a fuss until he was moved to another unit – where he had exactly the same reception. While the sparks were flying in the middle of 'Round Two' a message arrived, advising that Jack's commission had come through the system, and the whole organisation went into reverse. With menials now carrying his belongings Jack was ushered to an Officers' Ward of clean, tidy rooms with every convenience, including iced beer within easy reach of the bedside. In this ward Jack met the Sudetenland Me 109 pilot who had shot him down, before being knocked out himself. Jack found his recent opponent to be quite relaxed and philosophical about his situation, obviously enjoying the red carpet treatment in the hospital, and in no hurry to leave.

Jack took himself back to 249 Squadron after four weeks as soon as his leg felt fit, to add to his score four and a half destroyed, three and a half probably destroyed, and four damaged. He flew 30 sorties in 46 days. On occasions Me 109s and Spitfires actually chased each other around the streets and roof tops of Valletta, and the drill on landing during a raid was to dive out and into a ditch or shelter at the end of a landing run.

In early July small forces of Italian Cant bombers were being escorted by very strong formations of Me 109s, making it impossible to get at the bombers, which were thus delivering their bombs with considerable accuracy. It was noticed that if heavy flak came close to the German Me 109s on the run-up to the target, they tended to duck out of the way and leave their Italian comrades to get on with it. A late-night discussion in the bar produced a tactic which was put into effect next morning, but without any official blessing. As three Cants made their run-up to Grand Harbour surrounded by a swarm of Me 109 fighters, on a call from the CO ('Laddie' Lucas) a heavy barrage was thrown at the German fighter escorts, who obligingly moved off and allowed the section of four Spitfires – one of which was flown by Jack Rae – to destroy all three bombers.

Italian fighter pilots in their Macchi 202 and Reggiane 2001 aircraft sometimes turned on a spirited performance, and indulged in polished aerobatics in combat. Jack Rae and Allan Yeates bounced a mixed formation of Italian fighters, and Jack chased a Reggiane to Sicily, with the Italian displaying a pretty range of aerobatics en route. Jack turned for home at the Sicilian coast as he was out of ammunition, and the Reggiane pilot promptly turned about; keeping Jack busy for a good part of the way back to Malta with some very determined attacks of his own.

Luck, destiny or some other mysterious influence prevails so often in war that it almost becomes commonplace. 'Pop' Conway managed to be shot down four days in a row. The first time he was clobbered by our own barrage over Grand Harbour and baled out; the second time return fire from a Ju 88 crippled his aircraft and he baled out; the third time return fire from a Ju 87 did the trick, and he 'took silk' again. On the last occasion Jack Rae and other pilots were watching the action from the ground as a badly damaged Spitfire, running rough and trailing smoke, headed towards Takali. The onlookers were profanely willing the pilot to jump before it was too late, but the Merlin engine laboured long enough for 'Pop' Conway to crash-land on the aerodrome. This time, for a change, a Me 109 had shot him up, but when asked why he had not baled out as usual, he complained that he was getting sick of jumping out of Spitfires. When his parachute was taken from the wreck it was found that a shell, exploding underneath the cockpit, had completely riddled the parachute pack with shrapnel.

Jack Rae was leading sections of four in the Malta line abreast formation early in his time on Malta, and it is ironical that George 'Screwball' Beurling regarded himself as one of Jack's protégés. All George wanted was to be tacked on to the section to get near the action, and then left to fight his own battles. The last thing he wished was to be even a sub-section leader, where he would be partly responsible for his own Number Two, thus detracting from his own style of air fighting. So it is not surprising that he was a misfit in the squadrons operating over northern France, where teamwork and mutual cross-cover was the basis of success and survival. 249 Squadron pilots in Malta recognised the exceptional ability of the man, and that his mind was geared to no other way of fighting; so they just let him get on with it, and wondered how long he would last. His mastery of the instant, complex calculations required in air-to-air gunnery was matched by precise control of his aircraft in any attitude, and in assessing the unlimited combinations of two aircraft in the three-dimensional arena of airspace.

A fitting analogy of the art and skills of the top fighter pilots is the game of snooker. It would need a modern computer to calculate the number of possible combinations between the cue ball and object balls on the table. The correct solution to each snooker shot is a delicate balance of mental calculation and physical application, to which the snooker player can address himself at his leisure. Even world champions miss shots at the table, and top fighter pilots do not, of course, score with every burst from their guns. Those at the top of the ladder are the contestants who miss the least shots.

Jack Rae was very close to Ray Hesselyn and Paul Brennan, whose achievements in Malta hit the headlines at that time. Ray Hesselyn (from Dunedin) flew into Malta as a Sergeant Pilot in March 1942, and soon had the reputation of being 'the fastest thing in the air'; scoring twelve enemy aircraft destroyed before returning to the UK. His great friend Paul Brennan (Australian) had the same outstanding ability and also shot down twelve enemy aircraft in the same period. Gray Stenberg at Hal Far (a friend of Jack Rae from Auckland) was also in the same league, destroying eleven enemy aircraft during his stay in Malta. George Beurling, Ray Hesselyn, Paul Brennan, Jack Rae and Gray Stenberg between them destroyed at least 76 aircraft during the Malta siege, and probably destroyed or damaged double that number again.

During the war the Ministry of Information occasionally arranged – or authorised – the publishing of accounts of military actions which had particular historical significance. By such an arrangement Paul Brennan and Ray Hesselyn, in collaboration with a professional writer, produced *Spitfires over Malta* (1943), a book which is as vivid and unique as the circumstances which generated the text. Paul Brennan and Ray Hesselyn (with Jack Rae assisting) thus refought their Malta war in a London hotel room before they really began to unwind from the tempo and the tensions of that battle, which might best be described as a facsimile of the Battle of Britain itself.

11

SEADROMES

The excitement was starting to build in 485 Squadron as word was out that the long-awaited change to Mk IX Spitfires was not far off. Ironically, I had baled out of 602 Squadron in February because I knew that 485 was due for Mk IXs, but 602 had by now changed over to the Mk IX. Jack Rae's enthusiasm and operational experience gave a great lift to the squadron and, as I expected, particularly to the eager bunch of sergeants. Jack was no more interested in the distinctions of rank than we were, having travelled that same road himself. He used body language long before the phrase was invented, spoke like a machine gun – his blue eyes snapping – and switched the thrust of an argument this way and that, like the swirling and twisting action of an aerial dog fight.

I now had an ally who was fairly blunt in his criticism of the line astern and weaving battle formation, and Jack organised some practice in the Malta line abreast pattern, with the idea of at least using it for 'Rhubarb' operations. Headquarters, however, vetoed any suggestion of 'Rhubarbs' which – with hindsight – proved fortunate.

Vicki was now a welcome visitor in the Mess, and as one of the sergeants could still coax a tune out of the battered piano, she often sang the night away in a 'Request Session'. For a while she was puzzled by the rich voice and perfect diction of the person who usually answered the phone in our Mess and who chatted on academic subjects, which one does not normally expect in a wartime Mess. It was Jimmy Wetere, our Maori Typhoon pilot who, like most original New Zealanders, spoke the King's English in a way which put most of us to shame.

Jimmy had been educated at Te Aute College, and was a Maori All Black trialist just before the war. Several times we roped him into our squadron rugby team and, being five feet six inches tall and weighing fourteen stone, he was a sensational secret weapon as a wing threequarter. His style was based on the principle that the shortest distance between two points is the straight line joining them; and would-be tacklers simply bounced off him, as though hit by a runaway tank. A cunning New Zealand Fleet Air Arm pilot at Gosport, near Portsmouth, arranged a special challenge match against a navy team, to be played at Gosport on a Saturday afternoon when the squadron was stood down from flying. After an early lunch we travelled by RAF coach to the deserted ground, to be told that the navy was still trying to round up its players; but if we would not mind waiting in the pub up the road, they might be able to scratch up a team. At afternoon closing time we were summoned to the ground to find most of the navy waiting to see the humbling of these 'Air Force All Blacks' – which was by then more than a distinct probability. However, Jimmy won the game by thirty-odd points, while most of us just went through the motions.

On the last day of May 1943 we lost George Moorehead in a flying accident over the Channel, which cast more than the usual shadow in the crew room. The death of a friend in action was handled, in the only possible way, as that random touch on the shoulder which every fighter pilot knew he would never feel. Accidental death in an aircraft was something else altogether, and time never quite eased the sense of futility that a man should pass in that way. George, Max Sutherland and I had joined 485 Squadron on the same day in 1942; and it was particularly hard on Max as he was flying with George at the time, and they were the closest of friends.

Squadron Leader Reg Grant finally went on rest, which was to be a liaison tour with the United States Army Air Force and the United States Army Air Corps in the States. It was a

well-deserved break in the land of plenty of which we all
approved, even though with some envy. Reg Grant had been
continuously on operations since April 1941, beginning as a
Sergeant Pilot on 145 Squadron, where he won the DFM on the
recommendation of Douglas Bader, before joining 485 Squadron
as a NCO in October 1941. His score now stood at eight destroyed, and he held the DFC and Bar as well as his DFM. Reg
appeared quite unchanged despite his long, tough tour of duty;
and the only time I recall that he displayed any emotion was
when the squadron made him a presentation on his departure.

Reg Baker, one of the Flight Commanders, took over as CO;
a serious, courteous person and an analytical chemist before the
war who, at twenty-eight, was older than the average fighter
pilot. He also had a prolonged tour of operations behind him,
having joined 485 Squadron shortly after its formation in March
1941.

Right through June operations over France were cut right
back, and we spent most of the month on special training for an
interesting operational role. My log-book shows that I flew on
only three bomber escorts during the month, but nineteen
details on 'deck landing training'. The information we were
given was straightforward, and seemed logical in view of the
state of the air war in 1943. The first precept of the planners was
that maximum air superiority was essential over any attempted
landings in occupied Europe, as had been reinforced by the
experiences of Dunkirk, Dieppe, North Africa and Sicily.

Designers and scientists had produced the concept of Seadromes which could be anchored off invasion beach-heads, to
provide floating operational bases for close support aircraft. We
understood that the structure might consist of mammoth ice-
blocks cast from a sea water and sawdust mixture, each block
having built-in piping and refrigeration, on the basis that the
sawdust would retard the natural melt rate of pure sea ice. The
blocks or pontoons would be surfaced with steel mesh, and
joined by hinged steel plates to absorb the undulating effect of
the swell. Taxyways, with refuelling and re-arming bays, would
be on subsidiary structures linked to the Seadrome itself.

As the take-off and landing area would be very restricted in length, the intention was to train twelve nominated squadrons in the technique of short landings, as used on an aircraft carrier; but I do not recall any suggestion that arrester wire equipment would be fitted to the Seadromes. It was understood that model tests had proved the ideal to be feasible, and that the Chiefs of Staff had been given Mr Churchill's personal blessing to develop this project.

The long nose of the Spitfire produced real problems when we attempted to spot-land and to stop short from a conventional approach, so the Fleet Air Arm sent a Deck Landing Officer, or Batsman, to train us in the techniques used in the Seafires. A dummy deck was marked on the grass aerodrome, and the Batsman positioned himself, as in a carrier, on the port side near the landing point. The Mk V Spitfire used to stall at 73 mph, so a left-hand curving approach was made at 75 mph from a low-level circuit, with wheels and flaps down and the aircraft trimmed and angled nose-up in the three-point landing atti-tude. To keep the Batsman in view on straightening up over the last 50 ft or so of the descent, the cockpit access door was placed on half-lock, which opened the door about half an inch; and with one shoulder tucked against the door and head cocked over the side, it was possible to keep the Batsman in sight above the leading edge of the port wing, and below the exhaust stubs protruding from the engine cowling.

Once we got the head and body position right and were accustomed to the nose-high, slow-speed approach it was a comparatively simple procedure. By accepting that the Bats-man knew a lot more about it than we ever would – and by obeying his signals implicitly – each landing was precisely on the right spot. As confidence and skill increased the tempo was also increased, until the Batsman had twelve aircraft in his circuit simultaneously. As each aircraft touched down on one side of the simulated deck, thereafter to open up and take off again, the Batsman picked up the aircraft turning next on to its short final approach, to land on the other side – and so on. After ten hours of these dummy landings, thirteen trained pilots were flown in mid-June in a Harrow Transport aircraft to an isolated aerodrome in Scotland. For the next five days we were bored rigid, as apart from doing another hour of simulated landings in Mk Vc Seafires of the Fleet Air Arm, the Station was as dead as yesterday's news.

About the only relieving feature was that Blocko Jones was stationed there, having just returned to non-operational flying, on completion of his main round of skin-grafting at the RAF specialist hospital at East Grinstead. Despite the grafts on his face, eyelids and hands which were still raw and livid, the surgeons had done a superb job. Bill had crashed in a 253 Squadron Hurricane carrying two long-range fuel tanks, and that he survived was little short of a miracle. When flying in cloud the gyro-driven Artificial Horizon had toppled and he lost control of the aircraft, which emerged below cloud in a steep dive, which coincided with the angle of the hillside he hit. The cockpit remained intact, but fuel from the smashed long-range tanks had ignited; turning the wreckage and crash site into an inferno.

The training station was one of those places where the war was somebody else's problem, and had no right to disturb the peacetime cadence of each day. We did our best to liven the place up, which I think was appreciated only by my lonely, scarred friend. Even the Seafires seemed to have been affected by the malaise, and I have never seen such worn, weary, and shabby aircraft.

On our sixth day we were finally ferried out to the training carrier HMS *Argus*, to make four take-offs and landings in Seafires, using the Seafire's hook to catch an arrester wire on landing. One of the pilots had problems lining up on the Batsman's signals, so he was sent away to land back at the aerodrome, but the remaining twelve duly completed the four take-offs and landings. The most difficult part was to remember to drop one's hand off the throttle, after closing it to drop the aircraft onto the deck – which is contrary to RAF training and procedure. Several Spitfires pitched forward alarmingly with a great roar of power from the engine, as violent deceleration hurled the pilot forward against his safety harness, and his left hand rammed the throttle forward.

Johnny Pattison managed to be the one to be a little different by skidding sideways after catching a wire, to end up with the aircraft hanging nose-down over the ship's side; hoping the hook would not pull out before he did. Always the comedian, his excuse was that he was sitting lopsided in the cockpit, having forgotten to bring the cushion with which he propped up his right buttock, a chunk of which had been missing since the Battle of Britain.

Back home in the Tangmere sector near the end of June, the best of good news was that the changeover to Mk IX aircraft was on at last, and we were off to Biggin Hill on 1 July. Excitement was high, as the Biggin Hill Sector was running hot in the day-fighter stakes that summer, with the Sector Station commanded by Group Captain Sailor Malan, the top-scoring fighter pilot from the Battle of Britain; and the Wing Leader was Wing Commander Al Deere, the New Zealander serving with the Royal Air Force who was so well known for his survival rating, and who was also in the top sector of the fighter pilot scoring ladder.

It was known that Reg Baker was going on rest, and that he hoped to return to operations on multi-engine aircraft, which had been his original ambition anyway, before the Air Force had fitted with single-engine fighters. We were looking forward to the squadron being led by Johnny Pattison, as even if he used up a few more expensive aeroplanes, he could always make us laugh without trying. But we were surprised and disappointed when, at the last moment, he was promoted to Squadron Leader – and moved sideways and backwards into Training Command.

12

CREST OF THE WAVE

We flew our Mk V Spitfires into Biggin Hill on 1 July 1943 to take over the Mk IX aircraft of 611 Squadron pilots, who flew our old Mark Vs out the same day. The Sector Station was still celebrating the destruction of its one thousandth enemy aircraft, credited jointly to Squadron Leader Jack Charles (Canadian) of 611 Squadron and Commandant René Mouchotte, CO of 341 (Free French) Squadron. The main event of the festivities had been a gigantic party at a London hotel, and the London cabbies had made their own contribution to the night by providing free transport to and from the hotel where it was held.

485 Squadron picked up the crest of the wave which was carrying the high-performance Spitfire IXs of Eleven Group into frequent action against the peak of the Luftwaffe effort over occupied territory, right through that summer of 1943.

By this time the first expedition of Wingate's Chindits had entered Burma, and the German Sixth Army had surrendered at Stalingrad. In January RAF Mosquitoes had made their first daylight bombing attack on Berlin – during speeches by Goering and Goebbels celebrating the tenth anniversary of the beginning of Hitler's regime. Bomber Command had begun the Battle of the Ruhr, 617 Squadron had breached the Moehne and Eider dams, and the Battle of the Atlantic had peaked with Costal Command destroying thirty-six U-boats in the first four months of the year. The Allies had cleared the enemy from North Africa in May, and in June 1943 the RAF Second Tactical

Air Force was inaugurated in the United Kingdom, for operations directly concerned with the projected invasion of Europe.

When 611 Squadron departed from Biggin Hill, one of the Flight Commanders (Flight Lieutenant Johnny Checketts) was promoted to Squadron Leader in command of 485 Squadron. 341 Squadron also stayed on, so the New Zealand and French squadrons now constituted the Biggin Hill wing, invariably operating together as a unit. Group Captain Malan no longer flew on operations but supervised each briefing, and had a strong influence on the conduct of operations, and on tactics. Wing Commander Al Deere usually led by taking the place of the Commander of one of the two squadrons, who either stood down for the show, or led a section. When Al Deere himself stood down – which was not too often – a Squadron Commander led the wing; and with around twenty-four pilots on each squadron the operational flying was fairly evenly divided. Some shows were uneventful, while others were packed with excitement; so it was purely the luck of the draw which decided who was to get into the action.

The first week or so was used for both ground crew and pilots to familiarise themselves with the outstanding Mk IXB Spitfire. The reality of the flight performance was exhilarating, and I had a tremendous feeling of confidence from my first flight, which was shared by all the squadron. We were certain we could at last meet the FW 190 on even terms. The Mk IX performance, in fact, gave us a slight edge in most aspects, perhaps compensating for the disadvantage of always fighting over enemy territory, and the risk of running short of fuel.

Our Mk IXB Spitfires had Merlin 66-series engines which gave a significantly improved weight to horsepower ratio, with a climb rate at sea-level of 4000 ft per minute. The two-speed supercharger ensured that performance was maintained in the climb, and right up to operating altitude. The supercharger automatically changed into high gear at the correct altitude, but high-ratio supercharging could also be selected manually before the automatic cut-in height was reached, and the engine gave a great surge of power as the blower increased speed. Service ceiling was increased from 35,000 to 43,000 ft, and maximum level flight speed (according to the manuals) was 408 mph at 25,000 ft against 369 mph at 20,000 ft in the Mk V. Fuel tankage was unchanged, so the normal range of the Mk IX with its higher fuel consumption was slightly less than that of the Mk V; but on all Mk IX operations an auxiliary tank was used, which was jettisoned when the contents were exhausted, or before going into action. The capacity of the drop tanks was thirty, forty-five or sixty gallons; but as a general rule a thirty-gallon tank was used, which was sufficient to get us inside the enemy coast. The tanks were either shaped to follow the curve of the belly of the aircraft and termed 'slipper' tanks, or were bomb-shaped.

Armament was two 20-mm guns – usually (but incorrectly) called cannons – and four .303 in. calibre machine guns. This really was an excellent mix of weapons, and with the incorporation of a new and much more practical firing button either the 20-mm or .303 in. guns could be fired, although it would be usual to fire all guns together.

The Merlin 60-series engines were intended to be fitted into a redesigned airframe to become the Mk VIII, with a retractable tail wheel, two 14-gallon wing tanks of extra fuel and a 'tear-drop' canopy; but production on the Mk VIII was limited, and all of that model went to the Italian and Burma fronts. The Mk IX airframe was the basic Mk V frame strengthened and modified to accept the higher-powered engine; which says a great deal for the integrity of the basic Spitfire design.

The aircraft were in excellent shape and a fine tribute to the work of 611 Squadron ground crew, which was ably continued by our own people, whose first job was to replace the 611 identification letters with our own squadron designation of OU. As I qualified for a personal aircraft I claimed OU-V for myself. My ground crew painted a personal emblem on the cowling of OU-V, which was a facsimile of my pink elephant mascot over crossed swords, and a scroll titled 'Butch III'. Thus began an association with three friends, which was to be uninterrupted for over thirteen months. Each aircraft was cared for by the same team of ground crew, and their aircraft were the focal point of their lives. Knocker White, my engine fitter, was from Faversham, a solid and meticulously careful person; Vic Strange was the rigger, a fair-haired blue-eyed Welshman; and Paddy Fahy was the dark-haired Irishman who looked after the electrics. They were not only dedicated and reliable, but a trio of comedians who could turn any situation inside out with no effort at all. OU-V MH350 was as much their aircraft as it was mine, but I was the one lucky enough to do the flying.

The air of purpose and anticipation at Biggin Hill sharpened the senses – even the sun seemed brighter, the clouds whiter, and the countryside more beautiful. All the French pilots in the Sergeants' Mess had made their way to England after the fall of France, and many had gone through bizarre and hazardous experiences to escape and continue the fight. They had an intense dedication to their homeland, generated by the sufferings of their country which had been fought over so regularly in history, and now knew the humiliation of defeat and occupation.

In their distinctive dark blue uniforms with gold facings of rank, the French pilots provided a colourful and vivacious sprinkling amongst the RAF blue, and we soon found ourselves talking away with our hands like any Frenchman – the language proved to be no problem. Jacques Ramlinger was the archetypal dashing, handsome Frenchman, who had attended one of the famous public schools in England before the war, and still played an occasional game on the wing for the Wasps in London during the rugby season. Sergeant Bruno was a friendly, compact man who had the deepest of brown eyes to match his name.

During the settling-in period a new series of operational callsigns was allocated and the Wing Leader became BRUTUS, 485 became ANZAC which we thought was appropriate, and 341 was allocated POWDER. The French pilots were delighted with their callsign, taking from it connotations of gunpowder and battle. There was a fleeting international incident when a deadpan New Zealander commented idly that our Allies did seem to use a lot of talcum powder. French pride bristled, then quickly turned to laughter as they took the point.

The escorted daylight bombing raids (codenamed Ramrods) were by now the focal point of most operations, and the RAF planning and operations people had developed the technique into a complex and very accurately co-ordinated system. The main bombing force would be synchronised with diversionary raids by other bombers, each force having its own close-escort, high-cover, withdrawal cover and target support, while fighter sweeps hunted in pre-planned areas. The purpose was to draw the German fighters into combat, but by choosing a wide range of targets and thrusts, to divide the Luftwaffe and prevent its maximum concentration against any one force. Whereas in the Tangmere sector the squadron had been mainly employed in close escort to the smaller diversionary raids, now at Biggin Hill we were more often involved in the main feature of the programme.

Because of the still restricted endurance of the Spitfires, on deeper penetrations into enemy territory relieving or support forces of fighters would take over on the withdrawal of the bomber force. Usually a forward support or target support wing would be scheduled to be at the target, or turning point, just before the main force. Precise timing and accurate positioning for all units was vital on all these intricately patterned sorties. Briefings, therefore, were comprehensive, and, apart from having a picture of the whole operation in his head, most pilots usually wrote the return course to England (from the operating area) on the back of the hand, in case of becoming isolated from the squadron.

We had finally seen the last of the weaving formation, and from now on flew in the 'finger four' battle formation, which was simple and practical. The positioning was patterned on the related position of the fingers on one's hand with the leader holding the position denoted by the middle fingertip, and with aircraft about 150 yds apart – this was ideal for cross-covering and for either attack or defence. When breaking this formation on going into action, the object was for each pair to remain together. Sections of four maintained position with the other sections comfortably in sight; but with adequate space between to allow for sudden manoeuvring. Sections and squadrons were stepped up, usually away from the sun; so that the extra height of the top sections could be quickly converted into speed. The maxims of the First World War on the Western Front were just as valid throughout this war, and the aircraft with the greatest altitude, and positioned against the sun, held the initial advantage. While those pilots with better than average sight soon became known, a very large factor (which was only otherwise acquired with operational experience) was the ability to scan the sky carefully and efficiently for the enemy; and in particular to detect aircraft shielded by the glare of the sun. In the clear, upper air – and accentuated by reflection from white cloud below – the glare in the sun's eye was brutal, and every pilot developed his own way of surveillance. Like all facets of air fighting, a tremendous amount could be learned about the skills and tricks of the trade from the unending discussions, arguments and refighting of actions which were the main preoccupation in every bar of every squadron. Without that sort of background, I doubt if the intensity of purpose and nervous energy could have been sustained for months on end.

It was made abundantly clear from Command level at Biggin Hill that any Number Two who went hunting on his own, and left his Number One, could expect to pack his bags for Training Command the same day. The 'wily hun', as we used to refer to him, had his own repertoire of tricks and tactics, and was adept at the decoy duck ploy, especially when our formations were on the return journey and fuel was short. A few German fighters diving below our formations were always a tempting target; but they were often just bait for a strong force lurking above and in the sun, waiting to pounce on the backs of any Spitfires drawn by the decoys.

Once the familiarisation phase with the Mk IX was over, the squadron plunged into the action and flew almost every day, and sometimes twice a day, from early July through to the end of October. Shortly after we had taken over the 611 Squadron aircraft the boffins fitted a new device to help fuel conservation which worked well – just as long as it worked. The amount of fuel consumption depends on the throttle setting in relation to the pitch setting of the propeller – which controls the actual speed of the engine. At take-off, and in combat, both throttle and pitch levers are fully forward. However, for lower power and for cruising when fuel economy is important, the position of one lever in relation to the other (and the related readings on the engine instruments) is not that simple. For every position of the throttle lever, there is an optimum position of the propeller control lever to achieve the least fuel consumption without harming the engine. The device was engaged by pulling the propeller (or pitch) control lever right back, which brought a synchronising unit into action. From then on, for whatever throttle setting was made by the pilot, the correct, matching propeller control setting was automatically applied.

This device certainly functioned as intended until, on returning from one sortie, the control unit on Terry Kearins's aircraft went haywire, locking the propeller control into a maximum coarse pitch and minimum speed setting. There was nothing he could do about it. The failure occurred on approach to land, and Terry flew away round Biggin Hill, unsuccessfully trying to get more urge out of the propeller, while the aircraft tried to stop flying. He nursed the machine along in the valley below the level of the aerodrome, just zooming up and scraping in over the boundary to flop the aircraft down on the grass – regardless of the other traffic – while the Aerodrome Controller went ber-serk. As a result the device was removed, and the engine controls restored to their previous system.

On the first show I flew from Biggin the wing was high cover to a formation of Flying Fortresses, which were at their usual altitude of around 25,000 ft, while we covered from 35,000 ft. It became clear that we were still going to have problems with fuel shortages, as the bombers wandered around and the Spitfires were airborne for one and three-quarter hours, our petrol being very low on landing. The CO's section was in action that day and he damaged a FW 190; but sadly Captain 'Pappy' Walker (United States Army Air Corps) was shot down and killed, being one of several American guest pilots who flew with 485

Squadron in July and August 1943. They were from a rather strange set-up in which their American squadron was equipped with Spitfire Vs and based in Eleven Group; but the pilots were not permitted to cross the enemy coast, their operations being confined to Channel patrols. Naturally enough, they were completely frustrated, so it was arranged that one American pilot at a time should fly with 485 Squadron on four operations each, to gain experience. Their CO, Major Jim Haun, was the first – a quiet, impressive man who was a pre-war career officer. Captain Walker was one of his Flight Commanders, and later we had Lt 'Blackie' Travis, a slightly built, lively character who managed to persuade his CO to extend his own tour with 485 Squadron. Blackie had not fired his guns during his stay with us, and on the way out of France on his last trip the decoys below proved too much for him; so down he went and down came the hawks, which turned an orderly withdrawal into a shambles. The head count was only eleven when the squadron landed at Biggin Hill; but Blackie did make it back to England in a well-ventilated aircraft, having shot off all his ammunition. His cine-gun film showed aircraft flashing right and left – he had not hit anything, but he was happy.

Each of the Americans arrived complete with jeep and well loaded with cigars and cigarettes; but they really were popular squadron members in their own right. For all their keenness to get amongst the action, they were jumping in at the deep end, and it would have been wiser to have fed them into a squadron on escorts on the diversionary raids, such as we had been doing in the Tangmere sector earlier in the year.

The day after 'Pappy' Walker was killed I flew on a sweep round the Abbeville area – home of some of the crack German fighter squadrons – which was uneventful; but on the second show that day (which was a Ramrod to Poix) the squadron had its first real dogfight, in which Squadron Leader Checketts destroyed one FW 190; Jack Rae destroyed one and probably another; and Tommy Tucker scored a probable. Unfortunately Terry Kearins was missing, and there was no clear indication of what had happened to him.

During the earlier period we flew a sweep one morning, and Chalky White went off to London for two days on the first train he could catch after we landed. Frank Transom, Terry and I made straight for our quarters on landing to sit on our kit bags, and Chalk was a little hurt when he bustled in looking for a clean shirt and socks. As he invariably modified our shirts to meet round his own neck, and nylon stretch socks had not been invented, he had to settle for a bright blue civilian shirt of his own, and some rather unusual socks – he blacked his ankles with shoe polish.

Allan Mitchell, London Correspondent for New Zealand Press Association, was now a frequent visitor, and he was rather taken with the fact that Chalky was one of the top shearers on the New Zealand and Australian scene using, of course, the rapid shearing technique from 'down under', which was quite unknown in England in those days. During one of the happy, hazy Mess evenings Chalk had agreed to give a demonstration of his art, as Allan Mitchell confirmed when he rang to tell Chalk that the arrangements were all set. So away went Chalk to London, to be escorted to a corner of Hyde Park where some large, well-fleeced sheep were penned with some hurdles. There was a fair sprinkling of notables in the gathering and Allan had also arranged a contingent of news people, including a cine-camera team. After rolling a few smokes and chatting to the spectators Chalk said he peeled off his tunic, and ambled over to get on with the job. He was looking round for the machine and hand-piece, but someone handed him a pair of old-fashioned blade shears: 'Hell's teeth,' said Chalk. 'We only use those once in a blue moon to crutch a daggy old ewe out in the paddock.' But his assistants assured Chalk that hand shears were all that were ever used, and they did not know anything about any shearing machines anyway. So Chalk took the shears and advanced on the sheep.

'Two old fellas with caps on and waistcoats, and bits of string tied round their knees grabbed one of the sheep and stretched it out by its legs, like it was going to be crucified.' Assuring his helpers that he could manage, Chalk threw the animal against his leg in the accustomed style, and went to work: 'The shears were really bloody sharp and it's years since I used a pair anyway . . . I more or less murdered a couple till they looked like dog tucker – then gave it away, and we all went and had a few beers.'

For about twelve days in the second half of July we had one of those flat spots when the German fighters held off, and a brief spell of bad weather even caused a sweep to be cancelled. I had spotted an MG Midget sitting in the long grass beside the Biggin Hill Fire Station, and persuaded the owner to sell it for £15. The body was rough and brakes poor, but it ran like a clock, and gave me a lot of pleasure. It was a 1931 J2 Midget with a fish-tailed back, the same model (but supercharged) that had set the world speed record for that size of car at Brooklands around 1932, with a speed of 131 mph.

Apart from the first-class amenities in the tuned-up atmosphere of Biggin Hill Station, and the lovely countryside, it was only twenty minutes by train to London to see a show or have a day out, and even the local Police went out of their way to look after people from the Station. They even gave bed and breakfast to anyone arriving at Bromley Railway Station after the last bus had left for Biggin Hill, and sometimes early morning transport as well, back to camp. The food in the Sergeants' Mess was prepared and served to the highest standard I ever encountered – due to Corporal Brooks, who had been a chef at the Savoy before the war. Unlike many Messes where the kitchen doors slammed shut as soon as dinner was over, a range of supper dishes and hot drinks was set out every night.

Snow Clarke and Robbie Robbins had joined us earlier. Snow was a very pleasant but self-assured type, while Robbie took a fair amount of ribbing, as his very fair hair and smooth complexion made him look not a day over sixteen. He was not with us for long, and we were sorry to see him posted to Burma; but we had a letter later which began: 'Arrived at the forward airfield in the jungle last night, to be handed a spade and told to dig my own bedroom. . . . What a contrast from the comforts of Biggin Hill!'

As the quiet spell ended I flew on a Marauder escort to St

Omer – the other top Luftwaffe fighter base – but although German fighters were about, the sortie was again uneventful. Two days later the squadron had more success on the second show of the day, again when it was my turn to be on the ground. Acting as high cover to eighteen Marauders bombing the German airfield at Tricqueville (south-west of Rouen) 485 Squadron was one of nine squadrons supplying escorting cover, while four more squadrons flew a diversionary sweep to the north.

After turning for home the FW 190s came at the bombers, and a running battle began at 20,000 ft. Squadron Leader Checketts claimed two destroyed and one damaged while Bill Strahan had one destroyed. Jack Rae and Tommy Tucker shared one destroyed – as described in Jack's combat report:

'At approximately 20,000 feet several enemy aircraft approached from six o'clock slightly above. As a squadron we climbed into them. After manoeuvring for position, I picked out four menacing FW 190s above and climbed after them. One after another flicked away downwards attempting to lure us, obviously under instructions from their leader. I continued to climb up, however, and the FW 190 leading found himself alone and then, realising his predicament, nosed over and dived vertically down. I gave chase with Pilot Officer Tucker (my Number Two) still right with me. A long chase resulted, with extensive low flying. The FW 190 tried every trick from flying under high-tension cables to going round church steeples but could not shake us off. My cannons both had stoppages and, although I observed strikes with the machine guns and slight smoking I decided that Tucker, who had stayed with me magnificently, could finish him off. So I flew formation with the FW 190 and had the pleasure of watching Tucker blast him into the ground with a short burst.'*

341, the 'Alsace' Squadron was always in the thick of the action, as the other half of the Biggin Hill Wing; and in this period they were hard hit by the loss of their Squadron Commander, Commandant René Mouchotte, who, when he was

* From *New Zealanders with the Royal Air Force* by Wing Commander H.L. Thompson, p. 192.

leading the Wing as cover on a raid by 240 Flying Fortresses on a target near St Omer, became separated from his section and was killed. Mouchotte had been a symbol of the dedication of so many Frenchmen to the liberation of their country. The pilots of 341 Squadron were even a little in awe of this remarkable man, who lived and fought only for France, and for the freedom of man. He was very tall and slim, and radiated an air of austere and dignified self-possession. He had escaped from French North Africa as a NCO pilot by flying a Goeland twin-engine machine to Gibraltar with five other compatriots, which was an incredible feat in itself as the aircraft propeller controls had been sabotaged to remain in the low power range. He took the Goeland off in the deep shadows of first light before dawn, across an aerodrome cluttered with scores of aircraft haphazardly parked over its surface. This obstruction of the aerodrome had been ordered by bewildered French Commanders, at the behest of the Germans, to prevent Frenchmen escaping. He flew with RAF squadrons from September 1940 onwards, and was soon commissioned. Two years after his escape he had been appointed CO of 65 RAF Squadron, which he led until he was appointed to form the 'Alsace' Squadron as a Free French Spitfire unit.

After his death Commandant Mouchotte's personal diary was found amongst his belongings, and after the war was over it was returned to his mother. She passed the diary later to a close family friend saying: 'Here is all I have left of him. Will you read it? Will you publish it? Surely there is a lesson here for the young men of the country for which he gave all he had?'

The diaries were first published in France, and an English translation (*Mouchotte Diaries*) was produced in 1956. It is a personal and very moving record of one Free Frenchman's agony of mind following the defeat of France, his dedication to reversing that humiliation, and of his devotion to his mother – who was not aware that her son was flying and fighting with the Royal Air Force. The text of the diaries, reproduced in its original form, revealed the depth of emotion and determination which drove this outwardly aloof and self-contained man on to the point of exhaustion.

One of the last entries in his diary sums up the spirit of every pilot in exile from the occupied territories who refused to give up the fight:

'The other squadron on the wing got four, which makes nine altogether, perhaps more, without loss. A considerable success, which will further exalt our 'Alsace'. I received telegrams of congratulation, one of them from Churchill as follows: 'Please give my warmest congratulations to Squadrons 485 and 341 of Biggin Hill for their performance yesterday. Nine for nought is an excellent result.' And the sweeps go on at a terrible pace. I'm at the record figure of 140. I feel a pitiless weariness from them. It is useless for me to go to bed at 9.30 p.m. each night; I feel my nerves are wearing out, my temper deteriorating. The smallest effort gets me out of breath; I have a crying need of rest, were it even for 48 hours. I have not taken a week's leave for two years. Always at readiness to fly or stuck in the office on administrative work. Anyway, where can I go?

These last two days I've tried to hold myself back, fearfully anticipating the hard period of fighting ahead, for which I shall need all my strength and fitness. I have therefore cancelled all offensive work, confining myself to going nowhere but to the office. . . . But this three days' relaxation has softened my nerves and my will. I am still tired. Tomorrow morning I am flying again.*

The Bomber forces took heavy punishment from determined German fighter attacks and from flak; particularly the Fortresses on their long-range missions, where fighter protection was limited. The Fortresses were an impressive sight as they set off in close formation, usually around 25,000 ft; and leaving vast, streaming vapour trails across the sky. Only too often, on their return, great gaps had been clawed in the formations, with other aircraft extensively damaged but still flying.

One afternoon we escorted two badly damaged Fortresses

---

* *The Mouchotte Diaries* (1956).

back across the Channel as they could not keep up with the main force. As we could not talk to them on RT (having different frequencies) and the Spitfires were getting low on fuel, the Fortresses followed us in to land at Biggin Hill. There were several dead and wounded in the crews, and the aircraft were well shot up; so the balance of the crews spent the night on Station. After dinner the Sergeants' Mess and bar was packed with a lively crowd, including the American aircrew in their colourful jackets and insignia, who had already mastered the art of unwinding. They mixed happily with the Frenchmen and New Zealanders and seemed very appreciative of the fighter cover provided by the Royal Air Force as well as by their own American fighters. They even cheerfully agreed that their navigational skills were not all that good.

Later that night a crap game got under way, and we watched in fascination as this uninhibited demonstration of America at play echoed round the bar. Bill Strahan got into the game, and by the early hours had cleaned out our guests, who were rapt in the fact that someone – from a place that most of them had never heard of – could beat them at their own game.

The owners of one of the great whisky distilleries had generously handed over their English country home, Dutton Homestall (near East Grinstead), to the Royal Air Force, and it was being used as a short-stay rest house for operational pilots from Fighter Command, on a rostered basis. Bruno from 341 Squadron and myself drew the first week in August for a spell there; and it was certainly a pleasant, relaxing break. The stone mansion set in its own park, with shady woods and beautiful garden, was staffed by RAF orderlies under the control of a squadron leader; and about the only rule was that there were no rules, other than to treat the place as your own home for one week. Each fighter pilot was from a different squadron, and among the guests was Dave Bennett, whom I had not seen since Woodbourne. Dave was flying Typhoons in the Tangmere sector, and as the Typhoons were still heavily engaged in their anti-shipping and anti-flak role, casualties were still very heavy on those outfits. Sadly,

1 'Southern Cross', a Fokker F.VII B-3m, made the first transpacific flight from San Francisco to Brisbane, 31 May–9 June 1928, after the historic first crossing of the Tasman Sea

2 Vickers Vildebeest, the first aircraft in which J.H. was airborne. Designed as a torpedo-bomber it first entered service in 1933, and was used in action against the Japanese in 1941 during the invasion of Singapore

3 Sinking of HMS *Eagle*, during the convoy to Malta, 1.00 p.m., 11 August 1942

4 A Seafire taking off from HMS *Furious*, while on convoy-protection duty in northern waters, 1942

5 The tanker *Ohio*, lashed between two destroyers, limps into Valletta, August 1942

6 A Spitfire Mk V<small>B</small> being serviced by RAF and Army personnel on Malta while
   the pilot is seated at readiness. The aircraft is being fuelled from cans, re-armed,
   and the transmitter/receiver inspected

7 Paul Brennan (Aus) and Ray Hesselyn (NZ) at Takali, July 1942

8 Gray Stenberg (NZ) and a Harvard trainer, Canada, 1941

9 George Frederick Beurling, DSO DFC
DFM★, of Verdun, Montreal—known as
'Screwball' to his friends—on Malta,
July 1942

10 Jack Rae (NZ) in England during the win
of 1941

11 J.H. on his motor-cycle with pink elephant mascot, Tangmere sector, Sussex, 1943. His headlamp is fitted with special blackout shutters

12 J.H. in his Spitfire Mk Vʙ displaying his personal elephant emblem, Butch III

13 485 (NZ) Sqn pilots in the Dispersal Hut crew room, Hornchurch, 1943 (*l–r*): Al Stead, Bill Strahan, Doug Clarke, Chalky White, Tommy Tucker, Red Roberts

14 F/Lt Johnny Pattison, DFC ('B' Flt Cdr), Sqn/Ldr Reg Grant, DFC DFM (CO), F/Lt Reg Baker, DFC ('A' Flt Cdr), 485 (NZ) Sqn, Tangmere sector, March 1943. Both Reg Grant and Reg Baker were later killed in flying accidents

15 Harry Grant, who died while training with the pre-war RAF

16 Ian Grant, who was killed in action, February 1942

17 Celebrating Biggin Hill sector's thousandth 'kill', June 1943 (*l–r*): Sqn/Ldr
Jack Charles, DFC; Comdt René Mouchotte, Croix de Guerre DFC★; G/Capt
A.G. Malan, DSO★ DFC★ (Stn Cdr); W/Cdr Alan Deere, DSO DFC★

18 Hornchurch, November 1943 (*l–r*): Corran Ashworth, J.H., Ian Strachan,
Jack Yeatman, Al Stead

19 Terry Kearins in France during his escape

20 A Seafire Vʙ of 768 Sqn taking off from HMS *Argus* during deck-landing training, August 1943

21 Full-scale working model of a section of the 'Habbakuk' ice-block floating airfield under construction at Patricia Lake, Jasper National Park, Canada, 1943. A second layer of ice-blocks has been laid, and vertical pipes are in place

22 485 (NZ) Sqn, Biggin Hill, July 1943: visit of Bill Jordan, High Commissioner for New Zealand in UK. J.H. (*third from left*), like the three others in Mae Wests, was at readiness

23 Tailplane of Pat Patterson's Spitfire Mk IXB, hit by flak on a Ranger Operation over The Netherlands, May 1944

24 Pat Patterson, Selsey, June 1944

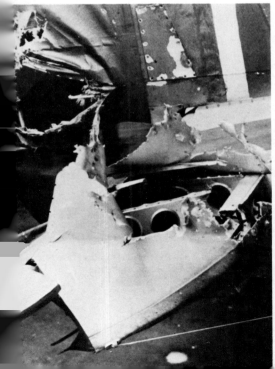

25 J.H. with his ground crew, Selsey, June 1944, shortly after shooting down a Me 109 over Omaha Beach (*back row*): Ron 'Knocker' White (fitter), J.H., Vic Strange (fitter), Michael 'Paddy' Fahey (electrician); (*front row*): 'Lofty' (armourer), 'Ginger' Gibson (radio)

26 Frank Transom and ground crew, Selsey, June 1944. Note individual aircraft code-letter N hastily applied over cockpit door, having been displaced by black and white 'invasion' stripes on fuselage

7 Aerial shot of Gold Beach, taken at 10.20 a.m., 6 June 1944, by Air
Commodore Geddes in a P.R. Mustang. Note wing with 'invasion' stripes in
bottom right of photograph

8 485 (NZ) Sqn, Maldegem, Belgium, 1 December 1944. Max Collett in his
Spitfire LF IX, named 'Waipawa Special', taxies out carrying a 500-lb bomb,
prior to dive bombing a target at Dunkirk

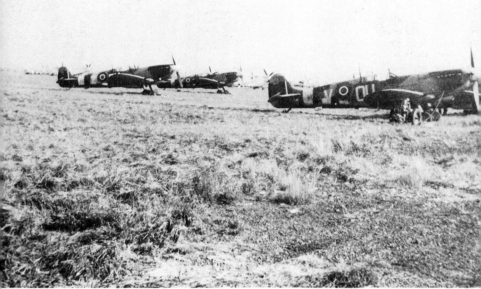

29 J.H.'s Spitfire ML407 OU-V (*foreground*) and other aircraft of 'B' Flight, Merville Airfield, Normandy, September 1944

30 Mac McGuiness, Lyndsay Black, Frank Transom, Bill Newenham and Johnny Niven (CO). The young Public Relations photographer asked if the Squadron had a motto; 'Hang on a minute and I'll paint it on the tent,' said the CO

31 485 (NZ) Sqn pilots examining a bombed 'no ball' (V1) site in France

32 Polish Army personnel inspecting devastation to German transport in the Falaise Pocket, July 1944

33 Spitfire ML407 OU-V, flown by J.H. on 27 August 1944, escorting RAF
Halifax and Lancaster bombers on a raid on Homberg, Lower Ruhr Valley.
Note 45-gallon auxiliary fuel tank under fuselage giving extra range needed for
escort duty; this was jettisoned before going into action or returning to base

34 J.H. with Spitfire ML407 OU-V, 12 June 1944

shortly after he returned to Tangmere, he was killed in action.

There were billiard tables in the house and all the usual amenities of a mess, but most of us just ambled about the grounds, dozed in the sun, or pottered about in East Grinstead. The townsfolk were very friendly, and showed great kindness and understanding to the many burn patients from the RAF specialist hospital nearby. One of the most important facets of treatment for burns is the integration of the patient into everyday society, and the worst hurdle for the patient is coping with the shock, and horror, which people can show when confronted with the effects of severe burning, where skin and tissue have been destroyed. Shock is understandable; but it causes the patient to shrink inside himself, as he is already deeply sensitive and over-conscious of his own disfigurement. An important part of the hospital's rehabilitation technique was to encourage patients to get about, usually in pairs or with a close friend from outside the hospital, and to come to terms with the inevitable reaction of strangers.

On the Saturday at the end of each week's stay at Dutton Homestall a publicly known person gave a luncheon address. Our guest speaker was Hannen Swaffer, the elderly stormy petrel of journalism in Britain, whose contentious opinions were matched by his flamboyant style of dress. He arrived for lunch in a black opera cloak, wearing a black velvet cravat and a large floppy black hat over long grey hair. He covered a wide range of topics, and the wheels within wheels of public affairs. He described the outlook of the former Prince of Wales, by then the Duke of Windsor, as: 'A Socialist in the morning, and a Conservative in the afternoon.'

The rest house had a permanently booked row of seats at the local cinema, and we had intended to see the film which was showing that afternoon. However, our guest was so interesting that we persuaded him to stay on to talk with us, and to take the evening train to London. The weather had deteriorated, and it was a miserable day with a low cloud base and steady drizzle, so it seemed like a false alarm when the air raid siren went in midafternoon. Then we heard the unmistakable, unsynchronised engines of a German bomber. I caught a glimpse of a Dornier low down (probably following the main railway line), then we heard the detonation of a stick of bombs.

A phone call from the Air Raid Warden Post in East Grinstead asked us to stand by to assist in recovery work, as the bombs had been dropped on the town, and the cinema had taken a direct hit. Hannen Swaffer, who was also active in investigating psychic phenomena, was quite sure in his own mind that his protracted visit – and its effect on us – was more than coincidence.

13

THE ACTION PEAKS

On the day Bruno and I arrived back at Biggin Hill we missed the first major engagement in twelve days, and the most productive fighter action in 485 Squadron's history. Al Deere led the wing, giving close support to thirty-six Marauders bombing St Omer airfield. Over Lille, Red Section bounced a formation of eight Me 109s flying straight and level in line abreast, with one lagging slightly behind. Squadron Leader Checketts was first in, and blew up the lagging machine from 200 yds – then a second, then a third; while Jack Rae and Bruce Gibbs also destroyed one each. The CO then damaged the seventh machine, but the eighth one escaped. The cine-gun films were as unusual as the episode itself, showing six Me 109s in succession being demolished,* virtually in level flight; and each of the three destroyed by Squadron Leader Checketts showed almost identical shots on his film. There was some speculation among us that this may have been a formation of newly trained German pilots on a familiarisation flight over the battle area, as there had been a steady toll taken by the Royal Air Force since the beginning of the summer, and the Germans by now must have been using a considerable sprinkling of inexperienced pilots in their formations – similar to the position in which the Royal Air Force

---

* The six Me 109s were in all probability of II./J.G.2 who lost four aircraft destroyed and two damaged (10% and 30%) in the St Pol area that day according to Luftwaffe Records.

found itself at the tail end of the Battle of Britain.

The Ramrod operation mounted on 17 August was a typical example of the complex pattern of the increasingly heavy strategic, daylight raids, when 376 Fortresses constituted the main offensive force directed against the German ball-bearing plants at Regensburg and Schweinfurt. Royal Air Force Spitfires and Thunderbolts of the US Command escorted this main force as far as Antwerp, and similar escorting formations picked up the bombers again at Antwerp on the way out. Mitchells and Marauders, with strong escorts, made diversionary raids against marshalling yards and airfields in Belgium and northern France, and the tactical plan succeeded in drawing a strong reaction from the German fighter force, yet still preventing it from concentrating on the main force of Allied bombers.

Once the Fortresses were beyond the range of the escorting fighters past Antwerp, however, the B17 formation was heavily attacked by fighters, no doubt from aerodromes in Germany itself, and thirty-six Fortresses were shot down.

The Biggin Hill wing flew top cover on the diversionary raid by thirty-six Marauders on an airfield near Arras, while two other wings flew close escort and escort cover, and another wing swept on ahead as target support. The whole diversionary force rendezvoused over Dungeness at 20,000 ft to give German radar every chance to latch onto the diversion itself, and it was a powerful-looking threat which headed across the Channel, as we climbed to our position above the bomber force and the other fighters. We could see the German fighters above when we crossed the French coast, and twenty-odd Me 109s made a pass, while others stayed upstairs. Once again it was Jack Rae who was in the right place, and with his Number Two went after a Me 109 diving away inland, which they lost sight of. Climbing back up they intercepted two Me 109s which were jumping some Spitfires below. Jack's combat report read:

We met them head-on and I had a short burst at really close range, and as one German shot underneath me I saw strikes along the top of his fuselage. Then, after just avoiding a collision with another

Messerschmitt, I turned to see the one I had attacked dive down with flames streaming from it. Then attacked the other German machine and after many violent manoeuvres and short bursts, I finally closed to within approximately 75 yds and opened fire again. The tail unit appeared to come to pieces and large flashes could be seen in the fuselage. I climbed away and watched the German machine skidding sideways through the air and burning until he finally crashed behind some woods.*

Two days later, on another high-cover escort to bombers going for an airfield near Amiens, the squadron was jumped by a mixture of FW 190s and Me 109s, and the attacks continued with the Spitfires breaking and reforming to stay in position covering the bombers; but Marty Hume was able to pour a close-range burst into a Me 109, which blew to pieces.

Having had our best day ever on 9 August, with six destroyed in less than one minute, the swing of the pendulum now handed out the squadron's worst day ever, on 22 August 1943. I flew on the morning show which was an uneventful sweep around Poix, and the afternoon shift flew as cover for a bombing raid on the airfield at Beaumont-Le-Roger.

When the aircraft arrived back over the Station I was taking a bath in my quarters, and for the first and only time rushed to the window to count the aircraft; then hastily dressed and raced down to the dispersal, to have it confirmed that four were missing.

It seemed that, when the Biggin wing was half-way in from the French coast, there could have been confusion over a large gaggle of aircraft approaching from head-on and above; and as a forward support wing was included in the plan of operation, it could have been a case of momentarily seeing what was expected to be seen. In the event, forty to fifty FW 190s slammed head-on and from all sides into the wing, followed by about twenty more. Our two squadrons disintegrated into a tumbling mass of aircraft mixed up with the Germans – the Spitfires and FWs

---

* *New Zealanders with the Royal Air Force* by Wing Commander H.L. Thompson, p.194.

twisting and turning in mad confusion all over the sky.

The Spitfires of Snow Clark, Max Sutherland and Chalky White were all hit hard in the initial moment of the German attack. Snow Clark must have died instantly, but Max Sutherland baled out. We learned later that he landed literally at the feet of ostensible collaborators, who had German permits for their vehicle, but who were actually leaders of an Underground cell. This courageous pair took off with Max to get him into hiding; but as his lower leg had been shattered by a cannon shell and he was bleeding to death, they rushed him to the nearest German military hospital. The Germans amputated the leg, and Max was eventually repatriated through the Red Cross Commission. Chalky White's aircraft had been seen diving vertically, leaving a heavy white trail, and there seemed little chance that he had survived. Jack Rae was last seen attacking a FW 190, and so the best pilot I ever flew with was also missing. Ironically, while the show was in progress, signals had arrived in the squadron to the effect that Jack had been awarded a Bar to his DFC; and he was promoted to become Flight Commander in another squadron. Jack was later reported as a prisoner of war and it transpired that, after destroying a FW 190 from very close range during the dogfight when the Germans pounced, his engine had stopped, causing him to force-land. His Spitfire's engine was probably hit by debris from the FW 190 which he destroyed.

My commission was notified in mid-August, and Chalk's was gazetted the day he went missing. I had taken a look at the Officers' Mess but went back down the hill again. Later, the Group Captain sent me a note, telling me to do either one thing or the other.

The navigation of the American bomber formations was still shaky, and after escorting a particularly prolonged ramble across the Channel every Spitfire in the Wing was gasping for fuel by the time we landed. The Wing Leader, Al Deere, flew up to the Headquarters aerodrome of the American Bomber Group that same day, as previously arranged with the Americans, to discuss the matter of escort tactics employed by the

Royal Air Force and bomber timings, so important to the success of a combined operation. The Americans, who were still comparatively new to operations, were most co-operative; and future escort missions went very much to plan.

Whether the US bomber forces borrowed RAF navigators or whether their own people were given the right training, the results were most satisfactory. Never again did we have cause to be critical of their navigation on these short-range missions over Western Europe.

Up to this point each pilot had been averaging about one show in two days, but the tempo now accelerated and several times I flew two in one day. Sergeants Herb (Pat) Patterson and Doug Clark arrived around this time, both very good pilots and keen to get into the action. Pat, in fact, had the aggressive drive and confidence of one who not only wanted – but expected – to win. I called him 'Pat the Pirate', as he was the type who would press any situation to its limits, and seemed to have no nerves.

Chris Martel was one of the Flight Commanders on 341 Squadron; a tall, powerfully built man with a pleasant personality, who was very highly thought of by the French pilots. Sometimes he was away for a few days at a time, then his absences ceased, and he seemed remote and withdrawn in the Mess. I saw a brief report in *The Times* stating that a considerable number (I think it was given as thirty) of members of the Martel family had been executed by the Germans for Underground activity, in a particular district in France. I showed the report to one of my friends on 341, who made no direct comment. However, he cryptically referred to the parachute emblem which Chris Martel wore on his uniform sleeve, and I inferred that during his absences Chris may well have been in and out of France on Underground work. If this was, in fact, his own family who had been brutally wiped out, one could but dimly comprehend his despair and his fortitude. In the comfortable Mess at Biggin Hill it was not always easy to grasp the dark reality of that secret war just across the Channel; but our own war in the clear air and bright sunlight seemed suddenly more vital, and more urgent.

Our only criticism of the handling qualities of the Spitfire Mk IX was the heavy load on the elevator control at high speeds. This was no great problem in just pulling out of a high-speed dive, as the elevator trim wheel could be eased backwards with the left hand, automatically deflecting a small tab on the trailing edge of the elevator downwards against the air flow, and forcing the elevator upwards. This relieved the force required by the pilot to pull the stick back. The main problem arose, however, in combat, with the aircraft being thrown into steep turns, and pulled in tight with harsh backward movements of the stick by the pilot. In dogfighting the aircraft is flung about rapidly and roughly, often with the throttle wide open and both hands on the stick, to exert maximum force and control. In these situations it was not usually possible for the pilot to make use of the trim tab to relieve the stick load. These high elevator stick forces not only posed limitations according to the physical strength and fitness of the pilot, but also caused split-second time-lags in maneouvring.

The Spitfire Mk IX brought the increased speed and climb performance which at last gave us the edge on the FW 190s; and the Mk IX is generally acclaimed as the finest in the Spitfire line to fly extensively in general service. Without the Mk IX the Royal Air Force would not have so decisively won the drawn-out battle of attrition fought out in the fighter sweeps and bomber escorts over Western Europe, from 1941 to 1944; or in the Western Desert and Italy.

However, the increased power, speed and weight of the Spitfire IX also brought an increase in elevator stick forces in combat, if it was not possible to use the trim tab. Early in August our aircraft were modified so that the elevator required much less backward force on the stick, when pulling into a steep turn without using the trim tab. We tested our aircraft and found that it certainly required much less effort now to reef the aircraft into a steep turn, and pull it in tight. For all that, several of us had some faint reservations, but could not put our fingers on the reason.

Every operation from Biggin Hill in that high summer of 1943 generated a tangible air of high-tuned expectancy. On 27 August the wing flew high cover escort to a formation of US Army Air Corps Flying Fortresses to bomb St Omer – the German equivalent of our own Biggin Hill Station, and the Luftwaffe reacted in strength.

As the Fortresses ran up to the target area at 25,000 ft in their usual impeccable, close formation the attacks began to come in. The radio came alive with Sector Control reports of radar plots of bandits above the stream, and with sighting reports from escorting fighters. Then came the calls for sections to break into attacks by the FW 190s, as the action began at the van of the bomber force.

I was flying Number Two to the Squadron Leader, and from our position at the rear of the formation could see the twisting vapour trails, and the glint of sun on perspex high above the leading bombers, as the top-cover Spitfires engaged. Steep, slanting streaks as enemy fighters dived for the bombers, the flurry of white puffs as they fired, then flashed on down through the Fortresses – this was the most effective method of attacking the heavily armed B17s, as the FW 190 built up speed very quickly in a dive, and could use that speed to pull up and make a second attack from underneath, before rolling out and away.

I sighted a FW 190 at 11 o'clock below, climbing very fast towards the rear box of bombers. I called the sighting to ANZAC Red One as the FW 190 fired and peeled away down. Red One called: 'I can't spot him – go down and I'll cover you'. At full throttle I dived steeply after the FW 190 which was now over 1000 yds away and going very fast downhill, while Red One swung over behind and outside me to watch my tail. Initially the FW 190 pulled further away, and I began to lose sight of his camouflage against the wooded countryside; but as we passed through 15,000 ft the ultimate speed of the Spitfire Mk IX started to pull him back.

At 10,000 ft the range was down to 800 yds and closing fast, when the FW 190 pilot surprised me by pulling round into a sweeping, descending turn to the left. I thought: 'Now we can get down to it', as it looked as if he was going to dice on a one-to-one basis. I pulled round into a matching turn above, which gave me a clear view of his smart camouflage markings and insignia, and slammed on full top rudder, slicing down to 8000 ft with the FW 190 then about 300 yds ahead in the turn, and slightly below.

Using both hands on the control column I pulled hard back, to cut my turning circle down inside that of the FW 190. Then several things happened at once: the stick shot hard back out of my hands, instantly tightening the turn to a degree which applied the effect of many times gravity on the aircraft and everything in it, including my body; my hands were snatched down by this invisible force hard into my knees, and my upper body buckled sideways and downwards inside the safety harness, with my head above the undercarriage lever on the right hand side of the cockpit. In a mental flash I recognised that there must, in fact, be a flaw in the modified elevator – which appeared to have taken over completely – locking the aircraft into a maximum rate turn.

I was virtually cemented in position, as it was physically impossible to lift hands, feet or head against that amount of g, and we just kept on careering around in a steep, left-hand descending turn; like winding down a giant, corkscrewing spiral.

Then Red One came up with several terse calls on the RT: 'Break Off, Red Two, six 190s coming down on us . . . Break off Red Two . . . Break off . . . Break off you clot – 190s coming at me – I'll have to leave you to it.'

The fact that my head and upper body were slumped well forward and to the right probably prevented a total blackout, and I could still dimly see the instruments just above eye-level. At 5000 ft the inside of the canopy fogged over with condensation, as we wound our way down into warmer air. At 2000 ft I gave up trying to lift my hands and attempted to push at the rudder pedals, which were hard against my feet. By flexing toes and feet alternately inside my flying boots I could just move the pedals, an inch or so at first, causing the aircraft to slip and skid in the turn. Some frantic tip-toe exercise washed off enough speed to reduce the g force, until I was able to lift my left hand and ease the throttle back.*

Hauling myself back upright again in the seat, I wiped the fog from the canopy, and there was the FW 190 still circling below me, right on the tree tops. At that point I blew a fuse. Five close friends had been shot down in this very area in the last few weeks. We had voiced our doubts about the new elevator modification which had damn near killed me. . . . Here in front of me was the German who had given me the worst three minutes of my life – so I was going to clobber him, if it was the last thing I did. The FW 190 pilot must have got the message, as he flicked out of the turn and shot away inland. At full power the Spitfire again proved her superiority in speed, and the range steadily closed. At 600 yds the FW 190 pilot pulled up steeply to about 300 ft, then rammed his nose down again. I turned hard left, then right again and – sure enough – he had tried to lead me over a German aerodrome with all its flak positions. Again the range shortened, again the FW 190 pilot pulled up over another airfield, and again I detoured.

About 30 miles from the start point the range was down to 400 yds, and the FW 190 pilot began to weave. At 300 yds I was tracking with the gunsight when his starboard wing clipped a power wire, and the FW 190 flicked into the ground and exploded.

At a rough guess I was somewhere south-west of Armentières, and suddenly there was no place like home. I set course for the coast at economical cruise power and at zero feet, but the day's surprises were not yet over. Not far ahead – flying

---

* It has always been my recollection that the elevator modification which gave me a bad time in August 1943 involved an increase in the 'horn balance' area of the elevator itself, and I also recall being both pleased and surprised when I was assured – the day after the incident – that the problem had been rectified. Servicing records from forty years ago have not usually survived, but Jeffrey Quill's *Spitfire: A Test Pilot's Story* (John Murray, 1983) includes a chapter on the complexities of longitudinal stability in the Spitfire. From the data in Jeffrey Quill's book, and his comments kindly passed to me through Hugh Smallwood, it appears that if an elevator of increased horn balance area was fitted, then adjustments would have indeed been necessary to the elevator control system as well.

in the same direction but at 1000 ft – was a lone B17 Flying Fortress. I thought: 'If the stupid clown stooges along at that height he's got no show of making it home . . . The light flak belt at the coast will get him, if he ever gets that far.'

So I pulled up abeam of the B17, waggling my wings slowly, hoping to entice him down to the deck where he might have a chance, and we could go along together. Fortunately I was 800 yds away, as the gunners let fly with everything they had so, cursing trigger-happy Yanks who did not know friend from foe, I dived back to ground-level and left them to it.

As the French coast came up I climbed to 500 ft and dived out fast, jinking amongst the farewell flak, and so out across the Channel. But I was still looking back over my shoulder, puzzled by that B17. In the first place no Allied aircraft at 1000 ft – especially one the size of a B17 – could hope to survive the light flak concentrated in the Pas de Calais; but all four engines were turning, and I had seen no signs of damage. How the devil did a single B17, seemingly intact, get down there from the formation height of 25,000 ft anyway? I had no conscious recollection of seeing the large, white star painted on all US aircraft. Then I recalled an Intelligence Report warning pilots that the Germans may try to infiltrate captured Allied aircraft into – or near to – our own formations.

I landed at Manston to refuel, then on to Biggin Hill where my ground crew were still waiting at the dispersal area. Their anxious faces lit up when they realised both OU-V and myself were all in one piece, and that we had one destroyed for the day.

'Spy', our Intelligence Officer, dutifully wrote down details covering the lone B17, but no comment ever came back down the line. However, nearly forty years later, when I was researching this book, I called on Jack Rae and his wife Vera, the sister of the late Wing Commander Reg Grant. Amongst Reg's effects which had been sent home to the family, I found the transcript of an interview of Squadron Leader Grant by the Air Technical Division, Office of the Chief of Naval Operations, Navy Department Washington DC, dated September 1943 when Reg Grant was on his liaison visit to the States. Included in this document is the following text:

Question: What do you think the Germans are trying to do with the US aircraft they've captured and are flying in our formations?

Answer: Well, I think they're only trying to confuse Allied pilots. After the fall of France on several occasions we found Hurricanes coming in. The Observer Corps reported them as Hurricanes, consequently they were considered friendly. They came in and machine-gunned aerodromes and went back out to sea again. After the Huns had pulled this trick several times, Spitfire pilots shot down some of our own Hurricanes by mistake. On a couple of occasions in 1941 we also ran across Hurricanes that had no British or squadron markings on them, though they still had our type of camouflage.

Question: B17s have been seen with BXO on the side, also BXU – Do you know anything about that?

Answer: They're probably copies of B17s that have been shot down from which the Hun has copied the squadron markings. There was a report of three B17s being landed intact in France by three ferry pilots who got lost.

So it remains a matter of conjecture whether the B17 I encountered was German – manned or not.

14

WALKABOUT'S RETURN

At about this time a flight of P47 Thunderbolts took over an unused dispersal area on the far side of the Biggin Hill aerodrome; but for what reason nobody seemed to know, as American fighter units were usually stationed to the north of London. The Thunderbolt pilots spent quite a lot of time practising close formation flying, at which they were very accomplished; but it ended in a tragedy. On a day of low cloud and heavy drizzle the four Thunderbolts made a shallow dive, in close formation, towards their dispersal. The leader failed to pull up in time, and the aircraft crashed together, killing all four pilots.

Although we were operating over France practically every day, there was again no real action until 6 September when, on a Marauder escort on the marshalling yards at Cambrai, twenty FW 190s and Me 109s tried to bounce us, as the formation turned after the bombing run was completed. I was a sub-section leader (or Number Three) in the down-sun section, and my Number Two lost contact in the dogfight as some of the enemy fighters briefly stayed to play. Twisting about in a swirl of aircraft I was sliding in behind a Me 109 which was in an easy diving turn, but had to break hard round as one of his friends slipped inside my own turn. Suddenly the sky was empty around me, but I caught a glimpse of aircraft up-sun. Moments later a Me 109 dived past with a Spitfire in hot pursuit, and as I swung out to one side and followed to give cover, I recognised the letters of Squadron Leader Checketts, the CO's aircraft. The Me 109 stayed in the dive, jinking violently right down to ground level, with the CO snapping off short bursts; then the Me 109 headed inland up a shallow valley. The CO closed right in to about 100 yds as I pulled up level with him on his right-hand side, then as he swung away to the left I realised he was out of ammunition. As I was sliding into position behind the Me 109 I saw that the CO had turned about and was heading for the coast. Conscious of the edict about staying with the Number One or being kicked off the squadron, I left the Me 109 to it, and set off after the other aircraft. As I pulled up again on his left side the CO called to the stray Spitfire to catch up and stay with him. Nearing the coast I could see that we were heading straight towards the large, white mud-flats of an estuary, against which our camouflage would be useless; and the sort of area where enemy fighters hang around to pick off stragglers, silhouetted against the bright background. I scanned above carefully, and sure enough there they were at 4 o'clock, and at about 7000 ft. While there was time I counted them even more carefully, making out fourteen Me 109s in a loose gaggle. As they started to dive the CO called that he had sighted them, then called a break to the right, when the Me 109 leader was flattening out of his dive about 1000 yds away. So up we went into a full-power climbing turn to the right, and the Me 109s used their diving speed to pull up underneath us. I pulled OU-V into a tight, near-vertically banked right hand turn with the nose cocked up and the air speed at 90 mph, which is like winding your way up a tight corkscrew. I knew that no Me 109 could match that sort of turn, let alone turn inside me to get a shot at me. Looking down, I counted the fighters in the spiral below me twice to make sure; and as there were now only twelve, I knew that there could be a problem coming up if the other two were climbing straight ahead instead of in a turn, as their climb rate would be much faster that way. The CO was climbing in a less steeply banked turn than myself, and was about 300 feet above OU-V when the thirteenth Me 109 drifted in at me out of the sun, and then as he pulled his nose higher to fire, his wings stalled and the aircraft fell away. Two more turns of the corkscrew and number fourteen appeared out of the glare, making an identical attack on the CO. The Frenchmen had the RT jammed with excited battle chatter, and there was not a thing I could do as the Me 109 drifted into position on a perfectly judged line. From 50 yds he poured a three-second burst into the belly of the Spitfire, before stalling out and falling away. The oil and coolant radiators under the Spitfire's wings were blown right off the aircraft, and when I completed one more turn the Spitfire was spinning down in flames. I decided to roll right over in the turn and take one of the Me 109s out on my way down, then keep going for home; but changed my mind when the CO's parachute opened. One by one the nearest Me 109 pilots pulled up and let fly at me; but each also stalled away as his guns fired.

The Wing Leader was calling the Squadron Leader, so I advised him that Red One had bought it, but had baled out OK.

By 10,000 ft all the Me 109s were out of the hunt, so I rolled my way out over the Channel, landing at 125 airfield on the south coast for fuel. For the second time in ten days I landed after dark at Biggin Hill to find my ground crew waiting at dispersal, along with Tony Van Dyck (Intelligence Officer) who noted the details of the incident. Marty Hume was now appointed CO, and one of his first duties was to tell me, very apologetically, that the sector hierarchy had ordered him to rip a strip off me – for coming back without my Number One! Marty was a popular choice as replacement CO, being an even-natured Maori who had been with the squadron for over eighteen months, and had very good long-range vision. Norm Rippon, the New Zealand Sergeant Armourer, tells of one incident heard over a ground radio set, on which the ground crew could sometimes listen to the squadron in action. A bunch of single-engined aircraft had been sighted in the distance, and speculation was going to and fro among the pilots as to whether they were friend or foe, when Marty called up with the clincher; 'They're Huns all right, they've got black crosses on them.'

About that time Bert Wipiti DFM, another Maori pilot, joined the squadron as a Warrant Officer, having fought in Singapore, and all the way back to Burma. Bert was a bundle of energy, intent on getting to grips with the enemy under any or every circumstance. Flying Brewster Buffalos, he and another New Zealand NCO destroyed the first Japanese aircraft shot down over Singapore, and he saw a lot of action under the atrocious conditions in that theatre. Bert's CO had apparently recommended him for a commission; but this was not forthcoming, and it was suspected it had been vetoed at the higher RAF command level for India and Burma, because of the colour of his skin.

Early in September a stray Thunderbolt pilot landed at dusk on his way back from northern France, after being separated from his squadron, and he then spent the night with us at Biggin Hill. He was a relaxed and laconic sort of American, who just sat back and took in the shop talk and friendly wrangling on anything to do with the fighter pilot's job. Inevitably, his Thunderbolt was the target of some sympathetic criticism from those lucky enough to fly Spitfires. The Thunderbolt was a massive aircraft, reputed to perform like a great brick with wings, and crew chiefs had been seen taxying them around tarmac areas with four or five people in the cockpit. Someone asked our American guest what evasive action a Thunderbolt pilot normally used in combat: 'W-aal,' he drawled, 'When the lead's flyin' too thick round our ears fer comfort, we j-eest git up and walk around.'

About this time Marty Hume advised squadron pilots of a report that the method of jettisoning the cockpit canopy – prior to baling out – was suspect. The recommended drill for abandoning the aircraft was first to unlatch the canopy and pull it back a fraction, using the metal handle at the top front, just behind the windscreen. We already knew that his could be a lottery, as above 200 mph the effect of the air flow tended to hold the canopy closed; and there was always the uneasy thought that, at high speed, the canopy might not unlatch, or one might tear the handle right off.

Having unlatched the canopy, the next move was to pull smartly on a black rubber ball (about the size of a golf ball) beside the handle. Anchored by a metal washer, two steel wires ran through the ball, down the rear frame of the windscreen, and through the mounting pins of the rails on which the canopy slid back and forth. The principle was similar to the ripcord of a parachute, in that when the ball and its steel lanyards were pulled free, the rails and the canopy would be released to fly clear of the cockpit.

We static-tested the jettison device in each of the eighteen aircraft, and in a number of them the steel wires and anchor plates pulled right through the rubber balls. This led to an immediate modification to the jettison system on our aircraft.

On 16 September the wing did a high cover escort for Marauders to Beaumont-le-Roger, and on the way out twelve Me 109s dived from directly behind straight underneath our section, and kept on going for the deck. It looked like the typical decoy gambit; but there were no aircraft anywhere above us. I led the section down, and caught up with the bunch just as they reached ground level. I was lining up on two Me 109s, which were very close together at the rear, and had eased the throttle back to avoid charging into the middle of them, when Murray Metcalfe and Bert Wipiti shot past and into the gaggle, which then split away to the left-right on the tree tops. Bert spotted six 190s coming in from the right, and pulled round into them. Murray dropped in behind a 109, a 109 turned in behind him, I fell in behind that one at about 600 yds range, and another swung in behind me, in a deadly sort of ballet routine.

We were all firing together except the 109 in front of Murray – which crashed into the woods – followed by Murray himself. I made some strikes on the one which got him, then I broke hard round to have a go at the one behind me – who was either a very bad shot or had been bouncing around in my slipstream. After some violent turns, with vapour trails streaming from the wing-tips, I saw strikes on the 109's wing, but had to break quickly again as one of his friends came at me. In the mêlée I got in a snap shot at another Me 109, then latched onto a FW 190.

We battled each other round and round in coarse, tight turns; and as the area was in deep shadow from low cumulus cloud, the white vapour trails from our wingtips showed starkly against the dark background of the woods. The FW 190 had a very fast rate of roll, and this pilot really used that ability well; swiftly reversing the direction of turn from left to right and back again, but staying right on the tree tops. I glimpsed a Spitfire wheeling around just above me (which turned out to be Bert) and could see the control surfaces on the 190 working rapidly as the aircraft was pulled round tight, to judder each time it hit the point of high-speed stall, so that our streaming vapour trails made a crazy pattern of irregular white arcs and angles. The amount of g we were both pulling in the turns was dragging hard, and as my own vision was hovering between grey-out and black-out it must have been much the same for the FW 190 pilot. I remember jumbled thoughts and images popping illogically to mind: 'This pilot must be one of those 'Strength through Joy' keep-fit fanatics – wish we had that canopy on our Spitfires – what a good-looking aircraft these FWs really are.'

As his turn rate momentarily slackened at the stall in a steep turn, I managed to pull through his flight path to fire a short burst, which produced a flurry of bright strikes on the wing-root. As the 190 pilot flicked away into an opposite turn he flew right into Bert's line of fire, and a short burst smashed the aircraft down into the woods in a great shower of debris.

Only a few minutes earlier twenty or more aircraft had been twisting and turning like demented bluebottles, but we now had the scene all to ourselves: as in most battles, we must have quickly spread out over a fairly large area. Setting course for the coast I was still gulping in pure oxygen from the mask, and suddenly felt very chilled; because I was literally drenched in perspiration from head to toe. My fuel was well down by now, so after crossing the Channel at economical cruising power, I refuelled at Friston on Beachy Head – which on that particular day was clear of low cloud. Bruce Gibbs had lost sight of the well-camouflaged Me 109s and Spitfires in the initial dive to the deck, and was heading for the coast at low level when a solitary

Me 109 crossed in front of him, which he promptly dispatched. Bert Wipiti's eyes were still flashing late that night as the action was relived and dissected in the bar – which is the way of all fighter pilots the world over.

Two weeks and about ten shows later Bert Wipiti was killed in action. The Germans had enticed some of the Spitfires down with decoys on their way out from the target; and Bert was last seen in the thick of a violent dogfight.

Another well-experienced, recent arrival who also went missing on the same day – but with a happier result – was Flying Officer Mortimer. After destroying a FW 190 he had to ditch his Spitfire close to the Somme River mouth, and only managed to free himself from the cockpit after the aircraft had dived to the bottom. After trying to sail his dinghy towards England, the strong tidal flow during darkness took him up the river, and into a muddy tidal creek; where he managed to struggle ashore undetected, but smothered with blood and mud. By good luck he avoided Germans in a camp near the coast, and local people gave him enough food to keep him going for five days, when he was put in touch with a group of the French Resistance Movement. After dodging around and getting involved in local activities, he was to return to England after an absence of eleven months.

When I joined the Officers' Mess I shared a room with Lyndon Peray Griffiths, which was an education in itself. 'Griff' was tall, dark and well-built, with a slightly high-pitched voice, and quite a range of mannerisms. He had been a foundation member of 485 as a Sergeant Pilot, and had just rejoined after a rest, having flown on a great number of sweeps during 1941 and 1942. If seniority or a pilot's experience came under discussion, Griff would nonchalantly tap the ash from his cigarette saying: 'Get some in, fellas.' The story is told that at Kenley in 1942 Griff bought a 1937 Ford V8 Coupé, and before heading off for a few days in London, topped the tank up from the aircraft bowser – a court-martial offence if caught. He became wedged in a line of stalled traffic near the main gate out of the station, and 100 octane petrol was overflowing from the tank, giving forth its distinctive and pungent smell. Spotting the Station Commander approaching, Griff lit a cigarette and dropped the match in the petrol, with fairly spectacular results.

After rejoining 485 at Biggin Hill Griff became separated on a show which had ended in a dogfight, and called on the radio: 'Hey boss, come and get me – I'm all on my own apart from half the bloody Luftwaffe.' Al Deere took his section back and found a lone Spitfire turning in a tight circle. Asked later where the Luftwaffe had gone, Griff said he thought they had gone home to get more ammunition.

Bruce Gibbs was now 'B' Flight Commander and was called to the telephone one evening, then came back to the bar shaking his head and looking very put out: 'Some people have a weird sense of humour – there's a bastard on the phone from London who says he's Chalky White.'

So we all trooped out to the telephone and I asked the profane character on the other end a question which only Chalk could answer – and disbelief turned to jubilation. The next day our walkabout shearer was back, and gave us a fascinating account of what was probably the fastest return of a missing pilot, without any help from the organised escape or evasion lines being run by the Underground movement.

Escapers or evaders were rightly cautioned not to reveal names or information which, if subsequently winkled out by the Germans, could bring death or disaster to people helping an evader in the occupied territories. In the same way they were warned not to speak of any incident en route which could place the escaper or evader himself in jeopardy, if taken prisoner later. So a few extra details did come to light later on; but he was able to give a fairly complete account at the time.

His formal report on the way he was shot down was given in *New Zealanders with the Royal Air Force*:

On the way in from the French coast to the target the wing was attacked. I was flying Green Three and was attacked from all directions by three or four FW 190s, and my aircraft was hit in the glycol tank. I rolled and headed back towards the sea but finding my radio telephone dead, I headed back inland and was intercepted by eight FW 190s, four of which immediately went onto another Spitfire which seemed to be in the same predicament as me. I went down from 12,000 ft to the deck with the four FW 190s behind me. A few moments later I saw one of them on the deck by itself so dived and attacked it from 150 yds. Glycol streaming from my engine caused the windscreen to mist up. I looked out the side and saw tree tops above me, so I pulled up and then saw the FW on the ground, crash-landed. After a few more manoeuvres I had a head-on with another FW 190 but my guns would not fire. My engine then stopped so I force-landed near Balbec with pursuing FW 190s still firing shells at me as I crash-landed.

We had been told that extra escape and survival rations had been added to our dinghy packs, to supplement those carried inside one's battle dress blouse, so Chalk tore the dinghy from the parachute, and was in the process of setting fire to the aircraft – in accordance with instructions – when some figures appeared on the far side of the field. With the heavy dinghy pack under his arm Chalk headed for the bush and took cover, only to find there were no rations in the dinghy pack after all.

The Germans mounted a concentrated search of the area, which kept him pinned down in the immediate vicinity of his forced landing for four days. He managed to obtain food by random calls at several houses to supplement the compressed food tablets and sweets of the escape kit, which were reputedly sufficient to keep a man going for up to fourteen days. At one stage he crawled under a mass of nettles in a ditch to rest; and suffered the indignity of a German soldier piddling down on him from a range of four feet.

Chalk was wearing an issue blue V-neck jersey with long sleeves under his battle-dress, and put that on over the battle-dress blouse, after some modifications. He cut the collar, lapels and patch pockets off the blouse, removed the New Zealand shoulder tabs, wings and sergeant's stripes which he put in his pocket; and carried his .38 revolver in one of the large, inside pockets of the battle-dress blouse. Cutting the gaiter tabs from the battle-dress trouser cuffs, he wore the trouser legs outside his New Zealand-made sheepskin flying boots. For the next three nights he slept in a haystack, a disused car and a stable respectively.

By the fourth morning the search parties had apparently given up, so at dawn Chalk marched up to the largest house or château he could see in the area, and knocked on the front door. By one of many strokes of luck the lady who came to the door spoke perfect English and recognised him for what he was straight away. She gave him food and some extra clothing, then pointed him in the right direction for the nearest railway station at Yvetot.

Stepping out smartly along the country road Chalk heard a horse coming up behind him, and looked back to see a two-man German patrol in a horse and trap; so he ambled into a field, shutting the gate behind him, to bend over a rusty plough – and the patrol clip-clopped past with only a casual glance.

At the railway station Chalk joined the queue at the ticket window amongst local people commuting to their day's work. He pushed a brand new one thousand franc note from his escape kit across the counter and said: 'Paris,' whereupon the ticket seller became quite agitated and shooed Chalk away from the window saying: 'Partez, Anglais – Partez, Partez.' Chalk gathered the chap was telling him to get the hell out of it, so he moved off to spend that night in the back of another car, and came back again the next morning. This time the man behind the counter pushed over a ticket to Paris without looking up at Chalk, who boarded the next train going in the right direction. The train was very crowded, and Chalk stood in the corridor until an Inspector's Control came through checking papers and travel permits. He kept moving along the corridor and, when the officials went into the last compartment, stood behind the half-open toilet door until they passed by.

In Paris he spent the day looking for help, and trying to find his way across the city to a station for the south of France; making his way, everywhere he went, through the German soldiers and airmen. He took a Métro ride to the terminus, then a bus trip, then another Métro trip, all with no success.

We had been briefed not to be out of doors after curfew in any town or city, so as curfew time was obviously getting close Chalk went into a small restaurant, and walked into the office of the lady manageress, or owner. Putting his wings, stripes and New Zealand tabs on the desk he mimed the reason for his presence saying: 'Spitfire . . . British . . . parachute' – which he reckoned was a word she should recognise more readily than any attempts to describe a forced landing. Madame indicated that he should stay in the office, then went out and locked the door, but returned with a French policeman. Chalk jumped to the conclusion that the lady was turning him in, and produced his .38; but the gendarme quickly reassured him that they would help him. This courageous Frenchman took Chalk to his own home for the night, fed and provisioned him for the journey, then next morning directed him across Paris to the right station, where Chalk bought a ticket as far as Bourges.

Leaving the train he walked on, using the handkerchief map from the escape kit, and laid low for a day near an aerodrome which he thought must be an Operational Training Unit for German fighter pilots. He was intrigued to see that most of the flying going on was by FW 190 pilots, practising steep turns and mock dogfights at zero feet.

Approaching the Vichy French border (into technically Unoccupied France) a French schoolboy cycled past Chalk, then waited by the side of the road. As Chalk walked by the youngster said: 'Good afternoon, Mr Englishman,' which stopped him dead in his tracks. Chalk said that all through his escape many French civilians had picked him for exactly what he was, and had helped with food, directions and encouragement; willingly putting their necks on the line by these spontaneous acts.

The French boy was delighted to try his schoolboy English on Chalk, and gave him directions for a place to cross the Vichy border safely. He then gave Chalk the bicycle to take him clear of the border area, asking only that it be left in a certain village for him to recover later.

Near Marmagne some children took him to a farm stable

where he slept for the night, and they also provided more food. The next day the English-speaking farm owner showed up and arranged Chalk's rail journey to Toulouse, paying for his ticket as well. He spent all that day on a variety of trains, before reaching Toulouse in the early evening. Chalk took a tram out of the city and was again lucky enough to find a house, at random, where he was given a meal; then he slept in a lean-to shed.

The following day he bought a ticket for Carcassonne, in the foothills of the Pyrenees, which we had been told was a likely area to locate a guide for the journey across the mountains. He left the train at Pezens, however, just short of his destination; and again he struck lucky by learning of someone who would be able to help him; but he had to wait around in the area from 1 to 10 September.

Chalk has been able to give me personally more details about his escape:

> I am sure the people I met in Pezens were not in any Underground movement, but they were certainly anti-German. . . . Every out-back farm around Pezens seemed to have a few Jews in hiding. In fact when I got back to England I was able to tell a number of Jews that so and so was safe, much to their astonishment. . . . I had to go through a German patrol at the foot of the Pyrenees and I could see they were arguing about me, so I stopped the argument with a revolver given to me by the people I met in Pezens.

Chalk said he gave his guide most of the money he had left from his escape kit, and a Promissory Note for £1000 on the British Government, before they set off to walk over the Pyrenees. He said it was tough going all the way, particularly as his guide did this journey often as part of his living, and was very fit and agile. Somewhere near the actual border they were challenged and fired on in the darkness by a patrol, but got clear by racing away on a goat-track along the side of the mountain.

Down in the foothills on the Spanish side, Chalk parted company with his guide to set off on the road to Barcelona, and his run of luck still ran hot. He was picked up by a Swiss millionaire and his wife, who had a summer home in Spain; and

they drove him much of the way to Barcelona in their luxurious
Buick convertible.

When he came down off the mountains the soles of his flying
boots had disintegrated, and with the help of his Swiss friends
Chalk acquired a pair of locally made rope-soled shoes. Having
arranged a rented room, they took a note from him to the British
Consulate, giving his name, air force number and address; but
when nothing had happened after several days Chalk took to the
road again, heading for Madrid. On arrival he got himself under
cover again, and sent a young boy off to the British Embassy
with another note; and after cooling his over-heated feet for a
few more days he was collected and taken to the Embassy.

No doubt the Embassy staff were quite accustomed to pro-
cessing escapers, and to them he was just another one passing
through; but Chalk was more than a little disgruntled at his
reception:

> I didn't expect to be treated like the King of England, but I
> hadn't done too bad to get out on my own, and thought they might
> at least offer me a whisky and a cigar. There was a sort of reception
> area where a clerk handed out clothing and so on, and when I asked
> for cigarettes, this bloke tossed over a packet of Players Weights
> . . . He had a fat looking smoke in his mouth, so I grabbed it and
> took the skin off his lip as well . . . The bastard was smoking Gold
> Flake which were probably meant for the escapers anyway, so
> when I gave him the message he handed some over.

Chalk is still critical of the attitude of the Embassy people:

> The whole trip seemed like a dream once it was done. . . . The
> biggest job I had was ingrowing toenails, and convincing the
> British people in Barcelona and Madrid that I was British and a
> New Zealander, as no one had done it alone before. . . . In fact, I
> think I was responsible for a Group Captain in Madrid getting the
> sack.'

He was escorted from the Embassy to the border by Spanish
police, then handed over to the authorities at Gibraltar, to be
flown back to England in a night-flying RAF Transport aircraft; arriving on 5 October 1943, six weeks and two days after

being shot down in France. His journey took him approximately three weeks to get out of France and about two weeks to pass
through Spain; with another week waiting around in Gibraltar.
Leslie Samual McQueen White was, and is, proud to be a New
Zealander of English, Irish, Maori and Jewish descent. While
there was a considerable element of luck in his escape, this was
well and truly matched by his sheer guts and determination. A
few days before he was shot down Chalk, Frank Transom and
Snow Clark had bought a Morris 12 hp car between them;
which Chalk had paid out on until they could pay their share
next pay day. His first words on walking back into the Mess at
Biggin Hill were: 'Where's my bloody car?'

My twenty-first birthday on 23 September 1943 was a double-
feature day, with two high-cover escorts for Marauders bombing at Conches and Evreux. The following weekend the squadron
had a stand down for twenty-four hours from noon on the
Saturday, with massive and memorable parties in the Messes on
the Saturday night.

Well-laden squadron cars made for the Old Jail – the ancient
pub near Biggin Hill village – after lunch on the Saturday, to get
into the right mood; and two of the very popular and pretty
waitresses from the Sergeants' Mess showed up on their sports
cycles to join the party. The Old Jail served Devon draught
cider, and I had already discovered that two pints of that
innocent brew was more than enough to paralyse one from the
waist down, while the top half was still fully operational and
having a great time. As we all made the move to leave Paddy and
Margaret discovered the trap, so they were hoisted into one of
the cars; while two big-hearted volunteers raced the bikes back
to the station . . . I went flat out down the hill and onto the
Mess driveway, where the brake cable snapped with a sheer
drop ahead over a retaining wall; so I laid the bike gracefully
down on the cinders to slide like a baseballer, right up to the
front door in a cloud of black dust. Corporal Brooks wheeled me
off to his kitchen to paint a yard of abrasions with iodine but I
didn't feel a thing, and it turned out to be one of the best parties

we ever had. Allan Mitchell came down from London to cover the event for NZPA; and was put to bed on a billiard table at about 3 a.m. The notes he had made during the evening were not much use, as he couldn't read them next day anyway.

Just over a month later the squadron moved on to Hornchurch, taking with it very fond memories of Biggin Hill Sector Station, having crammed a feast of operations into a three-month period, at the peak of Fighter Command's running battle with the Luftwaffe over the Occupied countries. The Squadron had destroyed 27 enemy aircraft with 4 probables and 5 damaged during the fourteen weeks of operations at Biggin Hill. Our tally of casualties was 4 killed in action, 2 prisoners of war and 4 missing, of whom one (Chalky White) had already evaded capture and returned to England.

15

HORNCHURCH

485 Squadron now became part of a four-squadron wing at Hornchurch under Wing Commander W. V. Crawford-Compton, another New Zealander. He and three companions had set out in 1938 to sail to England in a ketch, which was wrecked en route. After staying for some weeks with natives on a small island, Bill worked his way to England on a tramp steamer. Joining the Royal Air Force in a ground crew trade he then remustered to pilot, and was posted to his first squadron as a Sergeant Pilot early in 1941; then transferred again to become a foundation member of 485 Squadron.

Bill Crawford-Compton had been leading the Hornchurch wing since June 1943, and by the end of the year the unit had destroyed 41 enemy aircraft, with as many more damaged. Both Al Deere and Bill Crawford-Compton had the same number of enemy aircraft destroyed at that time (21½ each) and were up near the top of the scoring ladder in Fighter Command.

The atmosphere of Hornchurch was brisk and businesslike, very much as at Biggin Hill; and the operational role was similar, but with more emphasis on fighter sweeps than on escorts.

The Seadrome project* came alive again, and we made three trips to Ford, in Sussex, to work up to a full-scale demonstration of the system for the benefit of Mr Churchill and Senior

---

* See Appendix I for historical data concerning the Seadrome project.

Planning Staff Officers. The Seadrome and its service taxyways were marked out on the grass, and there were a large
number of aircraft on the aerodrome, with four squadrons of
Spitfires involved. In addition a collection of Beaufighters,
Mosquitoes, Hurricanes, Mustangs and Typhoons also made –
or attempted to make – landings in the marked-out area.

After lunch on the day of the demonstration the pilots were
returning to their parked aircraft, and I was ambling along with
Jack Yeatman and Griff, who were both well over six feet tall.
As we passed the Control Tower the pair grabbed me by the
shoulders and legs of my battle-dress and treated me to a hearty
sample of the old heave-ho swing – and I found myself gazing
upwards at a well-known face – complete with large cigar –
smiling down from the roof of the tower at their antics.

The Seadrome demonstration itself went off quite well, apart
from the frenzied enthusiasm of the sailors acting as taxying
marshals along the service strip parallel to the Seadrome. They
waved us faster and faster along the narrow lane: so fast that we
could not zigzag to check the position of the aircraft in front, or
stop in a hurry. As a result Pat Patterson ran straight up the tail
of Ken Lee's aircraft, chopping the tail and rear fuselage into
scrap, with the last propeller blade being stopped by the armour-
plate behind Ken's head. Frank Transom and others then
stopped and switched off their engines; refusing to respond to
the naval urging, which made *them* unhappy.

After the exercise was completed, I flew on three sweeps and
three high-cover escorts in the last six days of operations in
November, before the squadron was stood down for a rest over
the midwinter period.

Regrettably we were on the receiving end of an action which
happened on 20 November on a sweep round the Lille area. We
were still climbing out over the Channel with the sections in
loose line astern, and Control had just reported enemy aircraft
above us and in our vicinity, when a small formation of FW 190s
dived out of the sun onto the tower section, achieving total
surprise. The first sight I had of them was as they appeared from
the glare behind the up-sun section, and firing from close range.

Two newly joined pilots – Flying Officers Thompson and Baker – went down and were killed. Frank Transom was shot up, but made it back to the English coast before his engine seized and he baled out, to land safely in a paddock near the water's edge.

The attack by the enemy fighters was well executed, their shooting was excellent, and they did the right thing by keeping on going down and away, back into France. In fact the Germans had used some initiative in coming right out over the Channel to make the interception while we were still climbing and therefore vulnerable. In fact, we were caught with our pants down.

Ash had just returned from North Africa, and came to stay for a week with me at Hornchurch before starting his official rest period, and had also been commissioned. Since we had gone our different ways a year and a half before Ash had been flying strafing Hurricanes with four 20-mm guns, and 'tank busters' which were fitted with a 37-mm gun under each wing. The weight and drag of these artillery pieces pulled the performance of the Hurricane right down, and there were only a few rounds per gun, which had to be reloaded for each salvo by a remote control from the cockpit. When fired, the recoil of these heavy-calibre guns knocked 30 mph or more off the speed of the aircraft, but the results were often spectacular.

Ash had been on a convoy patrol north of Algiers in one of these tank busters when a Ju 88 dropped out of cloud in front of him, to begin a bombing run on the ships. Sighting very carefully Ash fired his two-round broadside, and the Ju 88 disintegrated, probably the only time those guns were ever used in the air-to-air role.

During Ash's visit a new pennant was presented to one of the Hornchurch squadrons, and the whole Station turned out in Number One uniforms for the day, which somehow seemed unreal, as though we were all actors in a play. That night there was a gigantic party, with visitors from all over Fighter Command; and I was particularly pleased to meet some of the Norwegian Spitfire Wing pilots from North Weald who had flown in for the occasion. Fighter Command was rather like a community of families, in that units were recognised as having particular characteristics, and it was generally agreed that the 'Norges' were in a class of their own. Apart from their high ability as fighter pilots individually, their squadrons had the reputation of absolute reliability, in whatever role might be allocated to them. The planning of the complex, co-ordinated segments of daylight offensive operations had almost become an art form. Unexpected actions by the enemy could always create situations to be dealt with by initiative in the air, but the first requirement on the RAF units was to do exactly what was expected under the briefing plan. We always knew that when the Norwegians were designated to be at a definite position, at a specific height and at a particular time they would be there; with a consistency second to none.

The similarities in physique amongst the Norwegians was quite noticeable; most of them being of lean but strong build, with their characteristic fair hair and fair complexion. Towards the Germans they had an attitude of controlled ruthlessness, but they were as staunch friends of the righteous as they were implacable enemies of the invader.

One incident indicates just how tough these men were. The pilot concerned had his sights on a FW 190 diving vertically at high speed, when the German half-rolled and started to pull up away from the vertical in the opposite direction from that in which the Spitfire was facing. The Norwegian trimmed his Spitfire quickly into the nose-heavy attitude and followed the FW 190, going into the bottom half of an outside loop – or bunt. This applied negative g to the aircraft and to himself, and as the blood was violently forced upwards into his head multiple blood vessels ruptured in his face, scalp and eyes. How he got back to base is some sort of a miracle, and he passed out in the blood-stained cockpit after landing. The doctors told him that his flying days were over; but six weeks later he was back on operations, and he was all present and correct at the Hornchurch party.

The tempo of the air war was still increasing, with the RAF heavy bomber and Mosquito raids reaching deep into Germany, and 40 out of 600 heavy bombers had been lost in an attack on Germany's Peenemünde Air Research and Development Station. The US Eighth Air Force lost 60 out of 300 Fortresses on 17 August operating against the ball-bearing factories at Schweinfurt and Regensburg, and in September RAF Bomber Command had used a 12,000-lb bomb for the first time.

In mid-October US Eighth Air Force had attacked Schweinfurt again, losing 60 Fortresses this time out of the force of 224. It was clear that, even if the German fighter force in France had been somewhat depleted, there were still very large numbers operating over Germany.

Looking back over the last four hectic months of our small segment of the war, it seemed that something like a pattern had formed around the outstanding pilots from the 1942 Malta period. Paul Brennan, Ray Hesselyn's friend and co-author of *Spitfires over Malta*, had already been killed in an aircraft crash in Australia earlier in 1943, but the three New Zealanders had returned to Eleven Group after the prescribed rest period, and had carried on with the same flair which they had displayed in Malta: Jack Rae had force-landed in France through engine failure on 22 August 1943 and was now a prisoner of war; Gray Stenberg had been killed in action with a Spitfire XII Squadron on 24 September, and Ray Hesselyn became a prisoner of war on 3 October 1943. Ray had been flying with 222 Squadron at Hornchurch, and in four months had added 7 more destroyed to his Malta total. The final, combined score of the three New Zealanders, one Canadian (Beurling) and one Australian (Brennan) was 87 enemy aircraft destroyed.

Shortly before we left Biggin Hill a Canadian Squadron had dropped in for a combined briefing – and stayed for lunch. George Beurling was standing in a corner of the anteroom very much alone, and we talked for a while before the Canadians flew out again. I knew he was one of the few survivors from the Liberator crash at Gibraltar on the way back from Malta, and asked him what had happened. He told me that when the aircraft was coming into Gibraltar he had an overwhelming premonition that it was going to crash, so he took his flying logbook out of his kit bag and put it inside his shirt, then positioned himself beside an emergency exit. He had been put on display all round Canada, which was torture for him, as he was basically shy and out of his depth as Guest of Honour, or Guest Speaker, at formal functions and parades. Nor was he too happy in his present squadron, for he could never be other than an individualist in the air; but I was startled when he said that his good eye was starting to weaken, and that the other eye had always been well below normal. He had wangled his way through the eyesight test for the Air Force by covering the weak eye both times with an envelope; but had changed the envelope from one hand to the other in full view of the examining doctor, who had fallen for this simple sleight of hand.*

As operations from Hornchurch were coming to a halt late in October 1943, one more event brought great cause for celebration, before we moved north for our rest period. The excitement of having Chalky White return to the fold had just subsided, when Squadron Leader Checketts and Warrant Officer Terry Kearins arrived back in England together. Squadron Leader Checketts made a brief visit to the squadron and we learnt that he had been concealed, and his burns cared for by French families, before being brought together with Terry Kearins. Their safe return was made possible through the dedicated work of the escape and evasion sections of the French Underground.

Although they both arrived back together, we had to wait for two more days before Terry turned up at Hornchurch, because he was being taken through an extensive debriefing by the Intelligence people. When word came that he had arrived in the Sergeants' Mess I went straight over, and could hardly believe my eyes. Terry had virtually turned into a Frenchman, and was still dressed in the clothing which he had worn for getting around in France. His black hair was long, thick and bushy, with a heavy moustache; and he was wearing a bright blue suit

* In 1944 we heard that George Beurling retired from the Air Force at his own request, and his total score of enemy aircraft destroyed is listed as 32. Some years after the war he was killed when ferrying an aircraft out to the Israeli Air Force.

cut in the French style, with a bright red tie and great, thick shoes with rope soles. He had been quite severely burned and, because of the parties of Germans quartering the area, he had to wander and hide in the area for two days, with whatever food and wine the local farming people could smuggle to him, until the Germans eased off the search and he could be taken indoors.

Apart from expressing his heartfelt admiration and respect for the courage of the French people who risked their lives daily to shelter him, and who nursed him through the effects of his wounds, we got very little out of Terry as to what had really gone on in the four months since he had been shot down. It was only correct to reveal nothing – even to his friends – which could possibly jeopardise the lives and work of the gallant French people involved. It seemed probable, however, from his extended debriefing in London and the odd comment which was prised out of him, that he may have been doing a little more than just quietly staying hidden until he could make his way out of France. Subsequently, he was awarded a French Croix de Guerre, and some time later we learned from another evader (who returned in the same party) that when a particularly hazardous set-up had arisen, Terry had taken some hard-nosed action which had held the situation together.

16

REST PERIOD IN SCOTLAND

We now exchanged our Spitfire IXs for the Mk Vs of a replacement squadron; then the aircraft were all flown north to Drem, near Edinburgh, for a rest period. It was known that this was to be a short break, and we would return to Hornchurch in the New Year, so I left the open cockpit MG in one of the garages attached to the Officers' Mess; and travelled in one of the other private cars heading north.

After we stood down from operational work I think most of us realised, for the first time, that we had been functioning at a higher level of stimulation and awareness since moving into the Biggin Hill wing at the beginning of July. Concentration on the day-to-day demands of the air war across the Channel and the North Sea now eased off, one's interests widened, and the mundane aspects of life outside the aerodrome gates seemed to drop back into focus. It was rather like going back to normal breathing after holding one's breath. It was a sound move to stand squadrons down and give them a change of scene, at times when weather conditions anyway reduced operational work to a low level.

Eight of us travelled by car, taking a leisurely four days for the journey; and relaxing at some pleasant watering holes along the way. At York our group joined a party in the hotel, celebrating the wedding of a young munitions worker. At closing time off we all went to the home of the bride's parents', where the party rolled on into the night. Around 4 a.m. a plaintive young man with confetti in his hair insisted he was newly wed but could not get to bed – and would we please shove off, as he was on early shift at 6 a.m.

Drem had been a Royal Naval Air Service Station in World War I, and there was a comfortable feeling of spaciousness about the station, the only other flying unit based there being a Polish Mosquito squadron. Apart from maintaining sections on Search and Rescue readiness, or on standby for any intruder interceptions, a reasonable level of flying activity was maintained on operational training, air firing and formation flying; while recently arrived pilots were able to be fitted into the pattern, under conditions which were far more suitable than when a squadron was fully operational.

Most New Zealanders felt very much at home in Scotland, particularly as the countryside – and especially the Highlands – is so similar to much of the back country in the South Island. It was a two-way attraction, many Scots who settled in New Zealand also found the similarity very much to their liking.

The squadron rugby team joined in the local round of competition, as had been the custom during each of the two previous winters, in whatever area the unit happened to be. After winning the early games we went down by one point to Edinburgh University, in what I believe was our first defeat ever. Pat Patterson proved to be a powerful, hard running three-quarter, and Lyndsay Black – the tall 'A' Flight Commander – also turned on an elegant turn of speed on one wing. Jack Yeatman was back again with the squadron and led the pack and the team in his usual driving style; while Al Stead had also joined us, and showed the brilliant flair of Maori rugby in mid-field.

The squadron was detailed to carry out service evaluation trials on a prototype g-suit – or to be more specific, an 'anti-g effect suit' which had been designed by a Canadian scientist, Dr Frank. The suit was, in effect, a pair of close-fitting trousers with a long waist and body section which extended to just under the armpits; but the garment was double-skinned and made from calico impregnated with latex to form a waterproof, hollow covering for the trunk and legs, right down to the ankles. The suit had laces down one side of the body and each leg so that it could be adjusted to fit the pilot's individual build, like a man-size corset. We were laced in with the suit over one's underwear; battledress trousers and blouse were worn on top, with the usual flying boots enclosing the suit on the lower legs. Next, the suit was filled with water through a filler tube and valve at chest level, which was done while the pilot was seated in the cockpit. The first fill was made with cold water, which raised a chorus of profanity on a raw mid-winter morning, and the verdict was: 'Hot water or no trials'.

The principle was that as g-force was applied to the body in a steep turn or pullout from a dive, the constricting jacket of water (which is not compressible), would restrict swelling of the body and legs as blood was dragged downwards from the brain and the chest, thus restricting the blood movement itself. We first tested our normal g tolerance with meters mounted at eye level in the cockpit, then measured the tolerance using the suit; and the results showed a significant increase in tolerance, measured at the grey-out to black-out point of vision. The meters were like a simple, spring balance scale; and I doubt if the instruments read actual g-forces; but the readings did indicate an increase in tolerance of the order of about 40 per cent. This would certainly confer a great advantage in a dog-fight, and it was confirmed in mock combats; but in our view – which was unanimous – the disadvantages far exceeded the anti-g benefit. The insurmountable problem was the serious restriction on mobility for the fighter pilot. Firstly, it was impossible to twist the body to any degree to either side in order to look back over one's shoulder, which was a constant require-ment in seeking to stay alive in a hostile sky. Secondly, with the suit filled with water, the extra weight and awkwardness which this imposed seriously hampered the pilot in attempting to abandon the aircraft, whether by parachute or after ditching. A third factor – which was less serious as a hazard, but nonetheless distracting – was that with the suit filled the pilot actually sat on a cushion of water, giving a sense of imbalance.*

Marty Hume was still CO when a signal arrived advising that Mac McGuiness had been turned loose from the glasshouse, and inquiring if 485 Squadron would take him back on its strength. The response from those who knew Mac brought a big smile to Marty's face, and the right reply was sent. Mac travelled north by a train which stopped at small rail stations, like Drem, only as required and, determined to arrive on time this time, Mac arranged for the guard to let him know when to dismount. So when the guard woke him in the early hours he slung his kit bag on his shoulder and stepped out into the darkness, to tumble head first down the steep embankment. Mac arrived on time all right, but with a broken arm encased in plaster.

Vicki came up on leave, and we spent ten wonderful days exploring the lochs and villages from our base at the Trossachs Hotel. On the Braes of Doune one evening at sunset we heard a lone piper in the distance, who marched up and past us into the dusk, then down into the valley below. We learnt next day that this elderly Scot piped that walk every night of the year, regardless of wind and weather, and was an accepted part of the local scene. Climbing a glen behind the hotel early one morning I walked onto a poised group of deer, and I could well have been in the fern and birch forest of the hills at home. The rugged beauty of the landscape, and the kindness of the people we met, are still just as real to us today as during that winter of forty years ago.

Ash had been posted to our old OTU at Annan as an instructor, and I flew over to visit him on a day which had quite a reasonable weather forecast for the area, but which clamped right down on me over the wild country in the centre. With wheels and flaps down I was map-reading along a single-track railway which disappeared into a tunnel, and I had a nasty five minutes casting back and forth in the murk, until I picked the

* The Frank g-suit was apparently dropped following these service trials but the principle was retained in the g suits which came into service after the war. In the later suit water was replaced by compressed air; which was admitted into the suit on a demand basis, according to the amount of g being applied.

line up again in another valley. In the coastal area between Dumfries and Carlisle even the sparrows were walking, and I sat down on the end of a runway which appeared under the wing tip, and which turned out to be Annan. I gave myself a good talking to for that effort, and only left the next afternoon after getting a more extensive check on the weather en route.

About ten days before Christmas a Flying Fortress landed at Drem late in the afternoon, on a delivery flight from the United States via the Azores; and the intended destination was Ayr, on the *west* coast of Scotland. Next morning one engine of the aircraft refused to start, but the pilot took off on the other three engines on a heading running up quite a distinct slope, at an angle from the main strip itself. The aircraft staggered into the air at the edge of the aerodrome; but stalled and dropped the wing carrying the dead engine, hitting an aircraft dispersal bay, and crashing with the loss of all on board. This tragic chapter of errors was deeply felt by the station personnel, as three airmen going on compassionate leave down the west side of the country were riding in the aeroplane; and it was further heightened when John Dasent – a popular recent arrival on 485 Squadron – was killed in a flying accident. We were very conscious of special sorrow for his family at home in New Zealand, as we buried him on the eve of Christmas.

Despite this, the New Year season was something special, with the traditional first-footing celebrations and hospitality north of the border. A few days later I went down with a heavy cold which turned into some sort of 'flu, which then had me floating round the ceiling of the Nissen hut for two lost days, and left me very wrung out indeed. Whether coincidence or not, I have not had another cold in the forty years since then.

Early in February 1944 we changed back to Spitfire IXs, and again I claimed OU-V. We farewelled Marty Hume as he left for a rest period after a long tour with the squadron, and the next CO was Squadron Leader Johnny Niven DFC, the first non-New Zealander to serve with 485 Squadron. Appropriately enough he was a Scot, having started out as a Sergeant Pilot in the Battle of Britain with 602 (City of Glasgow) Squadron. He was a dapper little man with bright blue eyes, and a happy knack of making a quick joke at the right time. I remember his account of an incident in which he was hanging on his propeller, as last man in a section of Spitfires clawing for altitude in a steep spiral, during the Battle of Britain. Al Deere was leading, and Sergeant Niven was getting left behind and feeling very lonely, and very scared. He called over the RT: 'Hey Al – how do you get out of a spin?' Al Deere came straight back: 'Are you in a spin?' and Johnny answered 'No – but I bloody soon will be.' Back in the crew room, however, Al Deere pinned Sergeant Niven to the wall and made a terse comment, and a lurid promise, to any idiot cluttering up the RT in a dogfight by trying to be funny.

The point is that, by recounting this story to a crowd of New Zealanders – which included some eager but relatively inexperienced pilots – he made everyone laugh, but the message was well received and recorded.

Another new pilot on 485 at Drem was Bill Newenham, a dark and dashing character who arrived as a Flight Lieutenant, complete with the DFC. His background was certainly different, as this was his first operational posting as a pilot, and he was fresh from pilot training in Canada, after completing two tours as a navigator in Bomber Command since 1940. His rank and decoration placed him in an awkward position in a squadron where he was senior to the other pilots with the exception of the CO and the Flight Commanders, most of them – including the sergeants – being reasonably experienced fighter pilots. Bill therefore had a rather wary reception in the squadron; but having survived a series of hazardous operations and incidents in his two tours on bombers, he had elected – when the opportunity arose – to remuster to pilot and change his operational venue; and he made it clear that he was starting out on the same footing as anyone else.

Returning in a Whitley from a raid on Hamburg in the winter of 1940, Bill Newenham's aircraft was still enveloped in a snowstorm, when about to run out of fuel. The crew baled out into the storm, and Bill landed in a cherry tree in the back garden of a doctor's house in York. He was most hospitably received, and later marked this happy landing by marrying Margaret, a daughter of his host.

Not long afterwards a special raid was laid on against Berlin, which had implications of international importance. It was understood that the Spanish ambassador in Berlin was being wooed by the Nazi leaders towards persuading Franco and Spain to join the Axis forces against the Allies; and the point had been reached where it was believed that Spain was wavering. So the RAF attack against Berlin, on this particular night, was intended to convince the ambassador that Britain was still capable of striking hard at the enemy. At the briefing the crews were warned that a front was coming down from Norway, and that they should be careful to avoid being trapped by weather on the return journey. Bill said it was clear and peaceful on the outward leg; but on the homeward journey the tell-tale high cirrus was already overhead, and the aircraft at 22,000 ft was soon above a solid layer of frontal cloud, which obviously contained the promise of severe icing conditions. Despite the natural inclination to try and get down quickly below the cloud mass and continue with 'one foot on the deck', the pilot and crew were persuaded to remain above, in the clear. When a large 'black hole' came up they let down into the gap, then through the lower cloud where the Whitley rapidly picked up a heavy load of clear ice, to break out at 3,000 ft near Middlesbrough Light, and only thirty miles from base. (Middlesbrough Light was one of two aerial beacons which remained alight throughout the war, for homing purposes.)

The pilot flew the iced-up Whitley onto the runway at 120 mph; but the undercarriage folded up to send the aircraft skidding down the runway and disintegrating, with the rear turret breaking away in the process. Bill said they got out of the wreck and were near hysterically congratulating each other, when he saw the detached rear turret move, and a stream of lurid language revealed the Irish air gunner to be more or less in one piece inside his cocoon.

That night the RAF lost 54 aircraft; and as the Germans

claimed to have shot down only 11, the remainder had presumably gone down in the North Sea, victims of the ice-bearing front. Had Spain aligned herself with Germany and Italy, however, the war would have taken a new and serious dimension for the Allies. If this raid did play a part in maintaining the status quo, then the RAF crews' efforts, and losses, had a real significance.

Returning from the long drag to Stettin one night in 1941 the Whitley had been well knocked about, and the pilot made a perfect ditching twenty miles clear of the Friesian Islands, the five crew all climbing into the dinghy without getting their feet wet. Bill said that their RAF base had been given an accurate position for the ditching; and they were quite comfortable, and confident of being quickly rescued. Then the dreaded North Sea 'fret' – icy, dense fog – rolled over and clamped down on the dinghy and its crew for the next five days. They were in real trouble, as the maximum that a man could be expected to survive under these conditions was set, by the medical people, at four days. Bill said they could hear aircraft searching overhead (presumably RAF) and sometimes also heard the typical, unsynchronised beat of German aircraft quartering the area. At other times they heard the drum of MTBs or German E-boats in the area.

At their base in Yorkshire the aircrew on off-duty nights used to drink at Betty's Bar, and then sometimes go off to the railway station for sandwiches at the all-night buffet. On their fourth day in the dinghy one of the crew stood up and said, 'Let's go to the station for a sandwich,' then died instantly; and a second crewman, who was asleep, failed to wake up.

On the fifth day a British destroyer found the dinghy; but one of the three survivors died on the ship, and the fourth man was already out of his mind. Bill was still in quite good shape, however, and by the time the destroyer put into Portsmouth at the end of the patrol ten days later, he was fully recovered. Bill put a phone call in to the Officers' Mess at his base, and when he gave his name to the receptionist she said, after a short silence: 'If you think that's funny, I don't.'

The next time Bill was late home he had a little more distance to travel, as the crew had baled out over The Netherlands. Presenting himself at a doctor's surgery, Bill walked straight into the care of one of the Underground Escape and Evasion Lines; and said that from there on it was a 'piece of cake'. He was taken out to sea in a fishing boat hidden under a pile of rubbish for dumping; then handed over to a Royal Navy patrol craft.

On the last trip of his second tour as a navigator – this time in a Wellington – the pilot was killed; and Bill flew the damaged aircraft back to England, landing it intact at an aerodrome in Lincolnshire. When the excitement and celebrations died down Bill was awarded the DFC, and he formally requested training as a pilot. When he arrived at an Initial Training Wing – or ground school – in Canada, the staff sent him off on a month's leave, telling him to come back in time to sit the end of course examinations. Returning to England with his new wings, Bill had decided not to push his luck any further in bombers, electing to return to operations as a fighter pilot.

The New Zealand Division had gone back into action on the Sangrove in Italy towards the end of 1943 and the German line was actually broken on 1 December. In mid-January 1944 the US Fifth Army landed at Anzio and Nettuno, and in mid-February the first air attack was made on Monte Cassino Monastery, with 450 tons of bombs. Despite the difficulties of snow and mud, the army had succeeded in keeping up some pressure, and as the weather improved we could expect their drive to accelerate, just as the air offensive over western Europe was expected to move back into high gear as the skies cleared.

Refreshed and recharged, we packed up and headed for Hornchurch again on 29 February 1944, and I look back upon Drem as a pleasant and stimulating interlude in a home away from home.

17

ACCIDENTS AND INCIDENTS

The next three months proved to be an odd period of accident, incident and little action. We flew south from Drem back to Hornchurch, but when we landed at Wittering to lunch and refuel, we were staggered to learn that Reg Grant had been killed in a flying accident. Once more the lingering impact of an accidental death sat with us.

After leaving the squadron in March 1943 Reg had spent some months in America and Canada on valuable liaison work with the US Air Force and RCAF, and had been promoted to Wing Commander on his return to England. As leader of 122 RAF Mustang Wing, based at Gravesend, he had just taken off to lead a sweep over France when he called up to hand over to his deputy, advising that he thought an oil pipe had burst, as oil was flooding back over the windscreen and cockpit. Reg baled out at about 1000 ft over the Thames Estuary, but although his parachute streamed, the canopy failed to open, plummeting him into the mud flat of the estuary.

There was a funeral service in the RAF chapel at Gravesend on the morning of 3 March, and I led one of three Sections of pilots from 485 Squadron who had known Reg, to fly in from Hornchurch for the service. About 4000 ft of thick haze or thin fog lay over Gravesend, and from above this layer the yellow sodium runway lights could be seen; but these were lost from view as soon as we entered the haze. By improvising a square let-down pattern using the gyroscopic Directional Indicator, we managed to pick up the glow of the runway lights again at about 300 ft.

The service was simple, with the Service Cap and silver medals on the flag-draped casket mute testament to the man who was gone. Reg was the last of the three Grant brothers to die in service with the RAF, Ian having been killed in action with 485 Squadron a year earlier, and Harry (the oldest) having died during air crew training in England before the war began.

Reg was buried in the late afternoon at the RAF cemetery and we flew a full Squadron salute. By then, an early March gale had created very turbulent conditions, and we really had to battle to avoid collisions and yet stay in tight formation at 100 ft in the run-up to the site. For those at the graveside it was a moving experience as the twelve Spitfires passed low overhead at the precise moment that the casket was being lowered to rest. That night we said our farewells in the time-honoured way of all air crew, and the next day went back to the war.

As part of the Hornchurch Wing, we picked up again where we had left off in November, with escorts and cover duties for medium-bombing raids into The Netherlands, Belgium and France. We escorted RAF or US Marauders, Mitchells or Bostons; but enemy fighters now rarely reacted against these sorties, although the long-range raids into Germany were still being heavily attacked.

Flying top cover on one of these short-range raids I eagerly set about making a climbing interception from 30,000 ft on two aircraft passing about 3000 ft above my own Section; and was amazed when they pulled up and swiftly accelerated away from the Spitfires, in quite a steep climb. The Intelligence people made non-committal noises when I mentioned the performance of these unidentified aircraft; but later on there was no doubt in my mind that this must have been an early visitation by Me 262 twin-jet aircraft.

One of our first escorts after returning to Hornchurch was to act as withdrawal cover for a bomber force returning over The Netherlands, on a bitterly cold day at the tail-end of winter. We learnt that the bomber force recorded an outside air temperature of 25° below zero at their altitude of around 20,000 ft, and we certainly experienced extreme discomfort in climbing to our assigned altitude of 30,000 ft. The cold gnawed deeply into the hands, knees and elbows in particular; and I can remember feeling almost grateful when numbness suppressed the worst of the pain; but there was, of course, a price to be paid. On the homeward journey descending across the North Sea we were headed for Bradwell Bay to refuel before returning to base, and at around 6000 ft feeling began to return in the warmer air, accompanied by increasing pain, which by the time we landed became excruciating agony.

Other escorting squadrons also put down at Bradwell Bay, and it was a bizarre scene as dozens of reasonably fit young men writhed on the ground, and cried from the effects of the thaw. One pilot of a squadron which followed us in virtually threw his Spitfire at the ground, to bounce sideways into a row of aircraft parked near the runway, demolishing his own and several other aircraft in the process. I spearheaded an approach through the squadron Medical Officer to be supplied with electrically heated flying clothing, which we knew was on issue to bomber crews. We won our case, but bureaucracy had its way, as we received this equipment in mid-summer of 1944, by which time we rarely flew above 10,000 ft anyway. The heated jacket, gloves and slippers certainly provided considerable heat; but as no one thought to fit variable heat controls to the electrical supply points in the cockpit, one either fried or froze.

On another return across the North Sea we closed up into tight formation at 10,000 ft in the normal way, before descending through a solid mass of cloud; and I was flying at Number Three in the left-hand Section. Normally, climbing or descending through cloud in close formation was quite a comfortable ride – like sliding along a rail – and one only had to concentrate on sitting steady, close under the tail of the aircraft ahead. On this occasion it soon began to feel all wrong, as the port wing-tip of the Number Three in the centre Section kept edging in towards me, and the Number Two ahead of me was wriggling about and falling back on to me, causing awkward control and throttle adjustments, and a rapidly increasing fear of collision in the cloud. Only the formation leader flies on his instruments in formation let-downs; the other pilots formate closely on the leader, or on the aircraft directly ahead. After several minutes we were more that 2000 ft down into the cloud and I was sitting in a pool of cold sweat pouring down my back, as the jostling and wriggling became more and more pronounced. A quick glance at my own instruments confirmed that the whole formation was moving left in an uneven, skidding sort of turn. I had an inane mental flash of one of the maxims of Pilot Officer Prune, that amiable idiot whose lofty pronouncements in the Air Crew magazine *Tee Emm* were pointers on what not to do in a service aircraft. Prune said: 'Descending through cloud is just like crossing an inter-section in your motor-car . . . the faster you go, the less time for accidents.'

When the pilot ahead of me again reduced power and wobbled back, and the wing tip I could see out of the corner of my right eye made a really determined lunge in my direction I panicked, wrenching OU-V violently out to the left, and vertically upwards on full power. Bursting clear of cloud into brilliant sunshine I was part of an unrehearsed aerobatic event, as five Spitfires shot into the clear together, at various angles over the vertical, like the air display manoeuvre known as 'The Prince of Wales feathers'. The other four aircraft then formed up on OU-V and we went down again to break cloud at 500 ft. Back at base the person leading the squadron that day hastily changed the subject, after hearing the profane and pointed comments on his sloppy performance.

The squadron accepted an invitation to visit the Ford factory at nearby Dagenham, but of the dozen private cars which rolled into the factory yard, Bill Newenham's 1938 10 hp was the only Ford in the fleet. Asked how the car was running, Bill said he was not too happy with the engine, which was supposed to have been recently overhauled. After looking round the plant and enjoying some liquid hospitality, the party left to find factory staff adjusting a brand new engine, which they had fitted to Bill's car during the visit. We were most impressed.

In the third week of March the squadron set off for a short armament course at Llanbedr, in Wales. The weather was atrocious when we left Hornchurch, with Johnnie Niven leading, and the journey turned into a saga of its own. North of London we were right down on the deck in close formation, and in driving rain and sleet which closed in behind us; so we groped our way into the American bomber base at Bobbington. The Americans made us welcome and found us beds for the night, as there was no improvement in conditions. The officers' Dining Hall intrigued us, as everyone lined up for food – including the two-star General in charge – and a choice of roast beef or chicken was served by a wise-cracking, white-clad Mess hand smoking a large cigar.

Next morning as we headed west again we tangled with a heavy snow storm, and landed at the RAF Station at Hullavington after half an hour in the air, to find we had descended on the Central Flying School of the RAF. Initially we were interested to realise that at this base top level instructors and staff officers were trained for the service; but our reception was far from cordial, quite unlike the ready acceptance found on an operational station. The weather lifted in mid-afternoon and we gladly moved on, only to meet even worse conditions in another snow storm, forcing Johnnie Niven to turn back to Hullavington, which thrilled us even less than our reluctant hosts.

There was no way of getting airborne again that day, and Hullavington was obliged to face up to the problem of accommodating a group of improperly dressed colonials. The Mess President had to make a major policy decision to allow us to eat dinner in battle-dress, scarves and flying boots; then excelled himself by ordering the bar shut for the evening. Full-length oil paintings of senior officers long gone graced the walls of the Mess, and I doubt if that museum and its attendants cared a great deal for our comments. The stiff-lipped, frozen-faced attitude of the few resident officers we saw in the Mess was matched by the regimentation on the station. Even the training aircraft were lined up on the tarmac in the morning like guardsmen on parade; which was an anachronism in war-time England, with aircraft normally well dispersed to minimise damage from air attack.

When the cloud base lifted next day, we managed to have the last word on leaving Hullavington. Taking off in echelon starboard each Section made a 'daisy cutter' take-off, lifting the aircraft just clear of the runway then retracting the undercarriage, but holding the aircraft level. As the air speed reached 100 mph, instead of climbing straight ahead in regulation Training Command style, each Section leader made a steep climbing turn to port right off the deck, with his three Section aircraft slipping into close line astern. This was a spectacular kind of departure, which would evoke severe disciplinary action at any training unit. No doubt it proved nothing – but at the time it seemed like an appropriate gesture.

Dodging round and through more areas of low visibility Johnnie Niven led us down to the south coast, where again we were boxed in by a storm, to land at Chivenor, a Coastal Command Station in Wiltshire, where we spent our third night. This proved to be a home away from home, as the Coastal Command people were a mixed bunch who had a generous approach to hospitality for stray fighter pilots. Their aircraft were white-painted Wellingtons, some of which were burdened with a large ring of rigid cable enclosing the whole aircraft. We gathered this device was meant to neutralise mines; but apparently it did nothing for the flying characteristics of the Wellingtons.

On the fourth day we finally reached Llanbedr which was a bleak, austere station on the coast of north Wales; then spent three days practising dive-bombing, low-level bombing and ground strafing at which we achieved a fair level of accuracy on the armaments range. We knew this would become our main role in close support to ground forces after the invasion of Europe.

At the end of March we vacated the comforts of Hornchurch and became part of 135 airfield of the Second Tactical Air Force which was to be responsible for direct support to the Army in the invasion of Europe. From this point onwards we lived almost continually under canvas – tangible evidence that the long-awaited day was approaching.

Our first base airfield was at Selsey, only a few miles from Chichester; which particularly pleased those like myself who had been stationed in the Tangmere sector a year earlier. The Selsey airfield was a private aerodrome on the country estate of Mr Norman Holden, whose house was built on the site of an ancient priory. Our aircrew tents were pitched on the tennis court, and the Officers' and Sergeants' Messes were set up in two cottages on the estate only a short walk from the dispersal area, where a large tent served as the crew room. The tennis court was surrounded by hedges; and naked, sunbathing pilots dived for cover one afternoon when the owners and their daughter strolled onto the court, obviously amused at the sudden display of modesty. Chalk, Frank, Terry and myself accepted their invitation to drop in for a drink; and when we nominated beer were handed very large goblets of ale, topped up with copious quantities of gin. Chalk asked if they always put gin in their beer, and the reply was: 'How else can you drink the stuff?'

The other Squadron on 135 airfield at that stage was 349 (Belgian) Squadron; and they were a keen and colourful bunch, one of the Flight Commanders being Jean Morai from my Hurricane OTU days. The Commanding Officer of the whole airfield was Johnnie Walker, who had been a Flight Commander in Number One Squadron (Hurricanes) in the Battle of France and the Battle of Britain; and had been part of the famous 1937 Formation Flying Team. Broad-shouldered, handsome, and tolerant, he also had the true art of command, without seeming to give an order. The Airfield Commandant (equivalent to Senior Executive Officer and Second in Command) was Wing Commander Fred Rosier, another veteran of the Battle of Britain, who had also fought with First Tactical Air Force in the Desert. Whereas Johnnie Walker was quietly spoken and radiated calm, Fred Rosier was a live wire of restless energy, a most popular Executive Officer, and yet very much one of the flying boys. With such men in charge, 135 Airfield was a very happy unit indeed.

18

NEW GUNSIGHT

Early in April 1944 I was detailed to attend a five-day course at the grass aerodrome near Southend, on a new (and at that time secret) gunsight, which was going into service in RAF fighters.

The problems involved in shooting under combat conditions are complex, as the pilot must make split-second assessments of a number of factors simultaneously to aim his guns (by aiming his aircraft) correctly. In the case where a fighter is attacking a target which is flying straight and level – or reasonably close to straight and level – and the attacker is able to shoot from directly behind, the pilot needs only to position his aiming point on the target, within effective range. That, however, is a simplified situation which rarely occurs in combat, where the attacker has to allow the correct 'lead' in aiming, so that his bullets and his target arrive at the same point at the same time. With both aircraft turning hard, and flying erratically, the chances of hitting the target hard and effectively are very slim indeed.

On a firing course at Martlesham Heath with 485 Squadron in 1942 we had practised deflection shooting at a 20-ft drogue, towed behind another aircraft. Incredible though it may seem I fired 5860 rounds but scored only 42 hits (0.72 per cent of the ammunition fired) and this was graded as an *average* result. In the intervening two years my accuracy had probably improved; but I doubt if it would have exceeded 2 per cent of hits in any sort of deflection shooting situation. As a Spitfire had approximately 8–10 seconds of fire power, and mindful of my own limitations in air-to-air gunnery, I rarely attempted snap-shots at fleeting targets during a mêlée. Most fighter pilots, in fact, practised the same philosophy of saving one's ammunition, in the hope of getting a close-range shot with some chance of success.

The introductory lectures at Southend disclosed the secrets of the British Mk IIc gyro gunsight which, if correctly used by the pilot, eliminated all the calculations or guess-work of aerial gunnery, under a fairly wide range of conditions. Reflected on a 6in. × 4in. glass screen, at eye level, the pilot saw two light images, or graticules. The left-hand graticule was the reflection of the conventional fixed ring and bead sight, which could still be used if the gyro failed, or in situations beyond the ability of the gyro sight. The right-hand graticule consisted of six diamond images arranged in a circle, with a central aiming dot image; and the diameter of the ring of diamonds could be adjusted by twisting the modified throttle control in the cockpit, like the twist-grip of a motor-cycle. On the back of the sight the pilot selected the actual wing-span of the target aircraft, then adjusted the diamonds to just enclose his target. The intricate mechanical and electrical functions of the sight computed and applied adjustments to the graticule's diameter – and to its position on the sighting screen – and when used correctly it was infallible. On a sizeable aircraft it could also be used accurately up to 800 yds, against the normally accepted maximum range with the conventional sight of 200–300 yds.

There were about a dozen operational pilots on the course, and after four days of practising on each other and assessing the cine-film taken in mock attacks, we had a live shoot against a towed drogue. As predicted by the instructing staff, we had to hang around in the air while the operator in the rear seat of the tug aircraft was streaming fresh drogues, because the towing cable was regularly being shot through.

The gyro sight was the greatest single advance in aerial gunnery since the first machine-gun was mounted on an aircraft; and there was much speculation on the probable grief to the Luftwaffe had this instrument been available during the Battle of Britain, for it was ideal for attacking bombers flying straight and level, or against fighters executing steady turns. We all agreed, however, that in a dogfight, with both aircraft violently turning and dodging, it was unlikely that the gyro sight could be of much use, because of a slight built-in time-lag as the graticule was adjusted by the pilot, or was adjusted internally by the computed factors read by the instrument itself. Also, in a steep turn at close range, the nose of one's own aircraft usually obscured the target in a deflection shot anyway.

From the background information supplied at Southend it was clear that the invention of the gyro sight was a major feat, accomplished by scientists and RAF armament specialists of the Royal Aircraft Establishment at Farnborough. In 1938, when the threat of war was looming, combat trials proved that the high speed of modern fighters required deflection shooting skill of such a high order that it was unlikely to be achieved by average pilots. Experimental gyro sights were produced for testing by late 1939, and development continued until mid-1943, when the prototype Mk II gyro sight proved to have resolved all the main problems, and was ready for mass production. The sight had also been developed and tested at Farnborough for use in bomber gun turrets; and full technical details were handed to the Americans, who produced the fighter version under their designation of K14 gyro sight.*

Back at Selsey I briefed the squadron on the correct use of the gyro sights when they were fitted to our aircraft, and arranged for a limited amount of training. However, there was no drogue available, and many of the pilots had real doubts whether a little black box could do something which we all found so difficult.

On 18 April 1944 I flew my first active dive-bombing sortie in France against a target near Crécy. We were shown an aerial

* In September 1944 I had a close look at an American K14 sight fitted into a US Mustang, and apart from one superficial difference it was identical to the RAF Mk II. The American pilot expanded at some length on the wondrous virtues of his gyro sight then added 'I'll bet you guys are just itching to get your hands on these babies. Yep, there's no doubt about it – you've gotta hand it to the ol' US of A.'

photograph of a short stretch of narrow-gauge rail line beside a wood, with a small building at the edge of the trees; and given its pin-point map reference. This was the first of many dive-bombing attacks, being a duplication of attacks on similar targets by many squadrons of the Second Tactical Air Force, during the run-up to the invasion. The settings were all very much alike, with the rails of the target appearing to be elevated and ramped. We carried one 500-lb bomb under the belly of the aircraft, and the run-in was made at around 8000 ft with the bomb carriers in echelon (angled slightly back from the leader). As we peeled off and dived, the momentary time-lag between each aircraft gave adequate separation in the dive.

The technique, as practised in Wales, was fairly straight-forward and a good proportion of direct hits was normally achieved. The excellent elevator and rudder trim, and stability of the Mk IX Spitfire in a steep, fast dive, enabled the pilot to fly very accurately to the point of bomb release; and the usual practice was to then keep going on down to the deck, and reform each section clear of the target area. Some of the targets were undefended, but others had a respectable concentration of light flak guns, which gave no encouragement to the 'Spit-bombers' to hang around looking at the damage. The German gunners usually held their fire until the aircraft were committed to the dive, probably not wishing to draw attention to their target area, in case we were just passing by.

We were given no information as to what we were bombing; but the code name for the targets was either a 'ski' site or a 'no-ball' site, so it was not difficult to imagine a weapon of some kind being launched from the rails. The betting was on large rockets with warheads, especially as the rails all pointed towards south-east England. Altogether I flew on eleven of these dive-bombing sorties in the six weeks before D-Day, and they made an interesting change from escorting medium bombers, as the Luftwaffe was not now reacting against raids into France – or at least not against the bomber raids which our squadron was escorting.

The 500-lb bomb was carried on a removable rack beneath

the aircraft, and released by a battery-operated solenoid when a button on the control stick was pushed; while on the run-up to the target the bomb was 'armed' by closing a switch on the instrument panel. During May we were told that, if the bomb did not release and could not be shaken loose, the pilot should point his aircraft out to sea and bale out; but no technical reason was given for such a drastic solution to what seemed like a hypo-thetical problem. However, on the next bombing trip my own bomb failed to drop away, and after I had wrenched the aircraft around in a variety of violent efforts to dislodge it, I was certain that the electrical release had failed. With the arming switch returned to 'safe' therefore, I went in to land at Selsey. Instead of the usual three-point landing, which can cause a jolt, I 'wheeled' the aircraft gently onto the ground with the tail wheel high, and then felt a solid thud while the tail kicked up a little higher – the bomb had dropped off as the wheels touched the ground, then bounced and dented the belly of the aircraft, right back near the tail.

My loyal ground crew were in a state of shock, but in my ignorance I was too furious to be frightened, as I could not understand it at all. Johnnie Niven tore a very large strip off me, and when Johnnie Walker – the Airfield Commander – came into the bar that night he called me some choice names too. Then be bought me a beer.

The lack of enemy reaction to the escorted bombing raids and dive-bombing sorties was becoming monotonous and, after some badgering, Group HQ finally approved my request to fly a Ranger exercise. This was a refinement of the 'Rhubarb', where the four aircraft now crossed into occupied territory at or above 8000 ft (to avoid the intensive light flak in coastal areas), then dived to ground level and followed a pre-arranged track, before turning for home and climbing again before crossing the enemy coast. Group Operations insisted that there should be adequate cloud above the area being penetrated, to provide cover in the event of being jumped by German fighters; and I planned a route into the north of The Netherlands which would take us past a group of airfields from which German night-fighters were operating. We knew that air tests were often flown in the afternoons by the Germans, ready for night operations, and it was hoped to intercept some of the air-testing aircraft. Otherwise there were always military ground targets, or transport, to be attacked.

We topped up with fuel at Manston and flew out over the North Sea and over the Friesian Islands, to find that the cloud cover ended at the Dutch coast, so I turned the section to fly in line abreast parallel with the coast, about ten miles inland at 8000 ft. Two large, stationary vehicles could be seen under the poplar trees lining a long, straight road, so I took the section down to ground level ten miles further on, then turned, and flew back to one side of the road, putting the section into long line astern. Pulling up at the right point I sighted two Tiger tanks parked close together, each with a wheeled fuel tanker behind, and fired a long burst into the four vehicles before pulling up over the poplars. The scene erupted in a dense, burgeoning cloud of black smoke laced with orange flame, and each of the other pilots also put a decent burst into the targets. Normally the Spitfire IXB armament of cannon and machine-guns was capable of only minor damage to the running gear of a heavy tank, and would not penetrate the tank itself; but these two would have been well gutted by the burning fuel.

Pat Patterson was flying as my Sub-Section leader with Doug Clark as his Number Two, and after the attack, for reasons which Pat never satisfactorily explained, he elected to break away in the opposite direction from where I was heading to reform the section. Some minutes later a light flak position opened up on Pat and Doug, so Pat turned in and took to the guns head-on. A shell exploded in the starboard half of his fixed tail-plane, opening it up like a large, ragged tin can and creating tremendous drag, or braking effect, on that side of the aircraft, and causing it to slew violently.

Doug Clark watched in awed fascination as Pat fought the aircraft upwards in a bucking climb, like a broaching Marlin on a deep-sea rod. The German gunners kept shooting, but they must have been confused by the gyrations of the Spitfire, and with its low speed, now back to 90 mph but still going up. Pat was an outstanding pilot, and physically very strong; which I am certain were the reasons for his survival that day. He nursed the Spitfire up to about 6000 ft, and dragged it all the way back to Bradwell Bay.

Pat found that below 120 mph with full left rudder he could keep it going in the right direction; but each time his stiffly braced left leg relaxed with numbness, the aircraft stalled and plunged nose down, requiring full power and strenuous juggling to regain something near level flight. He lowered the undercarriage whilst still high enough to bale out if necessary, then flew the aircraft down onto the runway at Bradwell Bay in a fast, wheel landing. Apart from a garbled burst of profanity I had heard nothing more over the RT and, failing to locate Pat and Doug, had headed back to Manston with my Number Two. By the time we learned Pat was down safely, the daylight was gone, so we had a pleasant forty-minute night flight back to Selsey, landing by the light of the paraffin flares. Pat was flown back to Selsey next day in an Auster, bringing with him a photograph of the wrecked tail-plane; which once more demonstrated the strength and durability of the graceful Spitfire.

A week or so later the 'Celestial Selector' had another look at Pat, when he was doing some aerobatics during an air test. The radio set in a Spitfire is quite weighty, and is mounted inside the fuselage behind the cockpit. Pat's set became detached from its mounting pins to lie across the elevator cables, jamming the control column; and he had to use more brute force, and considerable juggling, to get back on the ground in one piece.

Towards the end of April Air Transport Auxiliary pilots flew in a batch of brand new Spitfire IXs, to re-equip the squadron ready for the invasion.

Many of the ferry pilots were girls, one of whom was June Howden, a New Zealander. It was a diverting experience for the squadron pilots, and was food for thought in the competent way the girls brought the aircraft into Selsey – which had a fairly short landing strip – and in the realisation that they were proficient on a much wider range of aircraft than ourselves.

I selected an aircraft from the new arrivals, and air-tested it on a blue summer's day; but the second stage of the supercharger failed to cut in during the climb. Knocker White fitted a new aneroid control and this time it functioned correctly, so I gave the machine a thorough work out, climbing to over 30,000 ft. The cockpit clock indicated 12.15 so I decided to get down in a hurry for lunch, doing the 'Trim and Dive' test on the way down. This particular test involved trimming the aircraft into a fairly steep dive, then checking the 'upride' (or lifting) of the aileron on each wing. I half-rolled at 30,000 ft with about 70 per cent power, and trimmed the aircraft into a vertical dive, using a small wood beside the London road (near Bury) as an aiming point. The aircraft trimmed out perfectly, so that with hands and feet clear of the controls it arrowed down at the wood like a high speed dart, and the uplift of the ailerons was within the limits. What followed next arose from a combination of 'finger trouble' and ignorance.

Intent on checking that the Spitfire would maintain absolute stability at the highest speed likely to be reached, I misguidedly let the vertical dive continue much too far. In mid-1944 I personally had never heard of 'Mach Numbers' or the 'Sound Barrier'; nor of any serious problems in controlling a Spitfire in a high-speed dive, other than the obvious need not to pull out sharply and risk snapping off the wings. On the other hand I had read a 1943 article in the Air Ministry Intelligence Bulletin which circulated classified information to operational pilots, and which briefly reported on problems being experienced by American Thunderbolt (P47) pilots when pulling those heavy, high-powered aircraft out of a fast dive. It appeared that very heavy elevator forces and strange control responses were being experienced, and this phenomenon was referred to as 'compressibility'. The bulletin quoted these instructions issued to Thunderbolt pilots encountering compressibility; '. . . take one and a half turns back on the tail crank – and pray'.

The Spitfire IX had a sea-level climb rate of 4000 ft per

minute, or 66 ft per second; but when I started to pull out of the dive, the aircraft was flashing earthwards at about 1000 ft per second. As I eased back on the stick and elevator trim together, the nose of the Spitfire lifted about twenty degrees from the vertical, then the stick just 'fell free' – I moved it quickly in all directions, and felt only slight 'snatching' here and there. Simultaneously the aircraft began to roll very slowly to the right, and I flicked on two quarter turns of nose-up trim on the elevator trim-tab wheel.

I thought: 'What a stupid way to die, and on a beautiful day like this' and had a mental flash of Vicki waiting for me at the gates of Bishop Otter College. The elevator suddenly took over again and the Spitfire reared violently out of the dive, but the savage g force forced my whole body downwards. As my head shot below the edge of the cockpit I glimpsed, above me, the ridge-top north of the London road.

I was peering through a rain-blurred window at a vague and wobbly image: 'That's the instrument panel of a Spitfire . . . it's upside down . . . what the hell am I doing in a Spitfire?' The panel flopped right side up, and I levered myself upright, to find that the aircraft was back up at 9000 ft, and still making sluggish, upward rolls to the right. As I collapsed under the g force the split-type stick had folded across my right leg. My goggles were over my mouth, my oxygen mask was under my chin and I ached all over, particularly from the waist down.

The metal skin of the Spitfire's wings was badly buckled and was 'oil canning' freely, and the wing tips were twisted. I had heard that the wings would break off above 11 g, and if this had not been a new and unstressed aircraft, it might well have disintegrated.

When I taxied in at Selsey, Knocker and Vic stared in horror at the undulating wing panels and I had to get them to help me out of the cockpit. They had heard the banshee scream of an aircraft diving, and had waited, transfixed, for the terminal thud, only to hear the crescendo again die away. The repair Echelon removed the buckled wings, and the aircraft went away down the road on a 'Queen Mary' transporter. I was left with a permanent reminder of the incident, qualifying as a stand-in for Wun Hung Lo.

The next day I selected another new aircraft and it flew perfectly on air test. This was ML407, and the boys duly painted on the familiar letters of OU-V.

While I had flown two Mk Vs and two other Mk IXs carrying OU-V, ML407 was special, as it was my first brand-new personal aircraft, straight from the factory. With 24 pilots but only 18 aircraft on a squadron one's personal aircraft had to be flown by other pilots as well but there was a protocol involved, and the 'owner' could usually indicate who should – or should not – fly his particular aircraft. As every pilot and car driver knows, there are noticeable differences between supposedly identical aircraft and vehicles, and ML407 was in a class of its own. Any pilot of 485 Squadron was only too pleased to fly OU-V, and she served us well.

I flew only seventeen days in May, so Vicki and I were able to explore the beauty of Sussex and Hampshire during that glorious mid-summer. The build-up of troops, trucks and armour was reaching saturation point in many areas handy to Portsmouth and Southampton, and there was a tremendous feeling of vitality and expectation wherever one went. We spent an evening playing darts with a couple of Army sergeants who had been at Dunkirk, however, and it was solidly fixed in their minds that there was going to be as little help from the Air Force this time, as had been experienced then. The Army units camped in the area worked effectively at camouflage and concealment from aerial observation, and from the air I rarely sighted any obvious concentration of equipment, unless I knew (from ground sightings) where specifically to look.

Ten minutes before start-up time for a bomber escort sortie, the engine fitter on Terry Kearins' aircraft reported that the engine was not picking up fuel from the jettison tank. I told Terry to stand by to switch to a spare aircraft, while the ground crew made one more test run on his own machine. Then all pilots walked out to their aircraft.

The young fitter started Terry's Spitfire and two airmen seated themselves on the tail while the electric starting cable was being disconnected. (It was necessary to weight the tail when running up the engine against wheel chocks otherwise – even at only partial power – the Spitfire would nose over.) A dozen or so airmen were grouped round the aircraft and Frank Reeves, one of the Flight Sergeants, was standing at the left wing tip. In a matter of three or four seconds this normal, routine scene was transformed into a tragic nightmare, and Frank Reeves was dead.

The engine involuntarily went from ticking over to 3000 rpm and maximum power in one brief, roaring surge. The machine whipped nose-down over the chocks and the tail flicked high in the air, as I could see the fitter wrenching at the throttle in the cockpit. A great deluge of earth and debris exploded upwards as the four wooden propeller blades smashed into splinters against the ground, and the two airmen on the tail were catapulted high in the air, like helpless, tumbling puppets.

The stubs of the propeller blades clawed the Spitfire round to the left through an arc of ninety degrees, as the left chock held firm, but the right wheel pushed its chock clear. A body hurtled through the air out of the maelstrom, then the engine stopped dead, leaving a vibrating, shocking silence. I ran to the crumpled body, but Frank Reeves had died instantly; then I checked one of the airmen thrown from the tail, who had some broken ribs.

We had only a few hectic minutes left before start-up, and the hardest hit living casualty was the young fitter. He stumbled away from Frank's body in a state of deep shock, and I put him in the charge of Jack Yeatman who was a tower of strength in the aftermath of this hideous incident. The next day he was sent off on leave, in the care of two friends.

To this day it is hard to reconcile that docile Spitfire with the instant monster which savaged its devoted attendants. We heard only vague reports of a failure – or an omission – in the throttle control mechanism during assembly, which could have allowed a spring-loaded linkage to throw full power onto the engine.

Shortly after this, Royal Canadian Army Headquarters, which was in a commandeered house in wooded country, requested a mock attack to give their anti-aircraft gunners some practice. We duly obliged with a simulated low-level bombing and strafing attack; going in very fast, very low and very close. It was interesting to learn afterwards that the staff considered their HQ written off many times, and they doubted if their gunners could have hit any of the attacking aircraft.

All through spring and early summer the Typhoons had been pounding away at heavily defended targets along the French coast and inside France; but they paid a high price in casualties, particularly amongst the Section leaders. A general signal was received calling for experienced fighter pilots to transfer to Typhoons, and the last sentence of the signal said: 'Rapid promotion guaranteed'. Chalky White and I were both restless, and probably as ambitious as most; so we considered changing roles. The bait in the tail of the signal gave no guarantee of how long we might enjoy our promotion, however; and it seemed to make better sense to stay with 485 Squadron, at least until we saw what sort of reaction the invasion would provoke from the Luftwaffe.

19

D-DAY

By the end of May air operations by fighter elements of the Second Tactical Air Force had been scaled down, as the anticipated time for the invasion drew closer. For squadron pilots there was more time to relax in the heat of midsummer, while ground crews worked over their aircraft to ensure top-line serviceability for every machine on the day. Although we had been operating at reasonable frequency in April and May (my log-book shows 17 sorties in May) we had seen no sign of the Luftwaffe, and it began to look as though it might be a spent force in western Europe. On the other hand, it was already clear that there was going to be no easy road to Berlin, for enemy reaction against air operations inside Germany became more and more violent. In February the Royal Air Force had lost 43 out of 891 heavy bombers in raids against Berlin, and the first US daylight attacks had been made on the capital, with 800 Flying Fortresses bombing Berlin on 6 March.

The mounting viciousness of the Nazi reaction was demonstrated by the murder of 50 RAF and Dominion aircrew on 24 March, following the mass escape from Stalag Luft III. On 30 March RAF Bomber Command sent 795 aircraft to Nuremburg, and suffered its heaviest loss of the war, with 95 aircraft missing.

The pressure on Germany had tightened further when the Soviets entered Romania on 2 April; and during March, April and May RAF and US air operations had moved into high gear against strategic targets related to the invasion. Aircraft factories and oil refineries were bombed, and a wide-ranging assault had begun against the French railway system, to hamper German troop movements. In mid-April the direction of all strategic bombing was placed directly under SHAEF (Supreme HQ Allied Expeditionary Force) in order to co-ordinate the effort of the various Air Force commands.

In mid-May Allied pressure in Italy was stepped up with air operations against the Gustav Line, keeping German forces heavily committed in that theatre; and in the last days of May Allied bombing and rocket attacks had been launched against coastal defences and German command centres, ranging right through the Pas de Calais and down to Normandy.

Real risks had arisen from the concentration of aircraft in the Tangmere sector. About ninety fighter squadrons were crammed into that south-west corner of Sussex, and in some cases the landing grounds were so close that take-off and landing circuit patterns overlapped, and circuits were flown at different heights. Surprisingly, despite the congestion and tales of head-on confrontations between formations, there were no reports of actual mid-air collisions, and the Luftwaffe failed to attack the crowded airfields.

By 5 June a ruling was in force that the airfields were sealed, with all personnel to remain in camp. For the first time in the history of the squadron every pilot was in his camp bed by 9 p.m., only to be aroused at 10.30 p.m. for the D-Day briefing.

We can all recall incidents of high drama in our lifetime, and that is how I record the scene in the Operations tent that night. The Briefing Officers uncovered their maps of the Normandy coast, then laid out the broad outline of the entire operation. We were shown the sites of the five landing beaches, the airborne assault areas, the shipping lanes and the general tactical plan; all balanced against the forecast weather. As we listened, the vanguard of 5000 ships and 287,000 men was already on its way across the Channel*; the great forward move which had been

---

* Operation NEPTUNE was the cross-Channel phase of the Normandy landings; 'the immediate object of this Combined Allied Naval, Military and Air operation (was) to secure a bridge-head on the coast of France from which further offensive operations could be developed.'

fought for over the last four years since Dunkirk. I remember the stillness in the briefing tent; the awareness that, right then, history was in the making; and I had a vivid sense of a concentrated will for success going out to the soldiers and sailors of the invading force.

One thousand fighters were to patrol the invasion area at all times during daylight, and 485 Squadron was scheduled to carry out four patrols during D-Day itself, the first one to begin at first light. All squadrons were to split up into three Sections of four aircraft flying in line abreast, and each Section leader would have freedom of action within the overall patrol area, extending fifteen miles inland from the Normandy coast. In effect, the well-proven role of Desert Air Force giving air cover and close support to the Eighth Army was being handed over to the Second Tactical Air Force, now to over-fly the re-entry into Europe. An aerial corridor was established for all aircraft operating day or night in direct support of the landings, and these aircraft would set course over Selsey Bill and above our own airfield which, at 110 miles, was the shortest distance to the Normandy beaches.

At 11.30 p.m. a growling rumble from the night sky surged through the tent, and the deafening roar of hard-working engines effectively ended our briefing. The glider tugs and transports were passing overhead, precisely as planned, to deliver leading elements of the British Sixth Airborne Division into the vital left flank of the battle area. I was not the only one whose back-hair rose, not just because of the uncanny timing of the Armada setting course above us; but in visualising the cold courage needed to jump into the hostile darkness, or to ride down inside a plywood box with a gliding angle like a large brick and then – if physically capable of moving at all – to group up and fight a black-out battle, to guarantee a toe-hold on the Continent.

That background roar of aircraft overhead was to stay with us non-stop for days and weeks on end, a constant reminder of this high point in the tide of war.

But when I started up OU-V for my first patrol of D-Day, the engine failed to run at the first attempt, and I ended up chasing the other eleven aircraft to the take-off point. To reach my position with the second Section I swung wide round the tail-enders, then stamped on the brakes as the remains of a telephone, a wooden chair and my propeller tips sprayed up in front of me. The Flying Controller, carried away with the occasion, had planted a field telephone on a chair on the edge of the marshalling area. The Airfield Commandant leapt from his car using rude words; but was persuaded to drive me at high speed back to the dispersal area, where I climbed into a reserve aircraft and took off ten minutes behind the squadron. Altogether, it was a bad start to a very big day.

Climbing slowly across Channel I picked up the single line of ships heading for the beaches, fed by lines of ships sailing in from east and west, presenting an awesome impression of power and purpose. Landing craft were heading inshore towards the beaches, but from 10,000 ft it was difficult to pick up ground detail. Weaving gently along in the British Second Army sector I sighted countless Sections of patrolling fighters covering the whole area, and spent some time studying the airborne assault area astride the Orne River and the Canal running inland from Ouistreham to the city of Caen. Hundreds of parachutes were concentrated on and around the drop zone, proof of the high ability of the troopers and the crews of their transport aircraft, in one of the most outstanding feats of D-Day.

Back at Selsey after my one-hour solo patrol, all reports indicated that tactical surprise had been achieved, and this had been dramatically underlined by the total absence of the Luftwaffe.

In mid-afternoon I led Blue Section during the third patrol of the day, the other Section pilots being Maurice Mayston, Keith Macdonald and Eddie Atkins. South of Omaha Beach, below a shallow, broken layer of cumulus, I glimpsed a Ju 88 above cloud, diving away fast to the south. Climbing at full throttle I saw the enemy aircraft enter a large isolated cloud above the main layer, and when it reappeared on the other side I was closing in rapidly. Our aircraft were equipped with the gyro gunsight which eliminated the snap calculations or guesswork required to hit a target aircraft – especially one in a reasonably straight flight path; and it also enabled the guns to be used accurately at a far greater range than before. I was well aware, however, that most pilots were sceptical of the new instrument and preferred to use the conventional type of sight, which was still incorporated on the screen of the new sight. Normally one would open fire only at ranges below 250 yds; but I adjusted the gyro sight on to the target at 500 yds with a deflection angle of 45 degrees, positioned the aiming dot on the right-hand engine of the enemy aircraft, and fired a three-second burst. The engine disintegrated, fire broke out, two crew members baled out and the aircraft dived steeply to crash on a roadway, blowing apart on impact.

As I turned back towards the beach-head I sighted a second Ju 88 heading south and made an almost identical attack, which stopped the right-hand engine. This aircraft then went into a steep, jinking dive with the rear gunner firing at the other members of my Section who all attacked, until the Ju 88 flattened out and crash-landed at high speed. One of its propellers broke free, to spin and bound far away across the fields and hedges, like a giant Catherine wheel. As we reached the beach-head, radio chatter indicated that other pilots* were dealing with another German bomber, so this belated effort appeared to have been a costly exercise for the Luftwaffe.

By now, two lines of ships were ranged towards the beaches, with two more lines of unloaded ships heading back. As we flew back over the in-bound lanes, the two lines of ships advancing up and down Channel to the turning point for Normandy, stretched right back to the visible horizon. The Squadron's fourth patrol at dusk was uneventful. And so ended D-Day. Intelligence reports confirmed that the Army was ashore in strength, there was no doubt that the invasion had succeeded, and an overwhelming mood of relief had replaced the tension of the preceding days.

* 349 (Belgian) Squadron.

Supreme Headquarters nominated the first Ju 88 I had destroyed as the first enemy aircraft to be shot down since the invasion began, putting 485 (NZ) Spitfire Squadron at the top of the scoreboard for D-Day. Some days before the invasion I had casually suggested we should run a sweepstake for the first pilot to shoot down an enemy aircraft after the invasion began, and I duly collected a few shillings from the pool. When we later had time to unwind and celebrate, my modest winnings were well short of the cost of that party.*

From D-Day onwards, operations in support of the invasion continued at a high tempo, and for the first 24 days my log-book records 20 beach patrols, 4 shipping patrols and 2 escorts for heavy bombers. Second Tactical Air Force and RAF Fighter Command flew approximately 90,000 sorties during June 1944, by far the greatest monthly effort ever recorded in the history of air warfare, and around one quarter of that effort was concentrated directly above the Allied beach-heads. It was a massive reversal of the desperate shortage of air cover over Dunkirk, where the efforts of the British fighters were beyond sight and sound of the soldiers. I hoped that the constant presence of the Royal Air Force over the beach-heads in 1944 would have reassured those who fought their way out of France in 1940.

Enemy aircraft made sporadic appearances, mostly in fighter-bomber or fighter sweep roles; but with the mass of Allied fighters milling around in the area, the individual pilot's chances of intercepting these intruders were fairly slim. However the squadron continued to get its share of the action for the first few weeks, and part of the exhilaration of that time arose from the way all aircraft now operated in independent sections of four, well spaced out in line abreast. This was the formation which had been developed during the battle over Malta, and it certainly allowed each pilot to search the sky efficiently, and yet to cross-cover for the other pilots in his formation. Section

---

* By coincidence Flying Officer R.E. Lelong (later Flight Lieutenant, DFC and Bar) from Auckland destroyed a Me 410 on the eve of D-Day when flying a night intruder patrol with 605 (Mosquito) Squadron over the German aerodrome at Evreaux.

leaders could use a free-ranging initiative which had been impossible during the fighter sweeps over northern France, when German fighters had been operating in considerable strength over their own bases. The only operational restrictions were to patrol strictly within the beach-head area, and to keep clear of the Fleet elements now positioned off-shore, as any approaching aircraft would be treated as hostile by the Royal Navy.

On my first patrol on 7 June two bomb-carrying FW 190s dived past the Section towards shipping anchored off the British beaches, but I smartly broke off the chase when they disappeared from view amongst the violent barrage flung up by the Fleet. Our second patrol late in the afternoon of 8 June came alive when 222 Squadron reported enemy aircraft flying inland above the Ouistreham Canal. I was leading Blue Section below cloud, flying straight at the canal from the east, and called for the Section to make a steep climbing turn to the right up through the cloud layer. By sheer luck, three of us emerged behind a formation of twenty Me 109s, and ahead of some pursuing Spitfires which were out of range. Frank Transom and Pat Patterson were still with me, and as we latched on to three of the tail-enders the whole German gaggle – which was flying in three sections in loose line astern – began porpoising in and out of another cloud layer close above us. It was an unusual and frustrating sensation following these undulations, and trying to line up for a short burst each time the target briefly popped out of the cloud. By my fourth attempt I was about 50 yds behind and closing fast, as the Me 109 reappeared and pulled up again. This time I followed him into the cloud, firing a long burst as OU-V bounced around in his slip-stream, and just as I heard Frank's unmistakable yell over the RT, 'I've got the bastard', a great blob of black smoke and debris came back at me through the murk, and I half-rolled to break cloud simultaneously with the Me 109, which was trailing smoke and diving for the deck. Two other Me 109s were going down in flames – one destroyed by Frank and one by Pat – while the one I had hit started to flatten out of the dive, but crashed in a wood.

I called Blue Section to rejoin me at the coastal end of the Canal but, shooting out from below one of the cloud layers, I found myself below and ahead of twenty FW 190s. Calling the sighting on the RT I broke up into the leading aircraft, and the whole gaggle split outwards. Johnnie Niven – our CO – promptly arrived with his Section, and a hectic mêlée developed. I had used all my ammunition on the Me 109, but Al Stead destroyed one FW 190, and Johnnie Niven and Mick Esdaile damaged one each. The dogfight drifted out over the sea into an area of very bad light and poor visibility, caused by towering black clouds against the low sun. A multitude of orange flashes and 'flaming onions' from the gloom below revealed that the navy had, very sensibly, opened up on one and all – which rapidly broke up the party.

After four more uneventful beach-head patrols in the next three days, I suggested to the CO and Wing Operations that it would make better sense to have patrols sweeping inland in the direction of the German aerodromes, to intercept enemy aircraft before they reached the battle area. The umbrella of 1000 fighters over the beach-heads was no doubt excellent for the morale of the army, but the fact remained that some aircraft were arriving over the troops and dropping bombs.

Group headquarters insisted that we still confine our patrols to the prescribed coastal strip, so I quietly organised my own Section to make private sweeps inland. Each member of Blue Section was to keep strict RT silence, except in emergency, and we would slip away to search up to 50 miles inland. We would not be missed in the beach-head area, and reckoned that if we had any success, it would cancel out any rockets for being absent without leave.

Arriving over the beaches at first light on 12 June I took Blue Section away inland, as planned. It was a beautiful, clear morning; and we were flying over gently rolling country, very similar to the English Downs. Thirty miles south of Utah Beach I caught a glint on a lake 8000 ft below, then picked out a tiny speck moving north. Keeping my eyes locked on to the moving object I waggled my wings and went down in a wide, diving turn to identify two Me 109 fighter-bombers ahead of us and in line astern, flying towards the beaches at zero feet. I hit the rear fighter-bomber with a three-second burst from 200 yds and the 109 reared up, burning fiercely and disintegrating. At about 600 ft the pilot seemed to catapult outwards and upwards, his parachute opening immediately; the the wreckage stalled, fell, and exploded in a cornfield, which erupted in a sheet of flame. Unhappily for the German pilot, his parachute dropped into the heart of the fire. I then sent in my Number Two, Bill Newenham, who successfully attacked the other fighter-bomber, which crashed in the same area. As I expected, no awkward questions were asked as to how Blue Section happened to be so far outside the patrol area.

On 13 June the whole Squadron landed in France for the first time, to refuel following a patrol. The landing strip had been built by engineers inside the British beach-head and very close to the front line, where the airmen of the refuelling and re-arming parties were doing a great job in primitive and danger-ous conditions. There were no buildings at all, just a few earth walls and revetments, petrol bowsers and stacks of ammunition positioned at irregular intervals, and a few tents dotted around the perimeter. I had an unpleasant surprise as I switched off my engine near a petrol bowser. Nobody was in sight but a voice from a hole in the ground shouted at me to get out and get down. Joining some airmen in a large slit trench I drank some horrible-tasting black tea, as they explained that a sniper was active from a ragged wood about 500 yds away. After ten minutes a whistle signalled the return to work, and we wasted no time in refuell-ing and getting airborne again. Some days later I heard that a tank had been brought in to wipe out the sniper, who was reported to have been a young French girl, newly married to a German soldier who had been killed in the beach-head. I found it curiously reassuring, on this crucial battlefield, to glimpse both innocence and despair in that fleeting tragedy.

20

GREAT STORM

While 135 Wing was basically part of the very large force of Second Tactical Air Force fighters, giving constant cover over the battlefield, other Wings of Spitfires and Mustangs were operating deeper into enemy territory, and they took a heavy toll of the Luftwaffe in its attempts to operate into the beach-head area.

The rocket-firing Typhoons, with their four 20-mm guns, were heavily committed and they added to their already impressive record for accuracy and aggressiveness. One of the problems arising out of each Wing – or Airfield – operating as a self-contained unit was that we were isolated from personal contact with pilots from other Wings, and we necessarily saw the action, and recorded the impressions, through the relatively narrow spectrum of our own unit. To offset this to some degree, Second Tactical Air Force applied the lessons which had been learned the hard way by First Tactical Air Force in the Desert and in Italy; and daily briefings by the Intelligence Section made sure that we had some appreciation of the tactical scene and of the work being done by other units. Similarly, Situation Reports on the land battle, and identification of the enemy units involved, went a long way towards bridging the communication gap between all segments of the total effort.

Each Squadron and each Wing rightly took pride in its collective achievements, and in outstanding efforts by individual pilots; but the sensible policy of up-to-date, overall briefings ensured that one was made aware that there were literally thousands of other pilots playing their own part, in their own aircraft, in their own particular roles. A durable achievement of Second Tactical Air Force was the way in which the public image of the star-studded 'Ace' was played down and, without surrendering any part of his individualism, every pilot was subtly encouraged to recognise that he was rejoining all the other average people, when he climbed out of his aircraft at the end of the day.

The pilots were acutely aware that, while the war could be lost in the air, it could not be won in the air. Only the soldiers on the ground could finalise the conflict.

As the original schedule for break-out from the beach-heads fell further behind, the planned move of Second Tactical Force Units into Normandy was necessarily delayed, because of insufficient ground to build the forward airfields. While the delay meant that we continued to operate at long range from the UK, the comprehensive battle and tactical reports kept frustration in check, as we could see at first hand the main problems faced by the army. One did not have to be a Staff College graduate to appreciate the logic of firmly anchoring the left flank on the British beach-head area, then pivoting the whole front on that corner of the battlefield. Flying over the area, and later as we dropped more and more into the role of close support to the army, it was clear that the soldiers had a tough and unenviable job ahead, to make ground in country which was ideally suited to defensive operations by a determined enemy.

No military operation of any size ever goes completely according to plan, and from D-Day onwards there were foul-ups in plenty; but it never occurred to me at the time that the main objectives might not be reached, and I believe that every pilot at my level held the same view. Accustomed as we were to the excellent operational planning of Fighter Command and the RAF in general, I think the glimpse we had of the awesome complexity and detailed planning of the whole of Operation OVERLORD – translated into action right before and below us – stamped on our minds the idea of invincibility for our forces.

An extraordinary incident occurred in the middle of June, when the three Sections were patrolling a few miles apart, over the sea, between Sword Beach and Le Havre. Red Section, led by Al Stead, was in front above cloud, with the other Sections following below cloud, when Red Section reported two Spitfires flying parallel at the same level. One of them turned in behind the Section, and on command from Red Leader each aircraft executed a steep 360 degree turn then resumed course in their line abreast formation, as the single Spitfire turned away.

This was the normal way of identifying oneself to any inquisitive, friendly aircraft; as the elliptical wing of a Spitfire was clearly displayed during the steeply banked turn. The Section then continued towards Le Havre, but what had just been routine became deadly serious as the stranger made another pass at Al Stead, but this time firing, as could be clearly seen by the unmistakable puffs from the attacker's guns. The situation erupted as Al called: 'He's firing at me this time – what the hell do I do?' and the terse voice of Ray Harries – our Wing Leader – came back: 'Shoot him down.'

Alarm bells were ringing in our minds, as we had been briefed before D-Day that we might encounter captured Allied aircraft being flown by the Germans. The two Sections following behind went to full throttle to catch up with the action ahead; but it was all over very quickly. The aggressor let fly with another burst at Al, who promptly whipped round, out-manoeuvred him, and shot him down into the sea. The second strange Spitfire remained clear of the action, but had disappeared altogether by the time his companion had crashed.

Back at Selsey there was considerable excitement as the reports were made to Intelligence, and there was animated discussion amongst the pilots on the implications of the incident. It reminded me vividly of the unidentified B17 I had encountered at 1000 ft over France the year before.

The mood changed to shock, however, later that night when Group HQ advised that an Admiral was screaming for the head of the RAF pilot who had shot down a navy Seafire that afternoon. Apparently a very shaken Seafire pilot had landed at his

base, to report that his leader had been shot down into the sea by
Spitfires. We gathered that the Admiral refused to look at the
facts – which were irrefutable – and was demanding an immediate court-martial on his terms. Al Stead was shattered, despite
our insistence that each of us would have reacted in precisely the
same way. It says a great deal for his character that his chief
concern was over the tragic death of the pilot concerned, rather
than threats of reprisal from on high. The RAF took swift action
to protect its own, and Johnnie Walker – our Airfield Commander – sent Al away on leave the next morning. Group HQ then
informed the navy that the pilot involved had been relieved of
flying duties, and that any disciplinary action was strictly an
internal Air Force concern. We did hear that neither of the
Seafire pilots had any operational experience whatever, and had
not been authorised to fly into the invasion area. It was accepted
that there was grief enough already, without probing further
into the incident.

Meanwhile we continued to enjoy the best of two worlds;
with constant operations over Normandy, but returning to the
comforts of our tented base at Selsey every night. As a change in
routine, on 15 June we escorted a force of several hundred
Lancaster and Halifax heavy bombers to Boulogne, where they
hit German installations with great accuracy, and with no interference from the Luftwaffe.

As I took off from Selsey on 17 June the right-hand tyre burst
just as OU-V left the ground, and at the end of the patrol I
elected to land at Ford Aerodrome, as the short grass strip at
Selsey had interlaced steel rod on the surface, which might have
caused problems. When I landed on the grass at Ford, the
Spitfire again demonstrated what a docile yet sensitive aircraft it
is. By touching down on the left wheel with the left wing well
down into a cross wind from the same side, OU-V turned off to
the right only slightly, after the weight settled onto the damaged
wheel, and the tail came down.

It was about this time that 349 (Belgian) Squadron was short
of experienced sub-section leaders, and Doug Clark was
seconded from 485 Squadron to fly with the Belgians. He had an

enjoyable short tour, sharing the destruction of a FW 190; and the Belgian Command marked their appreciation of his efforts by awarding him the Belgian Croix de Guerre.

The 'Great Storm' which blew up on 19 June smashed large parts of the landing facilities and the prefabricated Mulberry harbours, sank dozens of vessels with considerable loss of life, and drove ashore 800 craft of all shapes and sizes, before subsiding again on 22 June. The storm itself, catching the meteorologists completely unawares, developed into the worst June gale for forty years, with north-east winds gusting up to forty knots. I flew on patrols over the shipping lanes and beaches on 19 and 20 June, and it was an awesome sight to watch the small craft battling to survive in the angry white water and fast-moving, steep waves. In fact, the storm destroyed far more vessels than German arms managed to sink, or damage, in the course of the whole of the invasion. When it was all over the beaches looked like the aftermath of a South Seas typhoon, but with derricks, masts and debris in place of romantic palm trees. We remained on stand-by at Selsey during 21 and 22 June, and there was some speculation that German forces would seize the opportunity to attack our beach-head forces, while they were preoccupied with the effects of the storm and deprived of air cover. Fortunately our ground forces had adequately stabilised their positions with the Germans on the defensive, and enemy effort seems to have been confined to rushing in reinforcements and supplies during the brief period they could freely use the roads in daylight, with Second Tactical Air Force grounded.

At the time of the launching of the invasion I had sensed an air of nervousness and worry at top level, probably because of the marginal weather conditions on 5 June; and, after the storm of 19–22 June, it was easy to visualise the kind of total disaster which had earlier been feared by the planners and senior commanders. In my opinion, however, one of the great unsung feats of the war came out of the Great Storm. The massive, sustained build-up of equipment and ammunition for the 600,000 troops already ashore came to a dead stop for four days, leaving a large part of the sea and shore equipment lost, wrecked or damaged in an area of great chaos. In ten days the Herculean efforts by the men of the Royal Navy, Merchant Navy and Engineers beach-head parties on the British and American beaches had restored the flow of equipment and supplies to the same level as the day before the storm broke. Also, three-quarters of the stranded vessels were repaired and refloated on the next extra high tide, in mid-July. Some monumental reminders remained and could be clearly seen from the air, such as huge caissons and other sections of the prefabricated harbours, and wreckage of all descriptions. Quite incongruously, a tank landing craft remained high and dry well beyond normal high water mark and, from the smoking chimneys and laundry displayed, appeared to have become home to some of the Beach Control force.

As a brief spell of similar weather blew up we spent the night on an emergency landing strip in the beach-head, to do a special patrol at first light the following morning. Having spent a very rough night on straw in the back of army trucks, after a meal of bully beef and hard biscuits; our briefing was to return to Selsey on completion of the morning patrol. Weather conditions deteriorated after take-off into a storm, with towering thunderheads, whirling cloud layers and heavy rain packing into the Channel and over Normandy. My Section became split up in the gloom, and at the end of the patrol time I let down into the cloud towards England, calling for a homing from Tangmere Control, as I had no real idea of my position. The radio remained silent, and I eventually broke cloud below 100 ft in torrential rain above steep seas, the crests of which were being blown into clouds of spray by the driving force of the gale. Forward visibility was down to about 100 yds as OU-V slipped along at reduced speed, and I was well soaked in perspiration when white cliffs reared up ahead. Turning hard right I followed the shore of the Isle of Wight, then across to the mainland and into base.

It transpired that all aircraft had been recalled to land again in Normandy because of the weather in the Channel, but my radio receiver was out. The transmitter was working, however, and Vicki was on duty that morning, and had plotted my homing call in her capacity as DF (Direction Finding) Teller. The homing course had been called to me by the Controller, and there had been a tense twenty minutes in the Operations Room before OU-V had been checked on to the ground. Heading for the kitchen, I protested bitterly on being directed to join a gathering of the off-duty pilots being addressed by the New Zealand Prime Minister – Mr Peter Fraser – who had the New Zealand Minister of Defence and Bill Jordan (the New Zealand High Commissioner) in attendance. Des Scott – now a Group Captain in charge of a four-squadron Typhoon Wing – was also sitting there, and looking as bored as the occasion demanded.

I was tired and hungry, and not interested in a litany of how well New Zealand was being administered in our absence, despite the many problems of war-time government. The Prime Minister was asked what would be the housing position for those of us who had married in the UK, as we had heard there was now a housing problem in New Zealand. Mr Fraser brightened up at this question and solemnly assured us there would be a house for every returned serviceman and his family – being an experienced politician, he neglected to say 'when'.

The air war slipped back into top gear again on 24 June and I flew two beach patrols; then on 25 June we escorted a force of Lancasters to bomb a 'no-ball' target in a wood. The real purpose of the 'no-ball' sites we had been dive-bombing in April and May had become unpleasantly clear on 13 June, when the first V1 – or flying bomb (aptly nicknamed the doodlebug) – crashed and exploded at Swanscombe, near Gravesend. It transpired that RAF and US Bomber Forces had been attacking these sites since December 1943, and the plastering the bombers could hand-out to these small targets made our own efforts look fairly insignificant. On this occasion we had a grandstand view of a copy-book display of precision bombing; with their bombs obliterating an area about 500 yds in diameter, and not a single burst outside the prescribed area.

After a shipping patrol on 27 June the Wing was released from all operations until a dawn patrol on 29 June; and we hurled ourselves into the celebration we had been promising

ourselves ever since D-Day. Although it seemed hard to believe
that we had headed off all the other squadrons of Fighter Command, our 'Spy' insisted we were still the top-scoring squadron
of the top-scoring Wing, for the three weeks since the invasion.
Whether this was correct or not I do not know, nor did it seem to
matter. The celebration really marked the certainty that the
Allied armies had successfully re-entered Europe, and that the
events and defeat of Dunkirk had been reversed.

My MG was part of the convoy which shot through to do the
rounds in Chichester, and found its way back that night to
Selsey; to repeat the process on the following day. We took as
many of the ground crew with us as possible, and they enjoyed
themselves as much as the pilots. My own three stalwarts –
Knocker, Vic and Paddy – turned on their non-stop comic act
and, crowded as the pubs were, they managed to keep me just
about helpless with laughter.

Wedged into a mass of uniformed humanity in the Nag's
Head a voice in my ear said: 'Hey, Johnnie, can you lend me a
quid?' And there was Frank Fahy from Woodbourne days,
quite unchanged – still grinning, and with no hat and no money.
His Spitfire squadron had landed on one of the local airfields to
refuel, but too late to fly back to base. It made my day to catch
up with Frank briefly, as by now not many of our original
course were still around.

After a late meal back at Selsey that night, the Officers' Mess
ran out of ale; which made a good excuse to visit the Sergeants'
Mess, where the unwinding process just kept on going, like an
end of season party at a Football Club. The patrol that morning
required us to cover the beaches at first light so, after a scratch
breakfast with the sergeants, we trudged through the dew-laden
grass to dispersal, to take off in the usual formation of fours –
and away to Normandy.

After completing the dawn patrol we landed on an emergency
strip in the beach head to refuel, then carried out a second patrol
before returning to Selsey. It was a morning with jumbled cloud
formations, towering build-ups and the sun mostly obscured,
with vast, black caverns between the pillars of cloud. I set off

after a remote object at 8000 ft, which I lost sight of after a couple of minutes; but in the gloom my Section also lost contact with me. So I spent some time banking, climbing and twisting between the huge masses of cumulus and through the caverns and canyons, which is an exciting way of pretending one is riding a great bird, alone in the upper air.

As I emerged from behind a towering cloud, a lone FW 190 flew out into a patch of sunlight half a mile away, and the pilot continued straight ahead as I turned in behind him. As I fired he went into the oddest evasion routine I ever encountered, slipping rapidly down and then slicing up, then down the other way and up, like slipping from side to side within a giant 'U' tube. I followed him through the first of these gyrations, which had a shocking effect on my already uneasy stomach, so I held the line of sight steady at the top of one side of the U he was creating, then fired as he came up into my sights on the return swing. There was a decent splatter of strikes on the wing, and the 190 pilot whipped round fast, to disappear into a handy cloud.

135 Airfield was moving to Coolham (near Billingshurst) that day, as a rehearsal for the expected movement to France, so I had arranged to take a 48-hour break while the unit took to the road. The pain in my stomach was acute by the time I headed out of camp in the MG; and I had to stop twice, as violent nausea took over, before I booked myself into a hotel. What I had planned as a happy two days turned into a very bad time as, once every hour for the whole two days, the violent retching recurred. Vicki called in when she was off duty and was concerned to find me in such a state, and worried because nothing would stay in my stomach. Dragging myself back to camp at Coolham, the MO took one look at me as I came into the Mess, then shot me straight off into the Canadian Army Field Hospital at Horsham.

The problem had apparently arisen from a contaminated brew of beer, which had laid low many people in the area, and one person actually died from the effects. The Canadian doctor soon sorted out the right treatment and, after five very comfortable days, I was cleared to return to duty.

135 Airfield made another short move in July to Funtington, and our role reverted to escorting RAF heavy bombers as they obliterated more of the flying bomb sites across the Channel. The V1 attack had by now become a well-sustained assault, with hardly a day on which the weapons were not launched against England. There were rarely any serious attacks by the Luftwaffe against these RAF bomber streams, and we repeatedly saw our bombers carry out their extremely accurate attacks on V1 sites, under what the bomber crews no doubt felt were ideal conditions. First of all they were flying in daylight, and secondly they had ample fighter protection to prevent distractions. If a crew was not satisfied with the run-in, they could turn back and regain the bomber stream for another run. I watched a Lancaster doing just that, and saw it rejoining the stream at an angle only to collide with another Lancaster as they both took violent last-moment evasive action. There was a violent bright flash, then just debris fluttering and tumbling down.

On 19 July a touring concert party put on an evening performance in the camp. I opted to turn in early, only to be rudely wrenched from deep sleep around midnight as I was dragged out of bed by an exuberant bunch of squadron pilots, and a bevy of attractive girls from the concert party. Johnnie Niven attached a piece of ribbon to my pyjamas with a safety-pin and noisy toasts were drunk, before the party returned to the bar.

Next morning Johnnie Niven showed me a signal detaching me for temporary duty with the Ministry of Aircraft Production. I was reluctant to go along with what I thought could be an attempt to prise me away from operations; but he assured me that this was not the case, and that the job ahead was important.

21

LECTURE TOUR

I reported to the Director of the Instrument Section of Ministry of Aircraft Production (MAP), Mr Alan Barker, in London. He explained that an analysis had indicated that the success rate of RAF fighters against the V1 was under threat, because of the slow production rate of the gyro gunsight from all the factories concerned, throughout Britain. This resulted from a combination of factors, including the direct effects of the V1 on workers' morale (particularly in south-east London) and the precise nature of the production work involved. Individual factories produced separate components, secrecy on the purpose of the various components was absolute, and only a handful of people had any idea at all of the identity of the finished article, or of its value against the aerial assaults on England.

On 13 July the defensive pattern against the V1 had been altered to define more clearly the area in which each Service had responsibility, and to avoid anti-aircraft gun attacks on our own fighters. The fighters now had a clear field of operations in the Channel to within ten miles of the English coast; then, from just inland, to the balloon barrage south-east of London itself. The main problem was that the speed of the V1 (350–390 mph) meant that only the fastest fighters at low level (such as the Tempest, Spitfire XIV and Mustang III) could operate against them with reasonable success.

As the V1 flew dead straight and level, it was an ideal target for aircraft fitted with the gyro gunsight. While the wing span of the V1 was smaller than a conventional fighter, if visibility conditions permitted and the gyro gunsight was correctly used, real accuracy was possible at ranges far greater than those usually accepted as practical. On the other hand, the very small span of the V1 meant that it would be difficult to see at long range against the countryside under sunlight conditions, as the aiming dot of the gyro gunsight could virtually obscure the target altogether.

At the time I was detached to the MAP, the V1 assault had reached serious proportions. There was no guarantee when the Pas de Calais launching area would be overrun by the army and, despite sustained bombing, the German V1 onslaught was being maintained.

Mr Barker said that at least fourteen RAF fighters fitted with the gyro gunsight were known to have fallen into German hands through crash landings in France, but he reckoned it would take two years for German scientists and technicians to duplicate it. The decision had therefore been taken to lift the secrecy on the gunsight in an effort to boost morale, and raise the production rate of the instrument. My job was to visit all the factories involved, to tell the workforces just what they were making, and how accurate it was; and also call for a boost in production.

Although I had been a reluctant starter in this Public Relations exercise, I soon realised the importance of the job, and that it needed to be done quickly. I could see the logic of detailing someone like myself to do this, as I was already familiar with the principle and construction of the sight, and I had used it successfully twice on D-Day – even though I did have private reservations as to its comparative success against targets one quarter of the size of a Ju 88.

I was given a free hand to prepare and present the lectures, and Mr Barker took me to his home at Much Hadham for the weekend, where I worked up the format. I was supplied with a complete gyro gunsight, samples of the various internal components, some enlargements of my cine-gun film from 6 June, and a Royal Air Force car and driver.

Mr Barker asked me to go first to a factory at Foots Cray in south-east London (Reyrolle Ltd) right in the V1 'Bomb Alley'. As I was completely new to speaking in public and have a low-level tone of voice, I asked for a public address system wherever a large audience could be expected.

Apart from the initial nervousness of having to stand up and speak to a sea of unknown faces, I found the lecture tour absorbing, and developed a deep respect for the technical ability of the various factories in solving intricate production problems, and for the dedication of the workforces who were performing boring, repetitious jobs over extended working hours.

At lunch beforehand with the Factory Manager at Foots Cray, I learned that practically all the staff had suffered, directly or indirectly, from the concentration of V1s landing in the area. Casualties were high, and four years after the Blitz it seemed that the V1 attacks were, indeed, having a very bad effect on morale.

The Manager offered me a large whisky before my debut, which I airily declined, having convinced myself that this would be no different from talking on the RT. Stepping out of the office on to a balcony above the Works cafeteria, the sight of a thousand up-turned faces brought on a rapid change of mind, and I quickly swallowed the whisky. Using the analogy of a duck shooter trying to hit a bird from a moving car, I stressed the way in which the gyro gunsight they were making took care of all the variables, to provide complete accuracy when correctly used; and asked for a big effort to lift production. To drive the point home, the Germans obligingly launched a wave of buzz-bombs, one of which snarled right over the factory roof near the end of my address. The message was enthusiastically received and, when I talked to some of the workers afterwards, it was clear from their excitement that everyone now knew they had a vital place in the war effort.

Other London factories I visited were Smith's Meters and the United Kingdom Optical Company – which incongruously bore the partly painted out legend 'Karl Zeiss 1912' above the factory entrance. This firm had solved the technical problem of plating the surface of the mirror attached to the gyroscope with a geometrically true layer of metal of microscopic thickness. The smallest group visited was at the London School of Photo Engraving, where I talked to six girl students who carried out the engraving of the glass graticule* inside the gunsight.

Next was a large Radio Factory near Newcastle, and the last visit was made to Ferranti Ltd outside Edinburgh, the only factory where the final assembly of the gyro gunsight was carried out – behind sealed doors. Barr & Stroud at Glasgow were also involved, but as that firm was having no real problems, we decided not to visit it.

Back in London Mr Barker asked me to draft a release for the Press based on my address at the factories, and I understood he intended to have it issued in the layout which I tabled.† By the time I rejoined on 6 August, when the V1 attack had reached its peak, 135 Wing had moved back to Selsey. 210 flying bombs had crossed the English coast on 2 August and over half actually detonated in the London area. By now an average of 15 day and 9 night (Mosquito) squadrons were involved on interception patrols. Eight hundred heavy and 1100 light guns of the Royal Artillery were in action; together with multiple rockets and 600 light guns manned by the RAF Regiment on Airfield Defence duties, and by the Royal Armoured Corps. The efficiency of the combined air and army organisations ensured that, by mid-August, 50–75 per cent of V1s were being destroyed. When the main attack ended in September 1771 had been destroyed by fighters, 1460 by the guns, and 232 by the barrage balloons.

Pilots on anti-V1 patrols had developed some unorthodox techniques (when out of ammunition) against the V1, and some

---

* Later replaced with slotted aluminium discs.

† Passing through London two months later I called to see Mr Barker, who was delighted to report a great upsurge in production of the gyro gunsights, which undoubtedly arose from the decision to lift the secrecy on the instrument. He showed me impressive production graphs, which dramatically emphasised the importance of morale and self-respect in the workplace. In some cases the increase was close to 100 per cent.

casualties were caused by aircraft being caught in the V1 explosion, or by being struck by debris. Two pilots collided and were killed when attacking the same V1. Jimmy Sheddan (ex-485 Squadron) had a unique accident while attacking a V1 when an empty shell case, ejected from another fighter flying close by, severed an oil pressure line in the engine of his Tempest. Jimmy crash-landed violently, and was slightly injured on being thrown clear of the aircraft.

Shortly after my return from the lecture tour Jack Yeatman put his head into my tent one night to say he had a message for me. Under the great arch of a starlit sky, Jack quietly told me that Ash had been killed in action. Strangely, my chief emotion was an overwhelming conviction of my own insignificance in the vast scheme of things.

22

BREAK-OUT

Early in August 1944 the long-awaited break-out from the Normandy beach-head began, with the aim of pivoting the Allied front on Caen and pinning the German forces back to the Seine, over 100 miles to the East. Out of this developed the Battle of the Falaise Pocket, which has perhaps been best typified by the title of a French book: *Stalingrad en Normandie*.

The Falaise battle is important as the first large-scale operation by Second Tactical Air Force and IX USAAF in close support of the armies – unique in that very large ground forces were involved in a very small area, with Tactical Air Force aircraft acting as airborne artillery, literally over the heads of the soldiers in the forward positions.

By 16 August the Allied armies had surrounded on three sides an area roughly 25 miles long and 15 miles wide, with the eastern end of the box still open towards the Seine. In the open-ended box were very strong elements of German VII Army and V Panzer Army, plus a Panzer Group. Titantic efforts were made by Allied troops to close this door to the east. By 19 August the door had almost been shut, to become the 'Falaise Gap' about two miles wide, which the retreating Germans aptly named the 'Corridor of Death'.

On 21 August the Gap was finally closed, and the tally of German casualties was approximately 10,000 dead and 50,000 taken prisoner of war (including three generals). German losses in equipment were 187 tanks and self-propelled guns, 157 light armoured vehicles, 1778 trucks, 669 cars and 252 artillery pieces.

Second Tactical Air Force's effort was spearheaded by the Typhoons with their four 20-mm guns and rocket projectiles; but the Spitfires and Mustangs also had a substantial part in the action. The orders were simple enough – to pinpoint the 'bomb line' from the marked map, then blast any target located in the pocket. Typhoons, Spitfires and Mustangs flew 9896 sorties in the pocket in fourteen days, and P38 (Lightnings) and P47 (Thunderbolts) of IX USAAF flew 2891 sorties in the same period. The wheel had turned full circle with a vengeance. Allied aircraft were now dealing out the kind of hammering which the BEF had taken in 1940, but this time the scale and sophistication of our air support far exceeded that of the Luftwaffe four years earlier.

We made a number of sorties into the Falaise Pocket at the height of the battle and, as much of the German transport and armour was using the winding by-roads which traversed heavily wooded parts of the area, it was difficult to be sure of just what damage was being inflicted beneath the canopy of trees. As soon as we arrived in Normandy Chalky White, Frank Transom, Terry Kearins and myself took a jeep into the area to make our own assessment. It was a very hot day, and we could smell the stench of the battle area long before we reached the killing ground. The German dead were being gathered up and buried, but the enemy had been using large numbers of horse-drawn carts, and the bloated carcasses of horses were littered throughout the area. At one point the winding, narrow road emerged into a small clearing where, with Teutonic precision, about fifty horses had been tethered in a row. The verges of the roads and by-ways were heaped high with shattered transport, armour and weapons where they had been thrust clear, first by the retreating Germans and then by the advancing Allied forces. Because of this congestion the roadways were mainly restricted to one-way stretches, and we could explore only a small area of the pocket; but it was enough to conclude that the damage inflicted by air attack was very great indeed. In many cases it was impossible to assess whether air strike or artillery had been responsible; but even along mere cart tracks there were shot-up half-track carriers and trucks, which had clearly been destroyed from the air.

In one small clearing we came across a large truck which had been opened up by a burst of 20-mm from above, and it seemed to have been the mobile Orderly Room of a German unit. The surrounding area – and the branches of the trees – were liberally plastered with official forms; and the paybooks of German soldiers lay scattered mutely on the ground.

As the Falaise battle reached its peak, on 19 August we flew into a beach-head airfield to stay overnight, so that we could carry out an armed reconnaissance at first light in the area between the pocket and the River Seine. A General Signal had just been promulgated instructing us to attack German ambulance vehicles in the battle area (unless in the vicinity of a properly marked Field Hospital) as Red Cross protection was being used to transport armed troops. The order caused considerable soul-searching amongst the pilots, which was somewhat alleviated when a pilot reported stopping an ambulance with a warning burst, then seeing a section of armed soldiers emerge and dive for cover. Nevertheless, it was an uneasy experience for me when I spotted a convoy of five ambulances racing along a narrow road, and I led the Section down in a low pass, hoping they would stop and bale out. There was no reaction, apart from white flags being held out the cab windows, so I put a two-second burst into the leading vehicle which somersaulted into a creek; then the other ambulances were also destroyed by the Section. Confirmation was not long in forthcoming that SS troops had been abusing the Red Cross flag.

Up to 50,000 German troops had escaped from the pocket before it was closed, and were fighting their way back to the Seine; but the weather broke the day after the Falaise battle ended, which hindered effective Allied air attack; but the British, Canadian and American troops followed up as fast as possible.

Four days later the colourful General Patton sent this telegram to the Supreme Commander, General Eisenhower: 'Dear Ike, today I spat in the Seine.'

The Battle of Normandy had ended in the rout of German forces whose casualties were in excess of 300,000. On the first day alone of the Battle of the Somme in 1916, 20,000 British troops had been killed. In less than three months of almost continual offensive action since D-Day against a determined enemy in country ideal for defence, the Allies had incurred 209,672 casualties; of whom 36,976 had been killed.

It was freely acknowledged by the front-line soldiers one met in those days that the success of the Normandy Campaign – and the comparatively low casualty rate – was very much due to the airborne effort, and particularly to the work of Second Tactical Air Force.

Since then the generals and the historians have written their memoirs or commentaries; but I believe that the mass of complex detail about the land battle of Normandy has effectively overlaid, and obscured, the real extent and the value of the Air Force contribution to what was the greatest combined operation of all time.

23

THE RAF RETURNS TO FRANCE

The day after Patton spat in the Seine, 135 Wing aircraft and pilots moved into Tangmere Station, while the ground crews were ferried across into Normandy. Like a fool, I sold my MG to a local garage owner at Selsey Bill, as I had the idea that I would not be back from Europe for a very long time.

After wallowing in the luxury of hot baths and soft beds in the Tangmere Mess for five days, we flew into Capriquet Aerodrome, (which had been the Municipal Airport for Caen) on the morning of 31 August 1944. The aerodrome buildings were virtually demolished, matching the great damage done to Caen by the artillery assault and heavy bomber raids; and the wreckage of war lay all around us. Coming into land I saw a flame-throwing tank incinerating a long, low mound under a row of trees; and my stomach heaved as I flew through the pall of smoke.

That afternoon we flew on an armed reconnaissance (using long-range tanks) all the way up to Abbeville, and I found a convoy of enemy transport, which we duly strafed and destroyed. The trucks were armed with the usual anti-aircraft guns, and as I made my second attack amongst the flak everything changed. I momentarily froze as the red and green balls curved up at me, and had an insane urge to wrench open the canopy and jump out.

Operational fatigue wrecks a pilot's decision-making and leadership ability, and I was well aware of the sometimes tragic

results when a time-expired Section leader refused to acknowl-
edge the problem and give up. All too often it is the pilots he
leads who pay the price for his lack of performance.

In Bomber Command a tour was arbitrarily set at thirty raids,
which was probably a wise decision in view of the close mutual
involvement of the crew; and the maxim that a chain is only as
strong as its weakest link. Fighter Command had a more flexible attitude, which quite often left the onus more squarely on
Commanding Officers to decide when a pilot was reaching the
end of his road.

Early in April Johnnie Walker and Johnnie Niven had tact-
fully suggested that perhaps it was time I had a rest from
operations; but I was still full of ginger and eagerly looking
forward to taking part in the invasion, which we all knew was
not far away. I offered them an undertaking that if I got the
'twitch' I would say so at once, and stand down. I was surprised
and touched when they agreed without hesitation, and we
shook hands on the deal. 'Twitch' was self-explanatory slang for
outward and visible signs of fatigue; which shows up in some
people, but not in others. It could be a facial tic, or jumping
muscles in the limbs, or sudden twists of the head. In some cases
the sphincter muscle would let go, leading to a very messy
outcome.

Back at Capriquet I was sitting morosely in the Mess when
Johnnie Walker, Johnnie Niven and Ray Harries (our live-wire
Wing Leader) came into the bar, and asked why I looked so
sorry for myself. When I glumly told them I had the 'twitch'
they let out a great shout of laughter, and told me they had been
waiting for this for a month or more. Johnnie Walker insisted on
putting on a Champagne party for the whole Mess, and a
depressing day ended with a wonderful evening. Before I
blacked out for the night Johnnie Walker asked me what I
wished to do while on rest, and I hopefully said that I would like
to attend Fighter Leader School and Central Gunnery School,
which were the top operational training courses in Fighter
Command. He surprised me again by stating that my wish
would be granted, and I must have fallen into my camp

stretcher that night with a very happy smile on my face.

Destiny clutches many marbles in her hand and sometimes, perhaps, her palming of the day's decrees may be subject to diversion. I was awakened in the pitch dark of pre-dawn, and in accordance with standing instructions the orderly remained with his lantern while I fitted myself into battle dress and flying boots, before remembering that I was now off operations. He then offered to wake one of the other Section Leaders, but when last sighted that character had been in a much worse state than myself.

So I led the dawn patrol, which was an armed reconnaissance in the Hesdin area, where we found and destroyed some transport. I did not experience the 'twitch' but OU-V collected a lump of shrapnel in the coolant radiator, the first time the aircraft had been damaged by enemy action. Later I recalled the prediction of Nan Inkster, the elderly Scots lady from my childhood. Perhaps I had been given a warning not to play games with Fate.

24

ONE FINAL BURST

Apart from relaxing on leave and attending the excellent Fighter Leader School and Central Gunnery School Courses, I spent two months as a gunnery instructor at a Spitfire OTU. A series of hair-raising incidents at that unit revived my conviction that Training Command was the dreaded end of the line; but some fast footwork enabled me to rejoin 135 Wing of Second Tactical Air Force at Nymegen, in The Netherlands, where I went to 274 Squadron (which had replaced 485 (NZ) Squadron) to fly Mk V Tempests. The Hawker Tempest was a sophisticated development of the Typhoon which was very fast down low, mounted four 20-mm guns, and was well suited to the ground attack role.

In April 1945 the Wing moved into an aerodrome in north Germany, thirty miles beyond the Dutch border; and continued its free-ranging attacks against enemy transport and airfields. This was the twilight phase of the war in Europe, and although large numbers of enemy aircraft were being shot up on the ground, none of the pilots in our unit had seen any Luftwaffe aircraft in the air for some months. One week before Germany capitulated, however, a Dornier bomber flew right underneath me at zero feet, heading in the general direction of Norway. A two-second burst from the four 20-mm guns put an end to the attempted escape, which meant I had accounted for the last – as well as the first – of the enemy aircraft destroyed by 135 Wing of RAF Second Tactical Air Force.

The period following VE-Day was a time of unexpectedly high tension and strange happenings – parallel, perhaps, to the 'phoney war' period between the German defeat of Poland and the attack on The Netherlands, Belgium and France. In fact, Second Tactical Air Force remained virtually in a state of full war-readiness for months, as the Western Allies faced the Soviet troops in Berlin, and along the designated demarcation lines.

Meanwhile the war continued against Japan, and in July I was advised of my promotion to command one of sixteen RAF squadrons destined for the Far East theatre, and to be re-equipped with the latest Tempest (the Mk 2).

Then early in August a signal reported that these reinforcements were not now considered necessary, so I remained with 274 Squadron.

On 6 August 1945 the atomic bomb, dropped on Hiroshima, explained why our services were no longer required.

Against quite formidable odds Spitfire OU-V ML407 (see Appendix V) has survived in England, and has been converted to a two-seat dual control configuration. She is being completely overhauled and reassembled for flight by Nick Grace, her dedicated owner today.

I am touched, and honoured, to learn that Nick is permanently restoring the markings, emblem and insignia of OU-V, exactly as they were when I flew the aircraft during the summer of 1944. So there is also a chance that I may yet fly again in that Spitfire, forty years on from our last flight together in Normandy.

I believe, however, that the survival of Spitfire ML407 had a historical significance which will long outlive the fighter pilots who flew her into action.

In wartime service this aircraft was flown, almost exclusively, by pilots from New Zealand, France, Poland, Belgium and Norway; during the crucial period when the Allied Forces were reversing the defeats of 1940, in the process of restoring freedom and security in the Western world.

All we have of freedom – all we use or know –
this our fathers bought for us, long and long ago.

Kipling, *The Old Issue*

APPENDIX I

Seadromes

INTER-DEPARTMENTAL SUB-COMMITTEE ON
FLOATING AIRFIELDS
REPORT ON FLOATING AIRFIELD DEMONSTRATION,
FRIDAY 15 OCTOBER 1943

INTRODUCTION

A demonstration was held at FORD before the Prime Minister, on Friday 15 October 1943, to demonstrate the operation by fighter aircraft, including refuelling and rearming, from a floating airfield of given dimensions suitably marked out on the surface of the airfield.

DIMENSIONS

The dimensions were as follows:

(i) A replica of the floating airfield was laid out on the airfield and marked by ground strips and flags in accordance with the drawing at Appendix 'A'. Dimensions were: length of landing strip 1800 ft, width of landing strip 175 ft, length of parking strip 1800 ft, width of parking strip 70 ft, distance between landing strip and parking strip 100 ft, width of communicating strips 50 ft.

(ii) *Parking strip.* The width of the parking strip (70 ft) was 20 ft greater than the originally planned measurement as it was considered that any lesser width would result in an unacceptable accident rate. This was borne out by experience.

(iii) *Repair strip.* In addition, it was considered essential that the landing strip should be kept cleared to allow the unobstructed take-off and landing of high performance aircraft. A third strip, or 'repair strip', to take damaged or unserviceable aircraft was accordingly marked out of equal dimensions to the parking strip and on the other side of the landing strip.

(iv) *Arrester gear.* As it was not known whether the use of Arrester gear would be necessary on the floating airfield, the landing strip was marked off at 300-ft intervals from the 1800 ft mark, in order to give an indication of the length of the run needed for aircraft taking-off and landing on the floating airfield.

CONDITIONS OF USE

(i)   There appear to be two distinct ways in which the floating airfield could be used for the operation of aircraft:
(a) As a 'floating home', or
(b) As a refuelling and rearming strip, aircraft returning to their home bases at night.

(ii) On the assumption that the floating airfield was to be used by aircraft as a 'floating home' it was estimated that not more than four squadrons (48 single-engined aircraft) could be operated. In this case the limiting factor being the number of aircraft that could be parked on and operated from the parking strip.

AIRCRAFT TAKING PART

(i)   Accordingly, 4 squadrons (48 aircraft) consisting of the following types took part in the demonstration:-
  12 F.A.A. Seafires — flown by Naval Instructors
  12 Spitfire IXs — No 485 (New Zealand) Squadron
  12 Spitfire Vs — No 416 (Canadian) Squadron
  12 Spitfire Vs — No 412 (Canadian) Squadron

(ii) *Loading.* All aircraft were fully armed and carried full fuel tanks. The twelve Spitfire IXs of No 485 Squadron carried full 30-gallon auxiliary long-range tanks in addition to normal fuel capacity.

(iii) *Pilot's experience.* The Fleet Air Arm Seafires were flown by Naval pilots experienced in actual deck landing conditions. In regard to the RAF Spitfire squadrons, it was not possible for the purposes of the demonstration to find sufficient pilots with previous deck landing experience. Out of the total of 36 RAF pilots, therefore, only 50 per cent pilots had had elementary deck-landing training, including landings on the deck of a carrier.

TIME-KEEPING
In order to find out the time taken for flying off, landing on and refuelling and rearming of the four squadrons taking part, a representative of the Operational Research Section, Fighter Command kept a detailed record of the timing of each individual operation and the results.

DECK HANDLING PARTY
This consisted of a party of 80 trained Naval ratings.

REFUELLING AND REARMING
This was carried out by a party of RAF Servicing Commandos. Refuelling was carried out from eight refuelling bowsers.

FLYING PROGRAMME
The programme was divided into two parts:

PART I was designed to demonstrate the maintenance of a standing patrol of two squadrons over supposed assault operations. At zero hour, therefore, two squadrons took off in quick succession. At zero + 15 – an interval to represent one hour's patrol over the beaches – the remaining squadrons took off in succession.

PART II was designed to demonstrate the operation of aircraft under conditions which might necessitate producing the maximum effort of four squadrons over the assault area. This part of the demonstration, therefore, showed the landing on, quick refuelling and rearming and flying off of all four squadrons in quick succession.

SPECIAL DEMONSTRATION
In order to demonstrate the landing and take-off of other types of aircraft in relation to the floating airfield, the following types carried out a special demonstration at the conclusion of the programme:

Beaufighter I
Mosquito VI
Fulmar II
Hurricane IV
Mustang II

Typhoon
Spitfire XII

Results are shown in paragraph 9 of Appendix 'B'.

CONTROL OF FLYING

(i) All landings were controlled by a FAA batsman.

(ii) All flying from the floating airfield was under the control of a Naval Commander Flying, assisted by a RAF Squadron Leader and Naval Lieutenants as executive officers.

(iii) When in the air all squadrons were controlled by R/T from pack sets situated close to the FAA batsmen.

RESULTS

A complete summary of the results and timing of the different operations is given in detail in Appendix 'B' to this paper. Briefly:

(i) *Take Off*. All aircraft took off safely. Average time 2¾ minutes per squadron.

(ii) *Landing*. 46 of the aircraft overran the end of the landing strip. Average landing time 4¾ minutes per squadron.

(iii) *Refuelling and rearming*. 46 aircraft were refuelled and rearmed in 26 minutes.

(iv) *Special Demonstration Aircraft*. All took off safely. Two ran over the end of the strip on landing.

CONCLUSIONS

(i) *Length of Landing strip*. Unless Arrester gear is to be provided, 1800 ft is too short for the safe landing of high performance fighters unless there is a wind speed of at least 15 – 20 mph over the deck. *50 of the aircraft taking part in this demonstration became casualties on landing*. (See para. 4 Appendix 'A').

(ii) *Parking strip*. Width of 70 ft is still not wide enough to allow safe taxying of aircraft. An additional 20 ft is considered necessary.

(iii) *Repair Strip*. A third strip, not necessarily the whole 1800 ft in length is required, for unserviceable aircraft to be removed to this strip immediately, otherwise operations are seriously delayed.

(iv) *Communicating strips*. These should be wider. Additional communicating strips about 300 ft from each end of the landing strip would improve speed and flexibility of operations.

18 October 1943

FLOATING AIRFIELD DEMONSTRATION:
TIMING OF OPERATIONS

RESULTS

Initial Take-Off

1. All the aircraft engaged – Seafires and Spitfires V and IX (the IXs only with long range tanks) – took off safely from the landing strip without overshooting.

2. With aircraft taking off singly and no hitches occurring the time taken for a Squadron of 12 aircraft to become airborne varied from 1 min. 38 secs. to 3 mins. 58 secs.

3. The time taken for the first pair of Squadrons (comprising 22 aircraft) to take off was 6 mins. 19 secs., and for the second pair of Squadrons (comprising 24 aircraft) 7 mins. 12 secs. These times were worse than those for the Practice Exercise due to a collision in the taxying strip between two aircraft of the second Squadron. The accident caused about 2½ mins. delay in the take-off of the second Squadron and probably had an influence on the pilots in the second pair of Squadrons in making them preserve a greater distance between aircraft while taxying.

Landing

4. The following aircraft overshot on landing:

   Seafires   – 4 out of 12
   Spitfire Vs   – 9 out of 24
   Spitfire IXs   – 8 out of 10

In addition, 1 Spitfire IX and 1 Spitfire V landed short of the landing strip.

   Thus, 23 out of 46 aircraft became 'casualties' on landing.

5. The time taken for a full Squadron to land varied from 3 mins. 46 secs. to 5 mins. 36 secs.

6. The time taken to land on the four Squadrons (46 aircraft) was 21 mins. 15 secs.

Second Take-Off

7   The four Squadrons (still 46 aircraft) took off without hitch in 12 mins. 58 secs., the times for the individual Squadrons varying from 2 mins. 15 secs. to about 3½ mins.

Re-fuelling and Re-Arming

8   The 46 aircraft were re-fuelled and re-armed in 26 mins. so that no delay was caused in the second take-off which commenced immediately after all the aircraft had landed. The re-armament party finished 1 min. ahead of the re-fuelling party.

Special Demonstration

9   The Beaufighter, Mosquito, Fulmar, Hurricane, Mustang and Typhoon and Spitfire XII (the last two with long range tanks fitted) took off safely. On landing the Hurricane and Mustang touched down short of the landing strip, and the Typhoon and Spitfire XII overshot. Thus 4 out of the 7 became 'casualties' on landing.

AUTHOR'S NOTES

1   The collision referred to was caused by the over-exuberance of the sailors acting as marshals on the taxying strip.

2   These trials were flown four months after twelve 485 Squadron pilots had completed basic deck landing training on HMS *Argus*. Six of those pilots had become casualties, and two had been posted to other duties.

3   The conclusion is drawn in the report that 1800 ft was too short for safe landing, *unless* into a 15 – 20 mph headwind. In my opinion this was not entirely valid, as 485 Squadron later operated successfully from airstrips of that length, in 2nd TAF. Also, by landing in these trials with almost full fuel tanks and carrying 30 gallons of extra fuel in our long-range tanks, our aircraft were at least 750 lb above normal landing weight.

4   It is my recollection – also confirmed by other 485 pilots – that the landing distance beyond which the landing aircraft were classed as casualties by the Fleet Air Arm judges was more like 600 ft which corresponds to the approximate length of an aircraft carrier deck at that time.

5   After studying this report one is left with the impression that the architects of the trials – and the report – may have been less than enthusiastic about the whole idea. If that was the case I am personally very grateful. One shudders to think of the shambles a couple of FW 190s could have created amongst 48 aircraft perched on a floating airstrip, all well loaded with 100 octane petrol.

FLOATING AIRFIELD DEMONSTRATION
FORD: 15 OCTOBER 1943 TIMING OF OPERATIONS

Sqdn.	Aircraft	INITIAL TAKE-OFF			LANDING (4 Sqns. in succession)			SECOND TAKE-OFF (4 Sqns. in succession)		
		First Aircraft Airborne*	Last Aircraft Airborne*	Time to Scramble Squadron	First Aircraft Landed*	Last Aircraft Landed*	Time to Land Squadron	First Aircraft Airborne*	Last Aircraft Airborne*	Time to Scramble Squadron
				Mins.Secs.			Mins.Secs.			Mins.Secs.
FAA	Seafires	00.05	01.43	1.38	30.50	34.36	3.46	53.48	56.03	2.15
485	Spit. IX	01.53	06.24†	4.31 (10 a/c. only)	36.02	40.09	4.07 (10 a/c. only)	56.18	59.28	3.10 (10 a/c. only)
			INTERVAL							
416	Spit. Vc	15.07	18.04	2.57	41.16	45.52	4.36	61.11	63.42	2.31
412	Spit. VB	18.21	22.19	3.58	46.29	52.05	5.36	63.59	66.46	2.57

* The times in this column represent minutes and seconds after zero-hour, which was 15 hrs. 6 mins. 40 secs.

† While moving along the taxy strip two aircraft of this Squadron collided and the taxy strip was blocked until both were moved off the strip. The first six aircraft of the Squadron were airborne in 56 secs. and the last four in 51 secs.

WEATHER
Visibility: 4 miles
Wind: Light southerly, 5–10 mph (Across landing strip)
Cloud: 2/10–3/10ths, base 3000 ft.

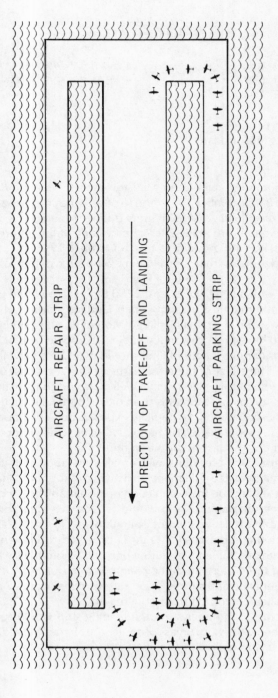

PROPOSED LANDING STRIP, PARKING AND TAXYING STRIPS

Scale: 1in = 275ft.

Appendix I

HEADQUARTERS,
ALLIED EXPEDITIONARY AIR FORCE,
NORFOLK HOUSE, ST JAMES'S SQUARE,
LONDON, SW1

12 January 1944

AEAF/Ms.13345/Air Plans.

Sir,

I have the honour to refer to Air Ministry letter, C.M.S. 393/D.Ops. (Tac.) dated 31 December 1943, and to offer some comments on the proposal to use floating Airfield Strips during OVERLORD.

My observations are made after careful study of the report on the trials undertaken at Ford airfield on 15 October 1943.

2 It would appear that the Floating Strips have the following limitations:

(i) Even with a length of at least 2250 ft, the strip would provide too little margin for safety when landing, particularly if the pilots were in any difficulties. Moreover, the parking strip would have to be very much wider if it is not to be blocked for a considerable length of time should there be a taxying accident. The effect of these increases in size and consequential strengthening involved, might well make the construction and operation of these airfields prohibitive, particularly if they are to be used in open, or partially exposed, sea conditions. The need for some degree of manoeuvrability to allow for change of wind must also be borne in mind.

(ii) The use of these strips will involve an additional training commitment the fulfilment of which cannot fail to have an adverse effect on the completion of the already heavy combat training programme, and would reduce the squadron effort available for active current operations.

(iii) The non-combat casualty rate is expected to be very high, even greater than it was during one of the Ford trials when 23 out of the 48 aircraft participating were casualties.

(iv) Maintenance and supply of aircraft would inevitably be more complicated and difficulties increased.

(v) The crash of an aircraft on the landing strip would seriously interfere with flying, unless of course the aircraft were 'ditched' to clear the runway.

(vi) The airfield would be vulnerable to air attack and the losses of personnel, aircraft, and equipment on this account might be very serious; even small damage to the surface might well render the whole Floating Airfield inoperative for a considerable period of time.

3 It is appreciated that during OVERLORD operations our short-range fighter aircraft will be operating at a disadvantage in the initial stage owing to the considerable distance of the assault areas from squadron bases. This factor is not however prohibitive and with extra tanks now being provided the handicap can be accepted. Moreover, the number of aerodromes available in southern England for the operation of fighter aircraft is adequate for our needs, and as far as can be foreseen the squadrons will not be called upon to operate in such overcrowded airfield conditions as will result in reduced operational efficiency. Further, the plan provides for the very early development of landing strips on the Continent and until they are available for use aircraft of all types can operate effectively from air bases in England.

4 For the foregoing and other reasons I am of the opinion that the employment of Floating Airfield Strips would afford no tactical or operational advantage and that there is no requirement for them in OVERLORD conditions. At the same time I can well visualise their profitable use in more favourable water conditions and where there is a serious paucity of available landing sites suitably located in relation to the assault area, such as might be experienced in the Far Eastern theatre.

I would therefore suggest that the Supreme Allied Commander, South East Asia, might well be interested in the development and potential use of these Landing Strips.

(Sgd.) T. LEIGH-MALLORY
Air Chief Marshal,
Air Commander-in-Chief,
ALLIED EXPEDITIONARY AIR FORCE

AUTHOR'S NOTE
Despite the agreed defects in using such floating airstrips under wartime conditions, the principle itself was valid.

With the advent of advanced technology in flotation materials, a good case could perhaps be made for seadromes in harbours; to operate feeder services between cities and airports etc.

It transpires that the deck-landing training in which I was involved in June 1943 was initially intended for specific operations in the Mediterranean and the Far East; such as BRIMSTONE (plan for capture of Sardinia), BUCCANEER (operations against the Andamen Islands), BULLFROG (amphibious assault on Akyab), FIRST CULVERIN (operations against N. Sumatra). The purpose was to provide relief squadrons for Fleet Air Arm units working from carriers, in support of amphibious operations. The initial training and subsequent landings on HMS *Argus* had been completed when it was recognised that the Far East theatre was more likely to require such protracted sea-borne support, in the war against Japan.

By October 1943, when the demonstration at Ford took place for the benefit of the Prime Minister, we had become part of the floating airfield – or 'Seadrome' – concept.

This concept arose out of a Combined Operations Headquarters analysis of the strategic situation, as it appeared in August/September 1942. This was one month after the Dieppe raid, when Eighth Army was stationed with its back to the Nile; and just holding its own in the El Alamein position. The wide-ranging 50,000-word-analysis document was deliberately quite imaginative, and put forward the idea of mammoth 'unsinkable' vessels having the function of floating airfields.

Originally, these floating airfields were envisaged in support of the ultimate invasion of German-held Europe; but when the 1942/3 view of the Japanese war is appreciated, the vital role of aircraft carriers – both conventional and fanciful – takes on very great significance.

In mid 1943 projected plans for the defeat of Japan involved a very long series of amphibious assaults on islands towards the coast of China, a land campaign against the Japanese then in China to secure airfields for the intensive bombing of Japan, to be ultimately followed by a number of amphibious assaults against the islands of Japan itself. The whole campaign was expected to last five or six years after the defeat of Germany.

Following a European victory vast numbers of aircraft and personnel could then be deployed against Japan; but an efficient means had to be devised of bringing them to the Far East and of maintaining them in the island combat zones. The Combined Operations analysis suggested that the use of floating airfields as well as conventional carriers might be the key, particularly in view of the extreme ranges at which any land-based aircraft would otherwise be forced to operate. American fighter aircraft had the enviable built-in fuel capacity for very long-range operations, as would be normal in the Pacific campaign. The comparatively short range of the RAF Spitfires, Typhoons and Tempests meant, however, that unless close-up airfield facilities could be provided, the RAF fighters were unlikely to get into action at many of the crucial, forward battle areas.

The functions of the 'carriers' of various types would be:

(a) To destroy the Japanese fleet, and to provide cover for Allied operations and communications
(b) To carry out raids on rear Japanese areas and in particular on shipping, bases, sources of raw material and on industries in Japan
(c) As convoy escorts
(d) To provide fighter and tactical bomber support in amphibious operations
(e) To enable long range amphibious operations to be supported by airborne troops flown from reasonably short distances, so that they were not unduly fatigued before being dropped into combat
(f) To augment or extend shore-based aircraft in support of defensive operations such as the holding of small island bases after they had been captured
(g) The supply of Naval fighter aircraft to the battle area, the aircraft carriers acting either as staging points or as ferries

Out of this emerged 'Scheme Habbakuk' which originally envisaged three types of floating airfields.

Habbaukuk I was perhaps the most conventional in construction, but relied on large quantities of wood which, unfortunately, was classified as too valuable a strategic material to divert in such enormous quantities and so this version was the first to be shelved.

Habbakuk III, made of about 70,000 tons of steel, would consist of a deck resting catamaran-style across two or more Liberty ships, and would be the fastest of the three designs, in transit.

But it was Habbakuk II which had the most adventurous touch. This vessel was intended to be made almost entirely of 'Pykrete', a substance named after Mr Geoffrey Pyke who was the originator of the Seadrome concept. Pykrete had the advantage of being made from non-strategic materials, buoyant, strong and easily repairable, and possibly proof against radar detection. Pykrete was in fact ice impregnated with woodpulp, and its viability was attested by H.T. Barnes in charge of 'Ice Engineering'. Attention was drawn to the longevity of natural icebergs, even when they had drifted into warmer seas, so the massive 'Berg Ships' began to look like a distinct possibility.

SECTION IV

TECHNICAL DESCRIPTION OF THE HABBAKUK II STRUCTURE AND METHODS OF CONSTRUCTION

From the constructional point of view, Habbakuk II is a vessel of 2,000 ft. length, 300 ft. beam, with an overall depth of 200 ft. and a draft of 150 ft.

The main structural material is Pykrete, and the essential structural principle of the whole hull is that of a massive hollow girder.

The Pykrete is protected from melting and erosion by an insulating skin, tough enough to withstand normal weather conditions and any battering which it is likely to receive from the sea. This skin also reduces the transmission of heat from the outside to the surface of the Pykrete, to an approximate level of .035 British thermal units per hour per square foot of surface area per degree Fahrenheit difference in temperature.

To maintain approximately 50 ft. freeboard and thus render effective air bombing operations possible, it was necessary, although the Pykrete is self-buoyant, to form a large internal cavity, which would raise 25 per cent of the hull above still water level.

The central section of this cavity is used for engine, crew and machine shop space, whilst other sections are available for tankage and similar requirements, but the main voids are simply filled with material or frame-work, having a total over-all density per cubic foot of the whole void in the vicinity of .5. The function of this construction is merely to absorb the loads formed by the under-water pressure on the bottom of the hull, and those produced by supporting the protective deck, and to remove the danger of flooding from any leak in the hull.

Throughout the construction 40 ft. thick bottom, walls and deck of Pykrete are provided, which will give the whole interior of the structure complete immunity from any present known form of air or under-water attack.

The bomb-resisting qualities of Pykrete are assessed, as the result of experiments, at approximately 2½ times less resistant than the best reinforced concrete, and so far, these expectations have been justified by experiment. The extent of any torpedo damage will be a crater not more than 3 ft. deep and about 20 ft. in diameter. Bomb damage, while the crater may be slightly deeper owing to better penetration, will be of the same order.

The main propulsion is formed by a large number of widely spaced electric motors in pressure hulls. These are powered by a series of Diesel electric generating sets carried deep in the main structure, and are believed to be capable of providing a speed of about 7 knots, and the required degree of manoeuvrability.

The complete elimination of a whole propulsion unit by enemy action will have a total effect on the propulsion available of less than 4%, and the breakdown of an entire Diesel electric generating unit will only result in an efficiency loss on the total output of about 6%.

AUTHOR'S NOTE

In the winter of 1943/4 the construction of the first of a series of full-scale sections of a Habbakuk II was initiated, in order to assess a range of different construction and insulation methods. The project was under the direction of Dean MacKenzie of the National Research Council in Canada, and the site was Patricia Lake, Jasper National Park. The test structure was 60 ft long by 30 ft wide by 20 ft deep and in the event took between ten and twenty men (employed at different times) three months to complete. A 30 ft by 10 ft by 8 ft cavity in the upper part contained three refrigeration units, and ice blocks cut from the lake were used, rather than set up a Pykrete manufacturing plant.

The exercise of testing whether it was possible to make and maintain an insulated ice structure floating in water was declared to be a success, with no insurmountable difficulties encountered. A schedule was drawn up for a full-scale production run for the following winter, to provide operational Habbakuk IIs for the spring of 1945, and a survey was made of possible manufacturing sites in North America.

However, despite all the testing success, the enthusiastic support of Mr Churchill and Chief of Combined Operation Louis Mountbatten and the strivings of the Habbakuk Committee under the Chairmanship of the Deputy First Sea Lord Admiral Sir Charles Kennedy-Purvis, hopes for a fleet of Habbakuks were melting away by the beginning of February 1944. The problem had begun when the Prime Minister, Admiral King (USN) and three American Rear-Admirals met with the President in his Washington study in September 1943. Mr Churchill's plans for Habbakuks received only a tepid response. The Americans had their own ideas, and felt that, in any case, there was simply not enough time to set up the manufacturing facilities without interfering with the flow of other vital equipment, such as Liberty ships. They felt that there would be plenty of escort carriers available shortly, and it would be better to stick to tried methods rather than start introducing 'novelties'. The US Navy officers also gained the immediate and vigorous support of the President for their own floating airstrip concept, which had the advantage of utilising conventional fleet lighter pontoons, four of which could be made into a barge, with eight of these barges lashed together to make a landing strip 1500 ft by 175 ft. Mr Churchill came away with a suggestion that the British might usefully investigate the possibility of making concrete floating airfields in India, but he immediately cabled General 'Pug' Ismay, his Chief of Staff, to organise in short order a demonstration of the ability of the Fleet Air Arm and RAF to utilise floating airfields. This was to be the October 1943 trial at Ford.

The Americans did not relent on the subject of Habbakuks, and they literally held the key to manufacture, owing to the acute manpower shortages in Britain and the Dominions; and as has been seen Air Commander-in-Chief Trafford Leigh-Mallory definitely ruled out Floating Airfield Strips for OVERLORD, after the Ford trials. However the US Navy project coded 'Tentacle Sock', and a parallel British effort under R.M. Hamilton coded 'Tentacle/Lily and Clover', did at least prove that it was possible to operate aircraft successfully from floating airstrips.

'Sock' was built at Davisville to the US Navy pontoon pattern and up to 90 aircraft of various types tested on it.

'Lily' and 'Clover' were built on a small scale at Rosyth, and in March and April 1945 successfully tested with an Auster and a Swordfish. 'Lily' had been designed in the first instance as a floating pierhead formed of hexagonal steel buoyancy units hinged together to make a flexible mat on the surface of the sea, whilst 'Clover' consisted of a wooden decking laid at right angles over steel buoyancy tubes. There was also a version of 'Tentacle' known as 'Wattle' which embodied features of both 'Sock' and 'Lily'.

In the event the war moved faster than all these projects, and particularly in respect of the campaign against Japan after the fall of Germany.

APPENDIX II

Analysis of Allied air-to-ground attacks by RAF fighter/bombers in Normandy

AUTHOR'S NOTE

1 The original of this document was produced by No 2 Operational Research Section for the Main Headquarters of 21 Army Group (General Montgomery) of the British Liberating Armies.

   The full report covers thirty-five foolscap pages divided into five parts, and includes five full-page detailed tables of damage to enemy vehicles and equipment, together with five maps of the area examined.

2 The Introduction and full text of Part I is reproduced below; with its Appendices A and B.

3 Parts II, III & IV are set out in much the same way; and it appears that Part IV – THE SEINE CROSSINGS – was a late inclusion in the surveys. Only selected items from these central Sections of the Report are reproduced below.

4 Part V – discussion of results and conclusions – is reproduced in full.

5 This was an Army Report for 21st Army H.Q., completed on 24 October 1944.

   The last Section of the conclusions deals with interdiction i.e. prohibition of enemy troop movements by use of the Air Force, as against concentrating only on destruction. The very last paragraph of that Section has a curious – if somewhat plaintive – flavour, the implication seeming to be that had the Air Force followed a successful policy of interdiction, no enemy forces would have managed to retreat across the Seine.

6 H.Q. 2nd TAF subsequently studied the Report and made some very pertinent comments, which were added to the report on 15 January 1945.

7 197 Infantry Brigade Battlefield Clearance Group later made an accurate census of the same areas covered by the Report, which increased the estimated total enemy vehicle and equipment losses by 22 per cent, and this is also shown in the ADDENDA; which is reproduced in full.

No 2 OPERATIONAL RESEARCH SECTION,
21st ARMY GROUP

REPORT ON ENEMY CASUALTIES IN VEHICLES AND
EQUIPMENT DURING THE RETREAT FROM NORMANDY
TO THE SEINE

INTRODUCTION AND PART I

INTRODUCTION
The primary object of this investigation was to ascertain the extent of
the enemy's losses due directly or indirectly to air attack and to assess
the effectiveness of different air weapons.

AREAS COVERED
The area involved can be divided into three portions, which we have
named the Pocket, the Shambles and the Chase.

I *The Pocket*
This is the area bounded by a line passing through the following
places: FALAISE, CONDE-SUR-NOIREUA, VASSY, TINCHEBRAY, GER, BARENTON, DOM-
FRONT, LA FERTE-MACE, ARGENTAN. In this area the retreat appears to have
been reasonably orderly, casualties were not particularly heavy but
increased steadily towards the eastern end.

The area immediately east of MORTAIN is not included as it was a
battle rather than a retreat area. It will be dealt with as a separate
report.

II *The Shambles*
This area is at the mouth of the Pocket and is bounded approximately
by a line passing through PIERREFITTE (on the FALAISE – ARGENTAN Road) –
ARGENTAN – CHAMBOIS – VIMOUTIERS – TRUN – PIERREFITTE. Here the retreat
appears to have become very disorderly, the density of the casualties
is high, and the area well described by the name given.

III *The Chase*
The area leading to the SEINE crossings, showing signs of a reasonably orderly retreat and with casualties lightly spread over a large
area.

PART I THE POCKET

1 *Collection of data*

The method of investigation in the Pocket has been to patrol the most likely roads and to record the following data:

(a) Type of vehicle or equipment.
(b) Cause of casualty.
(c) Date of casualty.
(d) Direction in which proceeding.
(e) Whether burnt or unburnt.
(f) Ease of visibility from the air.
(g) Degree of dismantling of the vehicle.

Local inhabitants were interrogated whenever possible.

In addition to the main roads a number of side roads were also examined in particular areas where it appeared likely that vehicles might be found.

Statements by inhabitants as to where vehicles were or were not to be found proved to be mainly correct when checked and have therefore been used to avoid searching every road in the area. Even so, we have no doubt that vehicles have been missed and that our totals are at the best only approximate. However, from the wooded nature of the country and the conditions in which the vehicles in side roads were found, we are confident that few of those had suffered directly from air attack.

There was difficulty in estimating the time at which a casualty had occurred. Local inhabitants informed us of many which dated from about D-Day. In many cases it was obvious from the appearance of the wreckage, and from the state of development of plants growing in burnt verges that the casualty was an old one. Further evidence of date was provided by the direction in which the vehicle was pointing and the degree of dismantling. It is assumed that during the retreat only a small number of vehicles could have been pointing west and that although wheels or tyres and possibly items of ignition systems might have been quickly removed as spares, it would hardly have been feasible to remove such items as engines and back axles. There was no evidence that any major dismantling was being carried out by the French or our troops; plenty of opportunities were still outstanding and were not being used to any appreciable extent while we were in the area.

2 *Results*

(a)   *At Appendix A* is a table giving details of the *total number of vehicles and equipments* that were found and examined. By comparing the numbers on side roads with those on main roads in a few areas, it is estimated that had all side roads been examined, the total would have been increased by not more than 50 per cent in the case of guns and AFVs* and 30 per cent for other vehicles.

The table is of general interest only; it contains all vehicles and equipments found, regardless of the date on which they became casualties. However it may serve as a comparison with other counts that have been or will be made.

(b)   The table at *Appendix B* includes only those casualties which occurred or might have occurred since the encirclement of the enemy. It is impossible to assess exactly what proportion of abandoned vehicles and equipments can be attributed to air action. Abandonment must often have come as a result of the extreme congestion and disorganisation which prevailed during the retreat; traffic was often totally blocked and petrol became scarce. Inasmuch as the congestion and disorganisation can be attributed very largely to the air, abandonment must in the majority of cases be attributed to air action. All abandoned vehicles and guns are therefore included in Appendix B.

A number of casualties attributed to air attack must first have been abandoned. Unless a vehicle had been set on fire or was in a traffic stream, there can have been no means of telling from the air whether it was already a casualty. Several cases have been quoted by local inhabitants of vehicles that had been shot up from the air repeatedly. One particular example was just outside PUTANGE where an armoured troop carrier abandoned in a somewhat conspicuous place with no petrol was said to have been machine-gunned twelve times. Its appearance and that of the roads and buildings nearby supported these statements.

(c)   *At Appendix C* is a trace showing the roads that were patrolled and illustrating the results given in Appendix B. It shows how the density of casualties increased progressively from the western to the eastern end of the Pocket, as would be expected. The assembly of guns around the point A (M.R. 846175) had all been abandoned at about that point, though they were actually found in a REME workshop. The concentrations around the points B and C, (MRs 9224 and

* Armoured fighting vehicle.

0626) were in for repair or had been stripped to provide spares for other vehicles.

(d)   Wherever possible the wheels of vehicles had been removed. Inhabitants invariably informed us that the Germans had taken them, and it has been subsequently confirmed through I channels that this was their normal practice.

(e)   The great majority of soft vehicles that had been hit by cannon and machine gun attack were burnt. In a sample of 153 lorries and cars near the mouth of the Pocket 77 had been hit and burnt, 7 hit and not burnt, 4 burnt but not hit, 65 neither burnt nor hit. It was found to be almost a rule that where the pock marks of strikes appeared in the roads, there a burnt vehicle was to be found.

(SGD).   P. JOHNSON

No 2 Operational Research Section,   *Lieut-Colonel,*
Main HQ 21 Army Group.   *A.D.S.R.*
B.L.A.

THE SHAMBLES

Horse-drawn transport was excluded from this survey for several reasons. Firstly it is so easy to destroy that it is difficult to tell afterwards what weapon was responsible; secondly the stench of dead horses was so overpowering that where there was any number of horse-drawn vehicles that area had to be passed with all speed. It is estimated that about a thousand carts and wagons, some belonging to the German Army and some farm carts impressed for the occasion, were seen in the area.

THE CHASE

On the south bank of the river to the west of the wrecked bridge in ROUEN was found a mass of burnt vehicles and equipment consisting of 20 AFVs, 48 guns, and 660 other vehicles. It appears that a traffic jam was formed owing to a misapprehension that there was a serviceable bridge. The RAF attacked the jam and started fires which destroyed the lot.

THE SEINE CROSSINGS

At all the crossings examined the inhabitants stressed the point that the Germans had travelled chiefly at night but that, in the vitally important week, there were three days when the visibility was very poor and during which they were able to ferry much traffic across in daylight without any interference from the RAF.

Appendix A

TOTAL DAMAGE TO ENEMY VEHICLES AND EQUIPMENT IN 'THE POCKET'
(from D-Day onwards)

Type	R.P.	Bombs	Cannon and M.G.	A.P.	H.E.	Mines	Destroyed by crew	Abandoned	Accident	Unknown causes	Total	%
Tanks	4	2	0	8	2	0	32	33	0	9	90	7.1
S.P. guns	5	0	0	2	2	0	12	4	2	4	31	2.4
Armd. vehs.	2	2	21	1	5	1	8	12	0	4	56	4.4
Lorries	5	36	283	0	40	8	11	192	9	75	659	52.
Cars	0	9	86	0	14	3	9	165	24	42	352	27.7
Motor/cycles	0	0	2	0	3	1	10	10	3	3	22	1.7
Guns	0	0	1	0	5	0	9	41	0	4	60	4.7
Totals	16	49	393	11	71	13	81	457	38	141	1270	
Percentages	1.2	3.8	31.0	1.0	5.6	1.0	6.4	36.0	3.0	11.0		

Note: Figures for guns and AFVs may be increased by not more than 50 per cent when missed side-roads and lanes are taken into account.
Figures for other vehicles may be increased by about 30 per cent for the same reason.

ANALYSIS OF DAMAGE BY AIR ATTACK TO ENEMY EQUIPMENT DURING 'THE POCKET' PERIOD Appendix B

Due directly or indirectly to Air (AP, HE, Mines, Accidents and Unknown Causes excluded).
(When it is not certain whether damage occurred in this phase of the battle or earlier, it is included in the table.)

Type	R.P.	Bombs	Cannon and M.G.	"Air" total	Abandoned or destroyed by the crew	Grand total
Tanks S.P. Guns Armoured vehicles	11	4	18	33	100	133
Lorries Cars Motor cycles	4	43	278	325	376	701
Guns	0	0	1	1	50	51
Totals	15	47	297	359	526	885
Percentages	1.7	5.3	33.5	—	59.5	—

Note: Figures for guns and AFVs may be increased by not more than 50 per cent when missed side-roads and lanes are taken into account. Figures for other vehicles may be increased by about 30 for the same reason. A further addition of 10 might be made to all figures to allow for those casualties which have been attributed to unknown causes but which were in fact due to air action.

Appendix II

NO 2 OPERATIONAL RESEARCH SECTION, HQ 21 ARMY GROUP

REPORT ON ENEMY CASUALTIES IN VEHICLES AND EQUIPMENT DURING THE RETREAT FROM NORMANDY TO THE SEINE

REPORT NO. 15
– PART V –
DISCUSSION OF RESULTS AND CONCLUSIONS

INTRODUCTION

The German retreat from Normandy to the SEINE and beyond is by no means the first occasion on which a large scale withdrawal, enforced by land action, has been laid open to air attack. The Turkish retreat through the pass at NABLUS, that of the Germans from ALAMEIN, and the British retreats to DUNKIRK and in Greece are all examples, but in none of these cases, as far as is known, has a detailed study of the resultant casualties been made.

The results of such air attacks are primarily of importance to the advancing army who may have to fight once more against the survivors; it therefore appears relevant to discuss from the military point of view the results of the survey that has been made and, notwithstanding the very great success achieved by the air forces, to consider how even greater success might have been achieved with the resources available.

1 *TOTAL CASUALTIES*

(a)   At *Appendix K* are two tables; the first shows the totals found during the ground survey and the second gives figures amended to allow for vehicles which were missed. The percentages added in the case of the Pocket were arrived at by examining two small areas in very great detail to compare side roads with main roads. In the Shambles area only a small addition had been made because the area was thoroughly searched. In the Chase, where the examination was not so complete, high percentages have been added. In round figures the amended totals are as follows:

Vehicles and Guns

POCKET	1500
SHAMBLES	3500
CHASE	5000
	———
Grand Total	10000
	———

This figure, in view of the nature of the estimate for the Chase is an approximation which however is unlikely to be in error by more than 2000 either way.

(b)   We have been unable to obtain a figure for the total number of mechanically-propelled vehicles that the German army had in Normandy, but there were known to have been 16 infantry and 10 Panzer divisions. Had these been up to strength, which they certainly were not, the figure would have been about 45,000 without including non-divisional transport. It is, however, known from captured documents that they were up to 60 per cent strength in artillery and it is therefore reasonable to assume that, including the great number of impressed vehicles used in the retreat, the Germans must have had at least 30,000 vehicles. It thus appears that two-thirds of this total was withdrawn to the far side of the SEINE and that had the number of casualties been doubled it would have made a considerable difference to the enemy's subsequent ability to retreat and resist.

2   COMPARISON OF CASUALTIES AND CLAIMS

As it is of value to the army to know how many casualties the enemy has suffered and pilots' reports are the only immediately available source of such information, it is interesting to compare the casualties due to air attack with the claims made.

(a)   *Total claims*

In the Pocket casualties directly due to air attack have been quite accurately assessed at 359, with a possible addition on account of missed vehicles which might bring it up to 500. In the Shambles an estimate of 800 has been made. For the Chase only a very rough estimate can be made, but as many as 2000 would be reasonable. This yields a total of over 3000.

Details of sorties by Spitfires, Typhoon and Mustang aircraft of 2nd

TAF and by P38s and P47s of the IX USAAF together with claims for vehicles destroyed in the areas which we have covered have been provided by ORS, 2nd TAF, and A – 2, IX USAAF respectively. The significant figures are as follows:

	2 TAF	IX USAAF	TOTAL
Sorties flown	9896	2891	12787
Claims for MT dest.	3340	2520	5860
Claims for Armour dest.	257	134	391
Total claims	3597	2654	6251
Claims per sortie	0.36	0.83	0.49

The above figures do not include the 531 sorties flown by medium bombers to attack the MT concentration near ROUEN when the pilots made no claims but we found about 700 vehicles which have been included in the 2000 mentioned above.

Although our estimate of over 3000 for the total casualties due directly to air can only be very approximate, the total is certainly less than the total claims made by the two air forces. However, there is no difference of order between totals of claims and casualties, and it is therefore reasonable to accept the former as having been a fair measure of the latter.

(b)   *Claims for Armour*
The particular claims for destruction of armour cannot be upheld. Of the available weapons bombs, cannon, and machine gun can only be expected to destroy heavily armoured vehicles on exceptional occasions and had they been a common cause of tank casualties we would not have failed to have observed it. 222 claims for destruction of armour were made by Typhoon pilots who presumably fired Rocket Projectiles (RP), but out of a total of 456 heavily armoured vehicles (tanks and SP guns) counted 301 were examined in detail and only 10 found to have been destroyed by RP. Even if armored troop carriers are included, it is found that only three out of the 87 examined were destroyed by RP. If armoured troop carriers destroyed by cannon or machine gun are included, a total more nearly approaching the claims might be obtained, but if such vehicles, which are readily distinguishable from AFVs, are claimed as armour,

this should be discontinued as militarily they are only of minor importance compared to AFVs.

It seems hardly to lie in our province to examine this discrepancy in further detail, nor from the military point of view is there much to be gained by doing so. The facts that remain are that 456 tanks and SP guns were actually counted, and the total is certainly greater, while only about 250 are estimated to have crossed the SEINE. It follows that owing to the conditions imposed by the retreat, and with the present state of reliability of German armour, a very large proportion of that armour was lost.

3 EFFECTIVENESS OF WEAPONS
The principal weapons used for the direct destruction of enemy vehicles and equipment were cannon, machine gun, RP, and bombs.

We have not been able to differentiate at all clearly between the relative effectiveness of the first two; both appear to have been very deadly to all except heavily armoured vehicles and the figures given in the preceding parts of the report speak for themselves. As indicated in 2 (b) above, RP have not produced the results against armour which might have been hoped for, whilst against soft vehicles they are clearly less suitable than cannon and machine gun fire. It is suggested that RP in its present form suffers the grave disadvantage of being virtually a 'one shot' weapon which even in the hands of the most skilful pilot has poor accuracy, whereas the protracted burst of fire from cannon or machine gun gives a far greater chance of scoring hits.

There was little scope for the really effective use of bombs as suitable area targets seldom presented themselves, but in the case of the one ideal target near ROUEN the results were highly satisfactory.

4 INDIRECT EFFECTS OF AIR ATTACK
Statements of PW have shown how traffic was disorganised by air action. The three principal effects appear to have been:
  i   Movement was restricted to the night until congestion and haste positively compelled day movement.
  ii Crews had to stop and take cover when aircraft appeared.
  iii Vehicles were driven off main roads on to the side roads.

It is hardly possible to assess these effects numerically in terms of casualties, but the delay resulting from them must have been largely responsible for the inability of the enemy to get away, and consequently for a large number of vehicles abandoned or destroyed by their crews.

5 INTERDICTION

In three places the densities of casualties were particularly high, namely near the mouth of the SEINE, near ROUEN, and in the Shambles area. Elsewhere the casualties were fairly uniformly spread along roads, and, although it is known that temporary obstructions did occur, they could be cleared and so delayed rather than prevented the enemy's escape. Where the densities were high, interdiction of enemy movement was virtually established, in the first instance by the natural obstacle of the River SEINE, and in the last by the action of ground forces.

It is considered that the evidence points to interdiction as being the primary task to be performed against a rapidly retreating enemy so that his retreat can be stopped and that infliction of casualties should in the first instance be of importance only in so far as it contributes towards interdiction. Once the interdiction has been established congestion must result and casualties can be inflicted at a very high rate by any weapon that can be brought to bear.

If the policy of interdiction followed by destruction could be adopted, it is considered that the total casualties resulting would in the end be higher than if destruction alone were concentrated upon. In the particular retreat which has been considered, what was a very severe defeat might have approximated to a complete rout. It should however be borne in mind that unless the interdiction is successful the results will probably be less satisfactory than if the effort has been concentrated only on destruction.

Main HQ, 21 Army Group
24 October 1944

Lieutenant-Colonel,
ADSR
No 2 Operational Research Section

APPENDIX K
TOTAL ENEMY LOSSES IN VEHICLES AND EQUIPMENT DURING THE RETREAT

A   *Totals found by No 2 Operational Section*

CATEGORY	POCKET	SHAMBLES	CHASE	TOTAL
Tanks and SP guns	121	185	150	456
Lightly armoured vehs	56	157	154	367
Lorries, cars, and M/Cs	1033	2447	3178	6648
Guns	60	252	166	478
Totals:	1270	3041	3648	7959

B   *Estimated totals allowing for vehicles not seen*

Tanks and SP guns	169 (121+40%)	222 (185+20%)	240 (150+60%)	631
Lightly armoured vehs	78 (56+40%)	188 (157+20%)	246 (154+60%)	512
Lorries, cars, and M/Cs	1239 (1033+20%)	2692 (2447+10%)	4449 (3178+40%)	8380
Guns	72 (60+20%)	277 (252+10%)	232 (166+40%)	581
Revised totals:	1558	3379	5167	10104

ORS/P6
SECRET
15 Jan 45
ADDENDA to No 2 ORS Report No 15

A   COMMENTS FROM 2ND TAF

ORS Report No 15, 'Enemy Casualties in Vehicles and Equipment during the Retreat from NORMANDY to the SEINE' has been studied by HQ 2nd TAF. The following is a summary of the comments that have been made:

1   It would be wrong to regard the data provided in the report as yielding information on which to make recommendations for changes in weapons, tactics or operational doctrine, although the factual side of the report can itself be accepted.

2   *Part V – Introduction*
Whereas the large-scale withdrawal is stated to have been 'enforced by land action', the ultimate cause of the withdrawal should more properly have been attributed to the factor of combined service action.

3   *Part V – para 2(b)*
(a) The air claims against armour are certainly too high if armour is interpreted as meaning AFVs. However, in close country and under operational conditions, it is not agreed that armoured troop carriers are readily distinguishable from AFVs.

(b) The circumstances of the examination did not make it possible to take account of the morale effects of RP. A lack of effectiveness in causing material damage cannot be accepted as a reason for abandoning RP as a weapon against armour until it can be replaced by something better.

4   *Part V – para 4*
The demoralising effect of air action is not adequately stressed and the report should be considered as relating only to the limited aspect of the material effects of air action.

5   *Part V – Introduction and para 5*
No conclusion aimed at deciding 'how even greater success might have been achieved with the resources available' can be based on examination of results of destruction alone. Other factors must be taken into account, such as weather, enemy flak, improper use of

Red Cross and limitations of bomb line. In fact, a policy of interdiction was followed in so far as it was tactically possible, and, with suitable terrain such as the crossings of the SEINE, it was successful.

B *ADDITIONAL VEHICLES*
Ref Part V para 1 (a) and Appendix K.

1 Since this report was published a census has been carried out by 197 Inf Bde Battlefield Clearance Group over an area almost identical with that which we named 'the Shambles'. The results of this census show that the percentages added for vehicles missed in this area were too small. The 197 Inf Bde results compared with the estimates given at Appendix K, part B, column 2, are shown below:

	ORS	197 Inf Bde
Tanks and SP guns	222	358
Tracked vehicles, lorries and cars	2880	4715
Guns	277	571
TOTAL:	3379	5644

2 As far as can be ascertained, the differences arise entirely from vehicles and equipment which we failed to discover in narrow lanes, orchards, farm-yards, and woods. Such vehicles were in almost every case abandoned, consequently the effect on the accuracy of the report is quantitative rather than qualitative.

3 The final estimate for total losses sustained by the enemy in the whole area, as given at Appendix K, should be amended to read '12369' instead of '10104'.

C *OMISSION*
Part V, para 3 – Effectiveness of Weapons
By an unfortunate oversight the following sentence was omitted from the final draft of the report:

'Whenever an RP was found to have hit an armoured vehicle, that vehicle was invariably destroyed.'

(Signed) P. JOHNSON
Lieutenant-Colonel,
ADSR,
Main HQ, 21 Army Group   No 2 Operational Research Section

APPENDIX III

Gyro Gunsight:
Detailed Background and Technical
Developments

Development of the Gyro Sight is an interesting example of technical invention being accelerated by war, and of the ability and energy of British scientists and engineers.

1917 W/Cdr Wackett suggested use of the inherent properties of the gyro as an aid to deflection shooting. Based at the same station was Major B.M. Jones, later Professor Sir Melvill Jones of the Royal Aeronautical Establishment at Farnborough.

1936 Dr L.B.C. Cunningham of the RAF Education Board, lecturing on mathematics, suggested that theoretically the complexities of deflection shooting could be solved by using a gyroscopically controlled sighting system.

1938 Analysis of a special tactical exercise conducted at Northolt proved that the general standard of deflection shooting was far from satisfactory, with the new generation of high-performance fighters. The Air Staff gave top priority to development of a predictor type gun-sight, for both fighter aircraft and bomber gun turrets.

Mid 1940 The Mk I Gyro Sight produced by RAE Farnborough solved computation of the correct deflection angle required to 'lead' the target aircraft.

Early 1941 Prototype Mk I Sights were fitted to a Spitfire and to the turret of a Boulton Paul Defiant. Test results were very satisfactory.

Spring 1941 Mk I Sights were fitted to twelve Spitfires and Hurricanes of operational squadrons.

July/August 1941 The Mk I Sight was used in the interception of German raids on southern England.

September 1941 The Mk I Gyro Gunsight was assessed as unsuitable in operational use. One of several reasons given was the need for the pilot to place one eye against a sighting eye-piece only .75 in. in diameter.

July 1943 The Mk II Gyro Gunsight made at Farnborough solved the earlier problems, and the image of the sighting graticle was now presented on an angled glass screen, at eye level, above the instrument panel in the cockpit. Displayed also on this screen was an image of the conventional 'Ring & Bead' Sight, for use in case of gyro failure, or at the choice of the pilot.

December 1943 The first production Mk II Gyro Sights were delivered by Ferranti Ltd from their Edinburgh factory, which had been specifically built for manufacture of the Sight.

The integrity of the design and development work behind the wartime Gyro Sight is such that – with no significant modification – it remained in service for over twenty years. Also, with the development of supersonic missile and cannon armed fighters; elements from the mathematics and construction of the Sight are still incorporated in the sophisticated aiming systems in use forty years on from the Second World War.

Scientists at the Royal Aeronautical Establishment Farnborough who were responsible for the invention and development of the Gyro Sight included Sir Melvill Jones, Mr A.A. Hale, Mr B. Sykes, and Mr R. Hancock.

APPENDIX IV

Data from Luftwaffe records and other German sources

1 *Ju 52 Aircraft Attacked off South Coast of Sicily- 28 Nov. 1942*
The Luftwaffe Quartermaster General's Loss Reports show that three Ju 52 aircraft of K.Gr.z.b.V. SII based at Brindisi in south-east Italy were totally destroyed due to enemy fighter action on 28 November 1942, while en route between Reggio in southern Italy and Bizerta in Tunisia. These three aircraft would almost certainly have been those attacked by the author on that date, which would effectively increase his personal tally to 8 ¾ enemy aircraft destroyed.

On the same day the German Records show that two more Ju 52s (possibly from the original formation of eight) were shot down by enemy fighters at Bizerta, presumably by RAF Desert Air Force fighters, which regularly swept and patrolled the German rear and support areas.

2 *485 Squadron Action on 9 August 1943*
The Luftwaffe Quartermaster General's Loss Reports identify the unit decimated in this brief action as being from II/J.G.2 Four Me 109s crashed as totally destroyed, and two force landed with 30 per cent and 10 per cent damage respectively. Two German pilots were listed as killed and one as missing. All six aircraft went down in the Lille/St Pol/Maisnil area.

3 *German Ejector Seat Research*
The pilot of the Me 109 destroyed by the author on 12 June 1944

appeared to be hurled violently upwards, and well clear of the aircraft. Researcher Hugh Smallwood learnt from Martin Baker Ltd (manufacturer of the first ejector seats fitted to post-war aircraft) that the groundwork for ejector seats was indeed carried out in war-time Germany.

The first successful ejection was from a German aircraft in 1942, following an emergency during a test flight; but there is no indication that ejector seats were ever fitted to operational aircraft. The Imperial War Museum holds documents from Focke-Wulf, Messerschmitt, Arado and Blohm & Voss relating to ejector seat development.

In his book *I Flew for the Führer* (Evans, London, 1953) Heinze Knoke describes kicking the stick hard forward with both feet (in a crippled Me 109) and being shot clear of the aircraft in a great, tumbling arc.

Use of that same technique would account for the spectacular, upwards departure of the Me 109 pilot from his aircraft on 12 June 1944.

APPENDIX V

Operational record of
Spitfire Mk IXB ML407

1 May – 31 December 1944 with 485 (NZ) Squadron, 135 Wing of 2nd TAF: Sqn letters OU–V

Personal aircraft of Johnnie Houlton, 1 May – 1 October 1944. During its eight months of service with the New Zealand Squadron, the aircraft was flown on the following sorties:

Fighter sweeps and escort to bomber formations 69
Dive-bombing with one 500-lb bomb   32
Patrols over the Normandy beach-head   30
Armed recce   6

Flown by 16 New Zealanders altogether, total: 137 sorties

Enemy aircraft claimed by OU–V include 2 Ju 88s (1 shared with the Section); 2 Me 109s destroyed; and 1 Me 109 damaged.

1–5 January 1945 with 341 (French) Squadron, 145 Wing of 2nd TAF: Sqn letters NL–D

Fighter support operations   3
Scramble   1

Flown by 2 French pilots, total: 4 sorties

22–24 January 1945 with 308 (Polish) Squadron, 131 Wing of 2nd TAF: Sqn letters ZF–

Weather recce   1
Dive-bombing   1

Flown by 2 Polish pilots, total: 2 sorties

8–13 February 1945 with 349 (Belgian) Squadron, 131 Wing of 2nd TAF: Sqn letters GE–P

Armed recce. Flown by 4 Belgian pilots and 2
English, total: 10 sorties

28 February–13 April 1945 with 345 (Fighting French) Squadron, 145 Wing of 2nd TAF

Armed recce. Flown by 7 French pilots, total: 14 sorties

16–22 April 1945 with 332 (Norwegian) Squadron, 132 Wing of 2nd TAF: Sqn letters AH–B

Patrols	3
Armed recce	2
Flown by 3 Norwegian pilots, total:	5 sorties

In her 12 months of operational service with 84 Group of the RAF Second Tactical Air Force Spitfire ML407 thus flew a grand total of 172 sorties. The homelands of all but two of her wartime pilots were outside the UK.

From May 1945 to July 1950 she was in RAF storage, then sold to Vickers Armstrong who converted the aircraft to a two-seater (T.Mk IX) for the Irish Air Corps, with the identity number of 162. She remained in active service until 1960 when, withdrawn from use, she was stored at Baldonnel. In 1968 she was sold to a private owner (Mr N.A.W. Samuelson) as a back-up airframe for the film *Battle of Britain* (in which she never appeared). In 1970 ML407 passed to Sir William Roberts' Strathallan Collection, Perthshire, until at last being purchased at the end of 1979 by her present owner, Nick Grace, who began the complete overhaul of the aircraft with the object of flying her again.

BIBLIOGRAPHY

I OFFICIAL HISTORIES and ACCOUNTS OF ACTIONS
New Zealanders with the Royal Air Force, Volumes I & II
   Wing Commander H.L. Thompson; War History Branch, Department of Internal Affairs, Wellington, New Zealand, 1953.
Malta Airmen
   J.A. Whelan; War History Branch, Department of Internal Affairs, Wellington, New Zealand, 1951.
The Air Battle of Malta
   Prepared for the Air Ministry by the Ministry of Information, 1944.

II ARCHIVE MATERIAL: AIR MINISTRY AND WAR OFFICE FILES
AIR 20/5336 contains the interesting investigation of proposed use of floating aerodromes. The summarised trials report & conclusions are shown in Appendix I.
ADM 116/4834 and adjacent numbers contain details of 'Scheme Habbakuk'.
WO 208/3118 includes the full report of Army investigations into air to ground attack effectiveness during the Retreat from Normandy to the Seine, and the comments of Second Tactical Air Force on the Army conclusions. This report is summarised and commented on in Appendix II. Other archive material included the 485(NZ) Spitfire Squadron Operations Record Books (AIR 27/1933) and Combat Reports (AIR 50/159).

III MEMOIRS & DIARIES containing or making use of original material
Andrews, C.F., & Morgan, E.B., *Supermarine Aircraft since 1914*, Putnam & Co Ltd, 1981.

Brennan, Paul, & Hesselyn, Ray, *Spitfires over Malta*, Jarrolds, 1943.

Henshaw, Alex, *Sigh for a Merlin*, John Murray Ltd, 1979.

Mouchotte, René *The Mouchotte Diaries*, ed. by André Dezarrois, translated from the French by Phillip John Stead, first published in Great Britain by Staples Press Ltd, 1956.

Price, Alfred, *The Spitfire Story*, Jane's Publishing Co Ltd, 1982.

Quill, Jeffrey, *Spitfire: A Test Pilot's Story*, John Murray Ltd, 1983.

Rawlins, John D.R., *Fighter Squadrons of the RAF and their Aircraft*, Macdonald & Jane's (Publishers) Ltd, 1969.

Richey, Paul, *Fighter Pilot*, Hutchinson & Co Ltd, 1941.

Scott, Desmond, *Typhoon Pilot*, Lee Cooper in association with Martin Secker & Warburg Ltd, 1982.

Smith, J.R., & Kay, Anthony, *German Aircraft of the Second World War*, Putnam & Co Ltd, 1972.

Vader, John, *Spitfire* Pan/Ballantine Illustrated History of World War II, 1972.

IV PERIODICALS

Aeroplane Monthly, vol. 11, no. 4, April 1983 and adjacent issues.
  'Drawing a Bead' by R. Wallace Clarke is an in-depth study of the development of aerial gun sights, leading up to the invention of the Gyro Gunsight, and beyond.

After The Battle Series
  Number 8, 'The Battle of the Falaise Pocket' Battle of Britain Prints International Ltd London. Edited by Winston G. Ramsey.

Purnell's History of the Second World War
  Number 65: 'D Day'. Editor Barrie Pitt

INDEX